# KNOWLEDGE ENCYCLOPEDIA
# SPACE!

**DK** S M I T H S O N I A N

**KNOWLEDGE** ENCYCLOPEDIA

# SPACE!

**DK London**
**Senior editor** Ben Morgan
**Senior art editor** Smiljka Surla
**Editor** Steve Setford
**US editors** Christine Heilman, Margaret Parrish
**Designer** Jacqui Swan
**Contributors** Robert Dinwiddie, John Farndon, Geraint Jones,
Ian Ridpath, Giles Sparrow, Carole Stott
**Scientific consultant** Jacqueline Mitton
**Illustrators** Peter Bull, Jason Harding, Arran Lewis
**Jacket design development manager** Sophia MTT
**Jacket designer** Laura Brim
**Jacket editor** Claire Gell
**Producer, pre-production** Nikoleta Parasaki
**Producer** Mary Slater
**Managing editor** Paula Regan
**Managing art editor** Owen Peyton Jones
**Publisher** Andrew Macintyre
**Associate publishing director** Liz Wheeler
**Art director** Karen Self
**Design director** Stuart Jackman
**Publishing director** Jonathan Metcalf

**DK Delhi**
**Senior editor** Bharti Bedi
**Senior art editor** Nishesh Batnagar
**Project editor** Priyanka Kharbanda
**Art editors** Heena Sharma, Supriya Mahajan
**Assistant editor** Sheryl Sadana
**DTP designer** Nityanand Kumar
**Senior DTP designers** Shanker Prasad, Harish Aggarwal
**Picture researcher** Deepak Negi
**Jacket designer** Dhirendra Singh
**Managing jackets editor** Saloni Singh
**Managing editor** Kingshuk Ghoshal
**Managing art editor** Govind Mittal
**Pre-production manager** Balwant Singh
**Production manager** Pankaj Sharma

First American Edition, 2015
Published in the United States by DK Publishing
345 Hudson Street, New York, New York 10014

Copyright © 2015 Dorling Kindersley Limited
A Penguin Random House Company
16 17 18 19  10 9 8 7 6 5 4
013–264881–September/2015

**THE SMITHSONIAN**
Established in 1846, the Smithsonian—the world's largest museum and research complex—includes 19 museums and galleries and the National Zoological Park. The total number of artifacts, works of art, and specimens in the Smithsonian's collection is estimated at 137 million. The Smithsonian is a renowned research center, dedicated to public education, national service, and scholarship in the arts, sciences, and history.

# CONTENTS

## THE SOLAR SYSTEM

| | |
|---|---|
| The Sun's family | 8 |
| Around the Sun | 10 |
| Birth of the solar system | 12 |
| The Sun | 14 |
| Mercury | 16 |
| Venus | 18 |
| Earth | 20 |
| Inside Earth | 22 |
| The Moon | 24 |
| Exploring the Moon | 26 |
| Impact craters | 28 |
| Eclipses | 30 |
| Mars | 32 |
| Valles Marineris | 34 |
| Exploring Mars | 36 |
| Red planet | 38 |
| Asteroids | 40 |
| Shooting stars and meteorites | 42 |
| Jupiter | 44 |
| Moons of Jupiter | 46 |
| Io | 48 |
| Saturn | 50 |
| Saturn's rings | 52 |
| Ring world | 54 |
| Moons of Saturn | 56 |
| Titan | 58 |
| Uranus | 60 |
| Neptune | 62 |
| Minor planets | 64 |
| Comets | 66 |

# STARS

| | |
|---|---|
| How stars work | 70 |
| Types of stars | 72 |
| Star birth | 74 |
| Exoplanets | 76 |
| Hot Jupiters | 78 |
| Lives and deaths of stars | 80 |
| Butterfly Nebula | 82 |
| Red supergiants | 84 |
| Neutron stars | 86 |
| Black holes | 88 |
| Multiple stars | 90 |
| Star cloud | 92 |

# GALAXIES

| | |
|---|---|
| The cosmos | 96 |
| Milky Way | 98 |
| Galaxies | 100 |
| Active galaxies | 102 |
| Colliding galaxies | 104 |
| Galaxy clusters | 106 |
| The universe | 108 |
| The Big Bang | 110 |

# EXPLORING SPACE

| | |
|---|---|
| Space exploration | 114 |
| Discovering space | 116 |
| Telescopes | 118 |
| Space telescopes | 120 |
| Rockets | 122 |
| First person in space | 124 |
| Space probes | 126 |
| Rovers | 128 |
| Crewed spacecraft | 130 |
| Space Shuttle | 132 |
| Apollo program | 134 |
| Lunar lander | 136 |
| Moon buggy | 138 |
| Spacesuit | 140 |
| Spacewalk | 142 |
| Space stations | 144 |
| Future exploration | 146 |
| The search for life | 148 |

# THE NIGHT SKY

| | |
|---|---|
| The celestial sphere | 152 |
| Practical stargazing | 154 |
| Northern star-hopping | 156 |
| Southern star-hopping | 158 |
| Star maps | 160 |
| Constellations | 162 |

# REFERENCE

| | |
|---|---|
| Solar system data | 196 |
| Exploring the planets | 198 |
| Stars and galaxies | 200 |
| Glossary | 202 |
| Index and acknowledgments | 204 |

# THE SOLAR SYSTEM

Our local neighborhood in space is called the solar system. At its heart is the Sun, an ordinary star that is so close it floods our planet with light. Trapped in its orbit by gravity are Earth and seven other planets, their many moons, and millions of comets and asteroids.

MERCURY   VENUS   EARTH   MARS   JUPITER   SATURN   URANUS

## THE SUN AND PLANETS

The Sun is huge compared to even the biggest of the planets, Jupiter, and it contains 99.8 percent of the solar system's entire mass. At nearly 870,000 miles (1.4 million km) wide, the Sun is ten times wider than Jupiter and over 1,000 times more massive. Yet even Jupiter is gigantic compared to Earth. The solar system's eight planets form two distinct groups. The inner planets—Mercury, Venus, Earth, and Mars—are solid balls of rock and metal. In contrast, the outer planets are gas giants—enormous, swirling globes made mostly of hydrogen and helium.

**1.3** million—the number of times Earth's volume could fit inside the Sun.

**SUN**

# The Sun's family

The solar system is a vast disk of material over 19 billion miles (30 billion km) across, with the Sun at its center. Most of it is empty space, but scattered throughout are countless solid objects bound to the Sun by gravity and orbiting (traveling around) it, mostly in the same direction. The biggest objects are almost perfectly round and are called planets. There are eight of them, ranging from the small rocky planet Mercury to gigantic Jupiter. The solar system also has hundreds of moons and dwarf planets, millions of asteroids, and possibly millions or billions of comets.

**NEPTUNE**

## ORBITAL PLANE

The orbits of the planets and most asteroids around the Sun are aligned, making a flat shape known as a plane. This means they rarely bump into each other. Comets, though, can be in orbits at any angle.

Sun

Jupiter

Comet

Neptune

### How orbits work

A fast cannonball escapes Earth's gravity.

A slow cannonball falls to the ground.

At the right speed, the ball keeps falling but never lands.

To understand how orbits work, English scientist Isaac Newton imagined cannonballs being fired into space. If a cannonball flies so fast that the curvature of its fall matches Earth's curvature, it will keep flying forever, orbiting the planet.

## MINOR BODIES

Besides the planets, there are so many other bodies in the solar system that astronomers have not been able to identify them all. Bodies more than about 125 miles (200 km) wide, such as dwarf planets and large moons, are round. Smaller objects are lumpy in shape.

**Asteroids**
There are millions of these rocky lumps, most of which circle the Sun in an area between Mars and Jupiter: the asteroid belt. A few asteroids have orbits that take them perilously close to Earth or other planets.

**Comets**
Comets are icy bodies that travel in from the outer solar system, forming a bright tail as they come close enough to the Sun for the ice to evaporate. Many comets are thought to come from a vast cloud called the Oort cloud, far beyond the planets.

**Dwarf planets**
The force of gravity pulls large objects into a spherical shape over time. Dwarf planets have enough gravity to become spherical but not enough to sweep the area around their orbits clear of other objects. The total number of dwarf planets is unknown.

**Moons**
Most of the planets and many of the other objects in the solar system have moons—natural satellites that orbit them, in the same way that the planets orbit the Sun. Nineteen of these moons are large enough to be round, and two of them are larger than the planet Mercury.

## STRUCTURE

The solar system has no clear outer edge and is so big that distances are measured not in miles or kilometers but in astronomical units (AU). One astronomical unit is the average distance from Earth to the Sun.

**Inner solar system**
Circling closest to the Sun are the four inner planets: Mercury, Venus, Earth, and Mars. Beyond Mars lies the asteroid belt, and beyond the asteroid belt is Jupiter (orbit in orange) at 5 AU from the Sun.

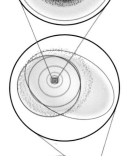

**Outer solar system**
Beyond the orbits of Jupiter, Saturn, Uranus, and Neptune is a ring of icy bodies known as the Kuiper belt, some 30–50 AU from the Sun. Two of the largest objects in the Kuiper belt are Pluto (orbit in purple) and Eris (orbit in red).

**Beyond Pluto**
One of the most distant solar system objects known is Sedna, a minor body whose elongated orbit takes it as far from the Sun as 937 AU. Sedna's journey around the Sun takes 11,400 years to complete. The Sun would look so tiny from Sedna that you could block it out with a pin.

**Oort cloud**
Far beyond Sedna's orbit is the Oort cloud—a vast ball of icy bodies reaching 100,000 AU from the Sun. Some comets are thought to come from the Oort cloud. The Sun's gravity is so weak here that objects in the cloud can be dislodged by the gravity of other stars.

**10**   the solar system ∘ **AROUND THE SUN**

**500,000** mph (800,000 km/h)—the **speed at which the whole solar system** is moving around our galaxy.

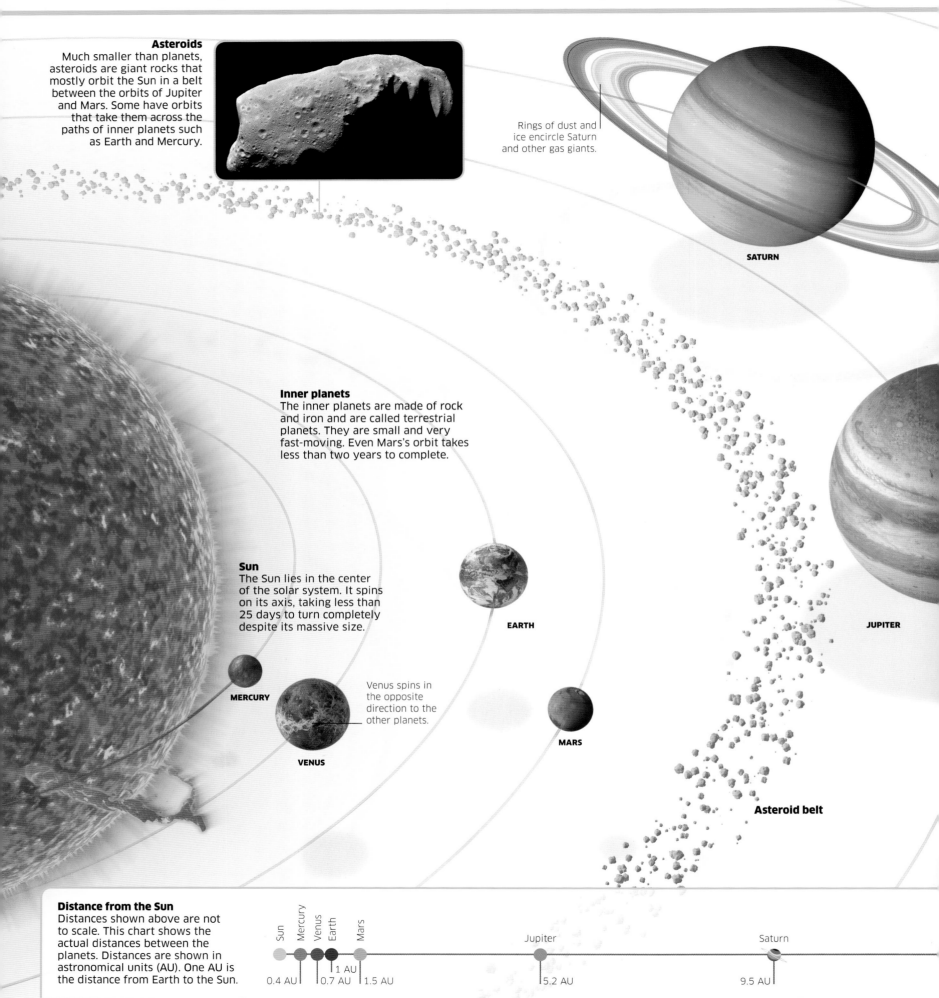

**Asteroids**
Much smaller than planets, asteroids are giant rocks that mostly orbit the Sun in a belt between the orbits of Jupiter and Mars. Some have orbits that take them across the paths of inner planets such as Earth and Mercury.

Rings of dust and ice encircle Saturn and other gas giants.

**SATURN**

**Inner planets**
The inner planets are made of rock and iron and are called terrestrial planets. They are small and very fast-moving. Even Mars's orbit takes less than two years to complete.

**Sun**
The Sun lies in the center of the solar system. It spins on its axis, taking less than 25 days to turn completely despite its massive size.

**EARTH**

**JUPITER**

**MERCURY**

Venus spins in the opposite direction to the other planets.

**MARS**

**VENUS**

**Asteroid belt**

**Distance from the Sun**
Distances shown above are not to scale. This chart shows the actual distances between the planets. Distances are shown in astronomical units (AU). One AU is the distance from Earth to the Sun.

Sun · Mercury · Venus · Earth · Mars · Jupiter · Saturn

0.4 AU   0.7 AU   1 AU   1.5 AU   5.2 AU   9.5 AU

**NEPTUNE**

Uranus, unlike the other planets, spins on its side, rolling around on its orbit.

**URANUS**

## Comets
Comets are giant lumps of ice and dust that have highly elliptical orbits. They can spend centuries in the outer reaches of the solar system before swooping close to the Sun and developing tails as they warm up.

## Kuiper belt
Beyond the planets is a belt of icy bodies, some of which are large enough to be classed as dwarf planets. These objects are so far from the Sun that they can take hundreds of years to complete one orbit.

## Gas giants
The outer planets are all much bigger than the inner planets. They are called gas giants because they are made mostly of hydrogen and helium. These substances are gases on Earth, but in the gas giants they are mostly in liquid form.

Jupiter spins round faster than any other planet, completing one rotation in under ten hours. The speed of movement at its equator is 27,000 mph (43,000 km/h).

# Around the Sun

**Trapped by the Sun's gravity, the eight planets of the solar system travel around the central star on nearly circular paths, spinning like tops as they go.**

The farther a planet is from the Sun, the slower it travels and the longer its orbit takes. The farthest planet, Neptune, takes 165 years to get around the Sun and moves at just over 3 miles (5 km) per second. Earth, meanwhile, bowls through space nearly six times as fast, and Mercury, the planet closest to the Sun, whizzes around it in just 88 days at a speedy 30 miles (50 km) per second. The planets' orbits are not circular. Instead, they follow slightly oval paths, known as ellipses, that take them closer to the Sun at one point. Mercury's orbit is the most elliptical: its farthest point from the Sun is more than 50 percent farther than its nearest point.

Every object in space is
**spinning around,**
from planets and moons to stars, black holes, and galaxies.

Uranus

Neptune

19 AU

30 AU

**New Sun**
The Sun contains 99.8 percent of the material now in the solar system.

**Rocky planets**
Grains of rock and metal collected in the inner part of the young solar system, which was much hotter than the outer zone. This material would form the inner planets—Mercury, Venus, Earth, and Mars—which have rocky outer layers and cores of iron.

# Birth of the solar system

**The planets of the solar system formed from gas and grains of dust and ice surrounding the newly formed Sun.**

The solar system was born inside a vast, dark cloud of gas and dust. About 5 billion years ago, something triggered a burst of star formation in the cloud—perhaps a nearby star exploded, sending a shock wave rippling through the cloud. Hundreds of pockets of gas were squeezed into clumps. Their gravity pulled in more and more gas, making the clumps larger and denser. This made them heat up inside and start to glow. Eventually, the cores of the clumps got so hot and dense that nuclear reactions began and they became stars. One of those stars was our Sun.

**Oldest rocks**
Meteorites are space rocks that fall onto Earth. They include the oldest rocks known to science. Many are leftovers from the cloud of debris that formed the planets.

The gas giants contain **99 percent** of the mass of the solar system outside the Sun.

About **100 small planets** in the early solar system collided to form just **four rocky planets**.

**13**

**Hot zone**
Closer to the Sun, gases are boiled away to leave just grains of rock and metal.

## Solar nebula
When the Sun formed inside a vast cloud of gas and dust, it was rotating, and a swirling disk of material collected in a flat plane around it. This disk is called the solar nebula.

**Cold zone**
The cold outer regions beyond the "frost line" are mostly grains of ice made from water, methane, and ammonia.

## The solar system forms
The solar system formed 4.6 billion years ago when a clump of gas and dust was pulled together by its own gravity inside a giant cloud. The collapsing mass gave birth to our Sun, surrounded by a flattened spinning disk (the solar nebula) from which the planets formed.

**Collapsing clump**
Within the giant cloud, a pocket of gas began to shrink, perhaps because a shock wave from a supernova (exploding star) disturbed the cloud.

**Spinning disk**
As the clump shrank, it began spinning, turning faster and faster until it formed a disk. Its center began to heat up.

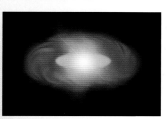

**The Sun is born**
Nuclear reactions began in the dense center, which began to shine as a star. The leftover matter formed a disk called a solar nebula.

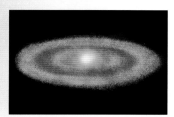

**Planetesimals**
Gravity caused the particles in the disk to clump together, forming billions of tiny planets, or planetesimals.

**Planets form**
The planetesimals crashed into each other, sticking together and growing into fewer, larger planets.

**Migration**
The orbits of the giant planets changed. Neptune and Uranus moved farther out, pushing smaller icy bodies into even more distant orbits.

**The solar system today**
By about 3.9 billion years ago, the solar system had settled down into its present pattern of planets.

**Leftovers**
Not all the material in the solar nebula formed planets—the leftovers formed moons, asteroids, comets, and dwarf planets.

## Birth of the giants
Vast amounts of icy debris collected in the cold outer part of the solar system. This material drew together to form planets so large that they had enough gravity to pull in gases such as hydrogen and helium. These planets would become the gas giants: Jupiter, Saturn, Uranus, and Neptune.

# The Sun

**Our Sun is a typical star—a vast, glowing ball made mostly of superhot hydrogen and helium gas.**

The Sun has been shining for nearly 5 billion years and will probably continue to shine for another 5 billion. More than a million times larger in volume than Earth, it contains over 99 percent of the solar system's mass. The tremendous force of gravity generated by this mass keeps the planets of the solar system trapped in orbit around it. The Sun's source of power lies buried deep in its core, where temperatures soar to 27 million °F (15 million °C). The intense heat and pressure in the core trigger nuclear fusion reactions, turning 4 million tons of matter into pure energy every second. This energy spreads upward to the seething surface of the Sun, where it floods out into space as light and other forms of radiation.

**Core**
The Sun's core is like a nuclear reactor. The nuclei (centers) of hydrogen atoms are forced together to form helium nuclei—a process called nuclear fusion.

**Sunspots**
Sometimes dark patches appear on the Sun, often in groups. Called sunspots, they look darker because they are about 3,500°F (2,000°C) cooler than the rest of the surface. They last only a few weeks and are caused by the Sun's magnetic field.

## FAST FACTS

**Diameter:** 865,374 miles (1,392,684 km)

**Mass (Earth = 1):** 333,000

**Surface temperature:** 9,930°F (5,500°C)

**Core temperature:** 27 million °F (15 million °C)

**Prominence**
Giant eruptions of hot gas sometimes burst out from the Sun. Called prominences, they follow loops in the Sun's invisible magnetic field.

**2** billion billion billion tons— the weight of the Sun.

In 1947 the **Great Sunspot** could be **seen** at sunset with the **naked eye**.

**15**

**Convective zone**
Below the Sun's surface is the convective zone, an area in which pockets of hot gas rise, cool, and then sink back down again. This movement carries energy from the core toward the surface.

**Radiative zone**
Deep beneath the convective zone is the dense, hot radiative zone. Energy travels through this part of the Sun as radiation.

**Spicules**
Jets of gas called spicules cover the whole Sun.

**Photosphere**
The outer part of the Sun is transparent to light, creating the illusion of a surface. This apparent surface is called the photosphere and has a grainy appearance, caused by pockets of hot gas rising from deep below.

**EARTH TO SAME SCALE**

## Speed of light

Traveling at the speed of light, it takes a mere eight minutes for the Sun's energy to travel across space to reach Earth. However, it can take up to 100,000 years for energy to travel through the star's dense interior to reach its surface.

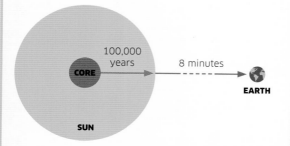

## Northern lights

As well as producing heat and light, the Sun flings out streams of deadly high-energy particles, forming the "solar wind." Earth's magnetic field protects us from these particles like an elastic cage, but when a strong blast of them disturbs the magnetic field, trapped particles cascade down into the atmosphere. They set off brilliant light displays near the poles, called auroras or the northern and southern lights.

## Solar cycle

The number of sunspots on the Sun varies in a regular cycle, reaching a peak every 11 years or so before dying down again. This happens because of the way the Sun rotates. The star's equator spins 20 percent faster than its poles, causing the Sun's magnetic field to get tangled up. Every 11 years it gets so tangled that it breaks down, before forming afresh.

| | | |
|---|---|---|
| The Sun spins much faster at its equator than at its poles. | The difference in speeds twists magnetic field lines out of shape. | The twisted field lines burst in loops from the surface, creating sunspots. |

# Mercury

**The planet Mercury is a giant ball of iron covered in a shallow layer of rock. It is the smallest planet and the one closest to the Sun.**

Mercury is the speedster of the planets, completing its journey around the Sun in just 88 Earth days at the brisk pace of 108,000 mph (173,000 km/h), which is faster than any other planet. Scorched by the Sun's heat, Mercury's dusty, Moon-like surface is hotter than an oven by day but freezing at night. Deep under the surface, a giant core of iron almost fills the planet's interior. The oversized core suggests that Mercury was once struck with such violence that most of its rocky outer layers were blasted away into space.

**Mercury's cliffs**
Among Mercury's most distinctive features are long, winding cliffs called rupes, shown in this artist's impression. They probably formed at least 3 billion years ago when the young planet was cooling and shrinking, which made its surface wrinkle.

Craters on Mercury, such as the Mendelssohn Crater, are named after writers, artists, and composers.

## Around the Sun

Mercury takes 88 Earth days to orbit the Sun. As it travels, its shape as seen through a telescope appears to change because we see different parts of the planet lit by sunlight.

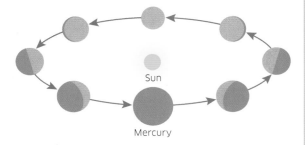

Sun

Mercury

## Deep impact

The Caloris Basin, seen here in false color, is one of the biggest impact craters in the solar system. The crater is 960 miles (1,550 km) wide, but the collision that produced it was so violent that debris was flung more than 600 miles (1,000 km) beyond the crater rim.

Caloris Basin

## Cracked planet

On the opposite side of Mercury from the Caloris Basin is a strange area of jumbled hills. Scientists think shock waves from the giant impact traveled all the way through Mercury and converged here, cracking the ground.

Impact

Hills

Large craters are surrounded by streaks of pale material blasted out by the impact.

Lange Crater

Eminescu Crater is 78 miles (125 km) wide.

**30** miles (50 km) per second—the **speed at which Mercury orbits** the Sun.

**806°F** (430°C)—the **peak daytime temperature** on Mercury.

**−292°F** (−180°C)—the **temperature during** the **coldest part of the night**.

**17**

**Core**
Mercury's gigantic core is made of iron. Because of the way Mercury wobbles a little as it rotates, scientists think the outer part of the core might be liquid.

**Mantle**
At only 370 miles (600 km) deep, Mercury's mantle is remarkably thin. Like Earth's mantle, it's made of silicate rock.

**Crust**
Unlike Earth's crust, which is broken into plates, Mercury's crust is a single solid shell of rock.

**Atmosphere**
Because Mercury's gravity is weak and its surface is blasted by solar radiation, its atmosphere is thin and contains only a trace of gas.

**Scar face**
Impacts billions of years ago have left Mercury thoroughly pitted by craters. Because the planet is small, it doesn't have enough gravity to hold on to a thick atmosphere, and there's no air to stop meteorites from crashing into it.

At the base of the mantle is a solid layer of iron sulfide. On Earth this mineral forms shiny rocks known as "fool's gold."

**1966** The year in which the Russian Venera 7 became **the first space probe to land on Venus**.

Venus rotates in the **opposite direction** of other planets.

# Venus

**Our nearest neighbor in space, Venus is very similar to Earth in size. However, the furnace-like surface of this rocky planet bears little resemblance to our world.**

Venus is cloaked in swirls of yellowish clouds. Unlike Earth's clouds, which contain life-giving water, these clouds are made of deadly sulfuric acid. The atmosphere is so thick that pressure on the planet's surface is 92 times that on Earth—enough to crush a car flat. At 860°F (460°C), the surface is also hotter than that of any other planet in the solar system.

## Volcanoes
Venus has more volcanoes than any other planet in the solar system. Half a billion years ago, the entire surface of the planet was remade by volcanic eruptions. We can't see if any of the volcanoes are active since Venus's thick clouds hide them from view. However, scientists have detected unusual heat from the largest volcano, Maat Mons (below), which suggests it might be erupting.

## Deadly clouds
Venus's dense atmosphere is about 97 percent carbon dioxide. A thick layer of cloud, about 35 miles (60 km) above the surface, hides the planet's surface entirely. These clouds are made of drops of sulfuric acid.

CELSIUS | FAHRENHEIT

1,000°
500° — 900°
Venus
Mercury — 800°
400°
— 700°
100° — 200°
— 100°
Earth 0° — 0°
Mars
— -100°
-100° — -200° — Saturn
Jupiter
— -300°
-200° — Uranus
Neptune — -400°

**SURFACE TEMPERATURE OF THE PLANETS**

## Hot planet
Venus is hot not just because it is close to the Sun but also because its air contains so much carbon dioxide. Like glass in a greenhouse, carbon dioxide traps the Sun's heat. This greenhouse effect warms Earth too, because of the water vapor and carbon dioxide in the air, but it is much weaker than on Venus.

Many craters on the surface, called coronas, were made not by impacts but by collapsing volcanoes.

Blank areas in the model of Venus are regions that the Magellan spacecraft did not survey.

The Dali Chasma is a 1,240-mile- (2,000-km) long network of canyons and valleys.

Venus rotates so slowly that **its day lasts longer than its year.**

**1,600** The **number of volcanoes** on the surface of Venus.

**5** miles (8 km)—the height of Venus's tallest volcano, **Maat Mons.**

**19**

**Surface gravity (Earth = 1):** 0.91

**Moons:** 0

**Year:** 225 Earth days

**Time to rotate once:** 243 Earth days

**Pancake domes**
Unlike volcanoes on Earth, those on Venus rarely erupt explosively. Instead, they ooze lava slowly. In some places, thick lava has piled up on the surface to form squat, rounded volcanoes called pancake domes.

**Core**
Like the other rocky planets, Venus probably has a red-hot core made mostly of iron. The inner core is likely solid but the outer part may be partly liquid.

The surface consists of bare rock and is so hot that an astronaut would be burned to a cinder in just a few minutes.

**Mantle**
Venus's mantle of rock is kept slightly soft by heat from the core. Over millions of years, the soft rock slowly churns around.

**Crust**
Unlike Earth's crust, Venus's crust is quite thick and rarely moves, merely bulging up in places now and then.

**Atmosphere**
Venus has the thickest, densest atmosphere of all the rocky planets, with a permanent blanket of cloud that covers the entire planet. The cloud-free view on the left side of this 3-D model was created from radar data sent to Earth by the Magellan spacecraft.

**67,000** mph (107,000 km/h)—the **average speed** at which **Earth orbits the Sun.**

# Earth

**Of all the planets so far discovered, ours is the only one known to harbor life and to have vast oceans of liquid water on the surface.**

Earth's distance from the Sun and its moderately thick atmosphere mean it never gets very hot or very cold at the surface. In fact, it is always just the right temperature for water to stay liquid, making life as we know it possible. That is very different from scorching Venus, where all water boils away, and icy Mars, where any water seems to be frozen. Life on Earth began around 3.8 billion years ago, soon after the newly formed planet cooled down, allowing water to form oceans. Since then, living organisms have slowly transformed the planet's surface, coloring the land green and adding oxygen to the atmosphere, which makes our air breathable.

**Life in water**
Water is essential to all forms of life on Earth because the chemical reactions that keep organisms alive happen in water. Most scientists think life began in water, perhaps at the bottom of the sea, where volcanic chimneys might have provided essential warmth and nutrients. Today, oceans contain some of the most diverse natural habitats on the planet, such as the coral reefs of tropical seas.

**Polar ice**
Because Earth's poles receive so little warmth from the Sun, they are permanently cold and are covered in ice. An icy continent sits over Earth's South Pole, but an icy ocean sits at the North Pole.

**FAST FACTS**

**Time to rotate once:** 23.9 hours

**Year:** 365.26 days

**Moons:** 1

**Average temperature:** 61°F (16°C)

Axis of rotation

**600** The number of volcanoes that have erupted in the last **10,000 years**.

**1,036** mph (1,667 km/h)—the **speed** at which **Earth rotates** at the equator.

**−136°F** (−93°C)—the **lowest recorded** temperature on Earth.

**21**

### Tilt
**23.4°**

Earth does not spin upright, as compared to its path around the Sun. Instead, it is tilted over at an angle of 23.4°. The planet also wobbles very slowly, causing its tilt to swing from 22.1° to 24.5° every 42,000 years.

Living organisms have been found in rock **3 miles (5 km) deep underground** and in the air 10 miles (16 km) high in the atmosphere.

### Continents
Most of Earth's land is concentrated in large masses called continents. Over millions of years, the continents very slowly move around the planet, colliding and breaking up to form new patterns.

### Orbit and seasons
Earth's tilt causes different parts of the planet to lean toward the Sun or away from it during the year, creating seasons. When the northern hemisphere leans toward the Sun, the weather is warmer and days are longer, causing the season of summer. When it leans away from the Sun, the weather is colder and nights are longer, causing winter.

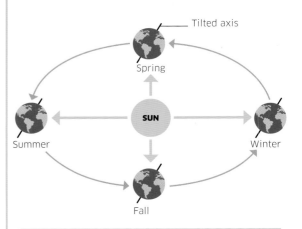

Tilted axis

Spring

SUN

Summer

Winter

Fall

### Human influence
In recent centuries, our species has changed Earth's surface so much that our influence is visible from space. As well as lighting up the planet's night side with electricity, we have changed the atmosphere and climate and have replaced large areas of natural ecosystems with farmland and cities.

### Life on land
For billions of years, life existed only in water. Then, 475 million years ago, tiny plants inched their way out of swamps and onto land. From this small beginning, life spread over the continents, covering the wettest places with dense forests.

### Watery planet
Water covers more than two-thirds of Earth's surface. Scientists think much of it came from comets or asteroids that crashed into the planet early in its history.

### Deserts
Not all of Earth's surface is covered by life. Deserts don't have enough water to sustain lush forests, and only special kinds of plants and animals can survive in them. Some of Earth's deserts resemble landscapes of other planets. The deserts of central Australia even have the same reddish color as Martian deserts, thanks to iron oxide in the soil—the chemical that gives Mars its color.

# Inside Earth

**If you could pull Earth apart with your hands, you'd discover that it's made of distinct layers that fit together like the layers of an onion.**

Earth is made almost entirely of rock and metal. When the young planet was forming and its interior was largely molten, heavy materials like metal sank all the way to the center, while lighter materials such as rock settled on top. Today, Earth's interior is mostly solid, but it is still very hot, with temperatures rising to 10,800°F (6,000°C) in the core, which is hotter than the surface of the Sun. This powerful inner heat keeps the planet's interior slowly moving.

**Volcanic action**
Most of the rock in Earth's crust and mantle is solid. However, pockets of molten rock form where plates collide or in hot spots where heat wells up from Earth's core. In such places, molten rock may erupt from the surface, forming volcanoes.

**Stormy skies**
Water from the oceans creates clouds in the lower part of Earth's atmosphere. The layer of clouds gives us rain, snow, and storms such as this hurricane near Florida.

**Oceans**
Earth is the only planet with a large amount of liquid water on the surface, making it possible for life to flourish here. About 97 percent of the water is in the oceans, but there is also water in the air, in rivers and lakes, and in ice.

**Atmosphere**
Earth is cocooned from space by a thin atmosphere of gases. The composition has remained unchanged for the last 200 million years, with 78 percent nitrogen, 21 percent oxygen, and small traces of other gases such as carbon dioxide.

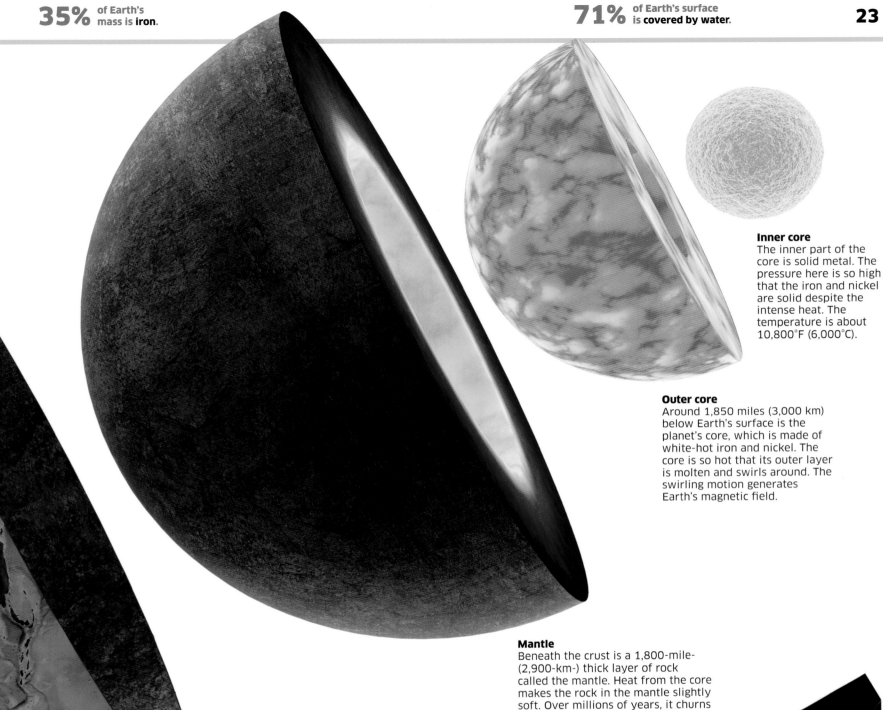

### Inner core
The inner part of the core is solid metal. The pressure here is so high that the iron and nickel are solid despite the intense heat. The temperature is about 10,800°F (6,000°C).

### Outer core
Around 1,850 miles (3,000 km) below Earth's surface is the planet's core, which is made of white-hot iron and nickel. The core is so hot that its outer layer is molten and swirls around. The swirling motion generates Earth's magnetic field.

### Mantle
Beneath the crust is a 1,800-mile-(2,900-km-) thick layer of rock called the mantle. Heat from the core makes the rock in the mantle slightly soft. Over millions of years, it churns around slowly like thick molasses, and this motion moves the rigid crust on top.

### Crust
The outermost part of Earth's solid surface is the crust, which is only a few dozen miles deep. Thick areas of crust form continents, while thin areas form the floors of oceans.

### Tectonic plates
Earth's brittle outer crust is broken into giant slabs called tectonic plates. There are seven or eight major plates and dozens of small ones. The plates move across Earth's surface at about the speed that fingernails grow, carrying the continents with them.

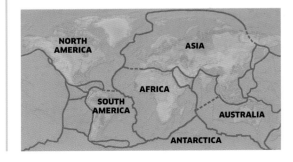

NORTH AMERICA

ASIA

AFRICA

SOUTH AMERICA

AUSTRALIA

ANTARCTICA

### Atmosphere
Earth's atmosphere has five layers, but only the bottom layer contains clouds and breathable air. Airliners fly above the clouds in the clear air of the stratosphere. The atmosphere has no upper edge, since it fades gradually, but the boundary between the atmosphere and space is defined as 62 miles (100 km) high, which is in the thermosphere.

Exosphere

Thermosphere

Mesosphere

Stratosphere

Troposphere

## How the Moon formed

Scientists have various theories about how the Moon formed. Most think it formed when a small planet smashed into the young Earth around 4.5 billion years ago. The impact destroyed the small planet and tipped over Earth's axis of rotation. Debris was flung into space to form a cloud. Over time, the debris particles stuck together to become the Moon.

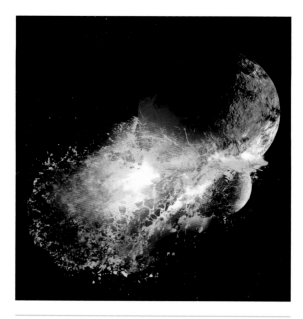

## Weak gravity

The force of gravity, which pulls things to the ground, is much weaker on the Moon than on Earth because the Moon has less mass. Astronauts weigh one-sixth of their Earth weight on the Moon and would be able to jump six times higher if they didn't have heavy spacesuits.

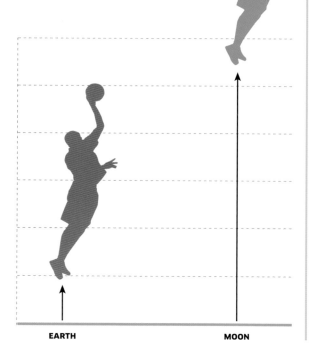

EARTH          MOON

**Inner core**
In the center of the Moon is a ball of incredibly hot but solid iron about 300 miles (500 km) wide. Its temperature is about 2,400°F (1,300°C).

**Outer core**
Surrounding the inner core is a layer of iron that may have melted, thanks to lower pressure. This outer core is about 430 miles (700 km) wide.

**Lower mantle**
Heat from the core has probably melted the bottom of the mantle, which is made of rock.

# The Moon

**So large and bright that we can see it even in daytime, the Moon is the only object in space whose surface features are visible to the naked eye.**

The Moon is a quarter as wide as Earth, making it the largest moon relative to its parent planet in the solar system. It is also the largest and brightest object in the night sky by far, and its fascinating surface—scarred with hundreds of thousands of impact craters—is a spectacular sight through binoculars or telescopes. The Moon formed about 4.5 billion years ago, shortly after Earth, but unlike Earth its surface has hardly changed in billions of years. The dark "seas," or maria, on its near side are flat plains formed by giant floods of lava that erupted about 3 billion years ago. Surrounding these are the lunar highlands, their ancient hills and valleys littered with the debris of countless meteorite impacts.

**FAST FACTS**

**Time to orbit Earth:** 27.32 Earth days

**Mass (Earth = 1):** 0.167

**Distance from Earth:** 239,227 miles (385,000 km)

**Average diameter:** 2,159 miles (3,474 km) wide

**49** The number of times the Moon could **fit inside Earth**.

**248°F** (120°C)—**midday temperature** at the Moon's equator.

**2,288** mph (3,683 km/h)—the **speed** at which the **Moon orbits Earth**.

**25**

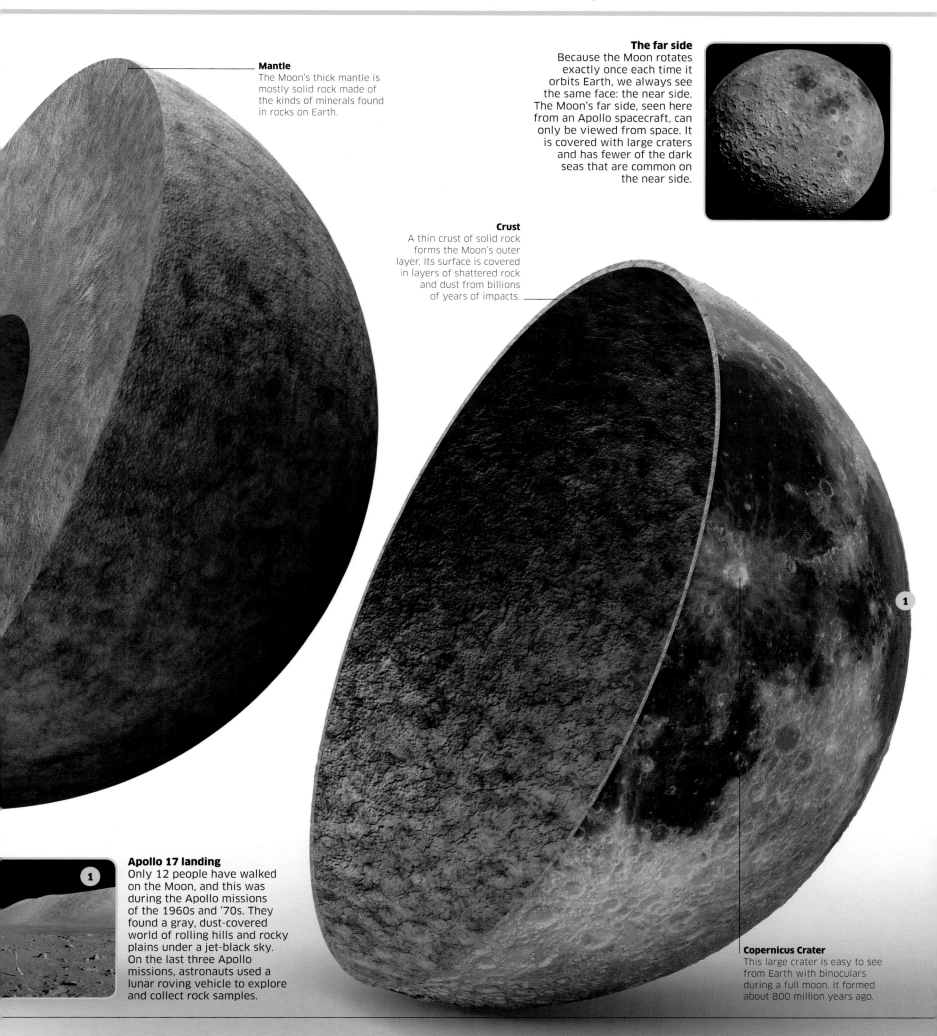

**Mantle**
The Moon's thick mantle is mostly solid rock made of the kinds of minerals found in rocks on Earth.

**The far side**
Because the Moon rotates exactly once each time it orbits Earth, we always see the same face: the near side. The Moon's far side, seen here from an Apollo spacecraft, can only be viewed from space. It is covered with large craters and has fewer of the dark seas that are common on the near side.

**Crust**
A thin crust of solid rock forms the Moon's outer layer. Its surface is covered in layers of shattered rock and dust from billions of years of impacts.

**Apollo 17 landing**
Only 12 people have walked on the Moon, and this was during the Apollo missions of the 1960s and '70s. They found a gray, dust-covered world of rolling hills and rocky plains under a jet-black sky. On the last three Apollo missions, astronauts used a lunar roving vehicle to explore and collect rock samples.

**Copernicus Crater**
This large crater is easy to see from Earth with binoculars during a full moon. It formed about 800 million years ago.

**Key**

☼ Failed

📍 Successful

*Pascal*

*Anaxagoras*

*Pythagoras*

**MARE FRIGORIS**

40

33

*Plato*

*Vallis Alpes*

*Aristoteles*

41

*Mons Pico*

*Landau*

23

*Mons Gruithuisen Gamma*

**OCEANUS**

*Mons Rümker*

*Mons Gruithuisen Delta*

**MARE IMBRIUM**

*Montes Alpes*

*Rima Calippus*

*Lorentz*

1 25

*Archimedes*

**MARE SERENITATIS**

30

29

*Vallis Schröteri*

13

42

9

8

**MARE INSULARUM**

7

*Lacus Doloris*

3

**MARE VAPORUM**

5

10

**PROCELLARUM**

12

15

16

*Kepler*

14

17

20

**MARE TRANQUILLITATIS**

11

21 24

*Hertzsprung*

2

*Grimaldi*

4

6

28

*Montes Rook*

*Mons Hansteen*

**MARE ORIENTALE**

*Gassendi*

**MARE HUMORUM**

**MARE NUMBIUM**

**MARE NECTARIS**

*Montes Pyrenaeus*

35

*Mendel*

18

*Schickard*

*Vallis Rheita*

*Phocylides*

*Clavius*

*Hausen*

*Bailly*

*Zeeman*

38

37

34

## Landmark missions

Most lunar spacecraft were launched as part of a series of similar missions. The US Ranger Program, for example, included nine missions, only three of which were successful. The first 20 or so years of Moon missions were driven by rivalry between the US and the USSR, who saw conquering space as a sign of military might or political strength.

## Ranger program

The US Ranger spacecraft of the early 1960s were designed not to land on the Moon but to crash into it. In the moments before impact, they beamed back stunning images of the surface, revealing craters of ever smaller size within larger craters.

## Lunokhod

Russia's Lunokhod ("moonwalker") rovers looked like bathtubs on wheels but were a great success. Lunokhod 1 was the first rover to explore another world. It traveled nearly 7 miles (11 km) in 1970–71 and took thousands of pictures. Powered by solar panels, it hibernated at night.

India's Moon Impact Probe of 2008 crashed at high speed into the Moon to throw up debris from the surface.

6 US Apollo missions landed astronauts on the Moon and brought them safely home.

27

# Exploring the Moon

**Spacecraft have paid more visits to Earth's neighbor than any other body in the solar system, and the Moon remains the only world beyond Earth that people have set foot on.**

It takes only four days for a spacecraft to reach the Moon, which makes it an obvious target for robotic explorers. More than 100 missions to the Moon have been attempted, and more than 40 spacecraft have landed on it—their landing sites are shown on this map. Making a controlled, soft touchdown on the Moon is difficult, so most landers have performed "hard landings," crashing into the lunar surface at high speed. The first hard landing was in 1959, and the first soft landing took place in 1966. Remarkably, just three years later, the US Apollo 11 mission placed two men on the Moon and returned them safely to Earth.

| | Name | Year | Country |
|---|---|---|---|
| 1 | Luna 2 | 1959 | |
| 2 | Ranger 4 | 1962 | |
| 3 | Ranger 6 | 1964 | |
| 4 | Ranger 7 | 1964 | |
| 5 | Ranger 8 | 1965 | |
| 6 | Ranger 9 | 1965 | |
| 7 | Luna 5 | 1965 | |
| 8 | Luna 7 | 1965 | |
| 9 | Luna 8 | 1965 | |
| 10 | Luna 9 | 1966 | |
| 11 | Surveyor 1 | 1966 | |
| 12 | Surveyor 2 | 1966 | |
| 13 | Luna 13 | 1966 | |
| 14 | Surveyor 3 | 1967 | |
| 15 | Surveyor 4 | 1967 | |
| 16 | Surveyor 5 | 1967 | |
| 17 | Surveyor 6 | 1967 | |
| 18 | Surveyor 7 | 1978 | |
| 19 | Luna 15 | 1969 | |
| 20 | Apollo 11 | 1969 | |
| 21 | Apollo 12 | 1969 | |
| 22 | Luna 16 | 1970 | |
| 23 | Luna 17/Lunokhod 1 | 1970 | |
| 24 | Apollo 14 | 1971 | |
| 25 | Apollo 15 | 1971 | |
| 26 | Luna 18 | 1971 | |
| 27 | Luna 20 | 1972 | |
| 28 | Apollo 16 | 1972 | |
| 29 | Apollo 17 | 1972 | |
| 30 | Luna 21/Lunokhod 2 | 1973 | |
| 31 | Luna 23 | 1974 | |
| 32 | Luna 24 | 1976 | |
| 33 | Hiten* | 1993 | |
| 34 | Lunar prospector* | 1999 | |
| 35 | SMART-1* | 2006 | esa |
| 36 | Chang'e 1* | 2007 | |
| 37 | Chandrayaan 1* | 2008 | |
| 38 | LCROSS | 2009 | |
| 39 | SELENE* | 2009 | |
| 40 | GRAIL* | 2012 | |
| 41 | Chang'e 3/Yutu | 2013 | |
| 42 | LADEE* | 2014 | |

*Lunar orbiters that impacted at the end of their missions.

### Apollo program
The success of Russia's Luna Program led their American rivals to invest billions of dollars in the Apollo program, which succeeded in landing six crewed craft on the Moon between 1969 and 1972. Later Apollo missions took a kind of car, the Lunar Roving Vehicle (LRV).

### Yutu rover
China's Yutu rover arrived on the Moon in 2013, the first lunar rover since Lunokhod 2 in 1973. Although successful at first, it became unable to fold up its solar panels in preparation for the freezing lunar nights and was damaged by the cold. It drove a short distance after landing with the Chang'e 3 spacecraft.

# Impact craters

**Asteroids, comets, and meteorites fly through space at such terrific speeds that they release devastating energy when they collide with planets and moons, vaporizing solid rock in an instant. The scars they leave behind are called impact craters.**

Meteorite impacts have scarred the rocky planets and moons with countless craters. Our Moon is covered with craters, but Earth has far fewer—on Earth, craters are destroyed by erosion and other forces, while those on the Moon remain preserved for billions of years. Many of the Moon's craters formed early in the solar system's history, when the inner planets were bombarded by asteroids. Collisions are much more rare today, but they still pose a deadly risk to Earth.

**Ejecta curtain**
After the meteorite hits, fragments of pulverized rock called ejecta are flung out in a vast cone and fall back to the ground far from the impact site.

**Lunar impact**
The explosive force of a meteorite impact comes not just from the object's size but also from its speed. A typical meteorite is traveling at about 45,000 mph (70,000 km/h) when it collides with a body such as the Moon, as shown here. This means it has 1,000 times as much kinetic energy as an equal-sized rock traveling at the speed of a car. When the meteorite collides, much of this kinetic energy turns into heat, causing rock in the ground to melt or even vaporize (turn to gas).

Below the Moon's surface dust layer is a deep layer of shattered rock fragments from past impacts.

**Impact site**
The meteorite usually vaporizes entirely on impact, but traces of telltale elements such as iridium are often left at the impact site.

Vredefort crater in South Africa—the largest crater on Earth—is around **2 billion years old**.

The Aitken Basin impact crater on the Moon's south pole is **1,550 miles (2,500 km)** wide.

**29**

## Barringer Crater

Barringer Crater (also known as Meteor Crater) in Arizona was the first site on Earth to be identified as an impact crater. Measuring 0.7 miles (just over 1 km) wide, it formed some 50,000 years ago when a nickel-iron meteorite only 160 ft (50 m) or so wide struck the ground at around 30,000 mph (50,000 km/h). The collision unleashed a thousand times more energy than the Hiroshima atomic bomb.

## How craters form

It takes a mere ten minutes for an impact crater to fully form, but most of the action happens in the split second after impact, when the release of kinetic energy causes an effect like a nuclear explosion. Small impacts leave bowl-shaped pits, but larger impacts create more complex craters with central hills or terraces.

Impact

Shock wave

**1 Contact**
The meteorite smashes into the Moon, compressing the surface dramatically and sending a devastating shock wave through the ground, pulverizing lunar rock.

Vapor    Ejecta curtain

Melt

Shock wave

**2 Transient crater forms**
Energy released by the impact vaporizes the meteorite and much of the surface rock. Debris is thrown out in an ejecta curtain, forming a deep but transient crater.

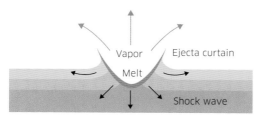

Uplift of crater floor

Ejecta    Ejecta

Material flow

Rebound

**3 Collapse and rebound**
The force of a large impact is so great that the pulverized ground flows like a liquid. The sides of the transient crater collapse, and the crater floor rebounds like water splashing, creating a central hill.

Central hill    Solidified melt layer

Collapse zone    Ejecta layer

**4 Final crater**
After a crater forms, its shape may remain unchanged for a long time, unless altered by volcanic or other geological activity. On the Moon, old craters frequently have younger craters within them.

Small meteorites usually make simple, bowl-shaped craters no more than 2.5 miles (4 km) wide.

The Moon's surface is covered by a thick sheet of fine dust from thousands of impacts.

# Eclipses

**A total solar eclipse is an amazing event. For a few minutes, the Sun disappears behind the Moon and day turns suddenly to night.**

Eclipses happen when Earth and the Moon line up with the Sun and cast shadows on each other. When the Moon casts a shadow on Earth, our view of the Sun is blocked and we see a solar eclipse. When the Moon swings behind Earth and passes through Earth's shadow, we see a lunar eclipse—the Moon darkens and turns an unusual reddish color.

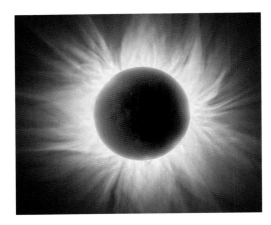

## The corona
During a total solar eclipse, the Sun's spectacular outer atmosphere, which is normally impossible to see, becomes visible. Called the corona, it consists of billowing streams of hazy gas surrounding the Sun like a glowing white halo.

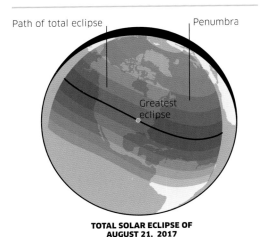

Path of total eclipse    Penumbra

Greatest eclipse

**TOTAL SOLAR ECLIPSE OF AUGUST 21, 2017**

## Eclipse path
Astronomers can predict eclipses years in advance. This diagram shows where the total solar eclipse of 2017 will be visible. It will pass across North America from Portland, Oregon, at 5:15 pm Universal Time to Charleston, South Carolina, at 6:45 pm Universal Time.

## Solar eclipse
On most of its monthly orbits around Earth, the Moon does not line up directly with the Sun. When the Moon's main shadow (umbra) does sweep across Earth, it is only a few miles wide, so a total eclipse is visible only from a narrow strip across the globe. People viewing from the outer part of the shadow (the penumbra) barely notice the eclipse because the Sun is not completely covered. As Earth rotates, the umbra sweeps across the planet's surface quickly, giving viewers in any one spot only a couple of minutes to see it.

**MOON'S ORBIT**

**SUNLIGHT**

**SUN**

**108** minutes—the **longest lunar eclipse** in the last century.

In 1504 Christopher Columbus amazed the native people of Jamaica by correctly predicting a **lunar eclipse**.

The eclipsed Moon can appear **red, yellow, orange, or brown.**

**31**

## Lunar eclipse

In a total lunar eclipse, Earth's shadow covers the entire Moon. The Moon doesn't disappear from the night sky altogether, though, because some sunlight is deflected by Earth's atmosphere. This weak light is reddish like the light from a sunset and so it changes the Moon's color.

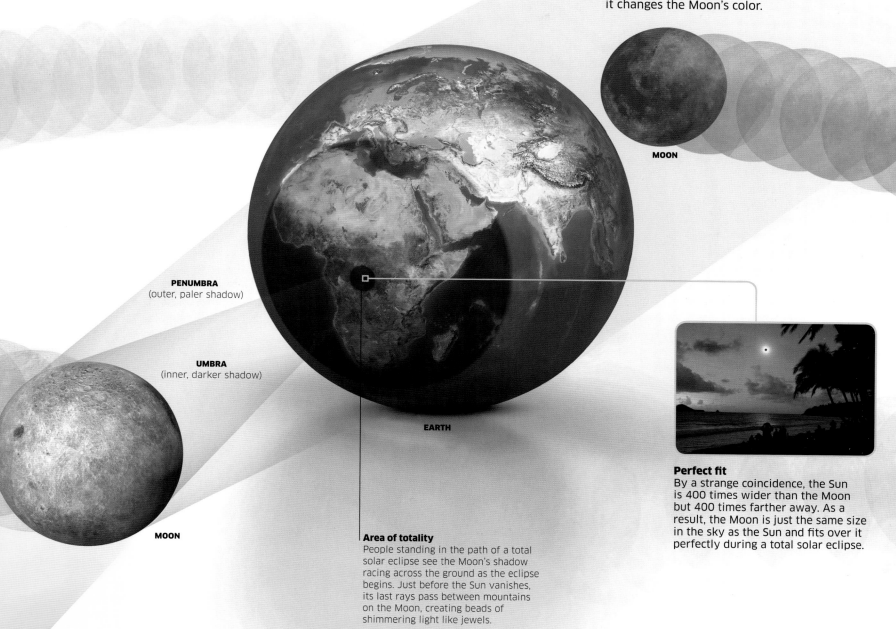

MOON

PENUMBRA
(outer, paler shadow)

UMBRA
(inner, darker shadow)

MOON

EARTH

**Perfect fit**
By a strange coincidence, the Sun is 400 times wider than the Moon but 400 times farther away. As a result, the Moon is just the same size in the sky as the Sun and fits over it perfectly during a total solar eclipse.

**Area of totality**
People standing in the path of a total solar eclipse see the Moon's shadow racing across the ground as the eclipse begins. Just before the Sun vanishes, its last rays pass between mountains on the Moon, creating beads of shimmering light like jewels.

**Red Moon**
Total lunar eclipses happen on average about once a year and are easy to see because anyone on Earth's night side can watch. Over several hours, Earth's shadow slowly creeps across the Moon's face, giving the remaining bright part of the Moon a peculiar shape. The period of totality, when the Moon turns red, can last nearly two hours.

**Surface temperatures** on Mars can plunge to **-225°F (-143°C).**

The **most recent volcanic eruption** on Mars happened 2 million years ago.

# Mars

**Earth's second nearest neighbor in space is Mars—a freezing desert world that may once have harbored life.**

Mars is half Earth's size and much colder, but its arid surface looks oddly familiar, with rocky plains, rolling hills, and sand dunes much like those on Earth. The dusty ground is tinged brownish red by rust (iron oxide) and makes Mars look reddish from Earth, which is why the ancient Greeks and Romans named the planet after their god of war. Mars may have been warmer and wetter in the past, and there are signs that water once flowed across its surface, carving out gullies and laying down sedimentary rock. There may even be fossils of alien life forms hidden in the ground.

**On the surface**
The first soft landing on Mars was made by the Soviet probe Mars 3 in 1971. More than 20 spacecraft have successfully flown close to, orbited, or landed on Mars. Seven of these were landers that successfully returned data. Many missions to Mars have ended in failure, but some successful missions have placed robotic rovers on the planet, such as the car-sized rover Curiosity (above), which arrived in 2012.

**Core**
Mars's small, hot core is mostly iron, but unlike Earth's core it is largely solid. Only the outer layer is partially molten.

Like Earth, Mars has permanent caps of ice at the poles.

**Surface**
The desertlike surface is made of rocky plains and valleys, rolling hills, mountains, and canyons. Sandy areas are pale; areas of bare rock look darker.

**Valles Marineris**
A gigantic canyon system called Valles Marineris is etched deep in the planet's surface near the equator.

**Olympus Mons**
Mars is home to the largest volcano in the solar system: Olympus Mons. Its summit is 22 km (14 miles) high, making it three times taller than Mount Everest, though its slopes are so wide and gentle that a visitor would barely see it. Unlike Earth's volcanoes, those on Mars can keep growing for millions of years because the planet's crust doesn't move about.

Mars has the **largest dust storms** in the solar system.

Only **18 out of 40** missions to Mars have been successful.

**33**

## FAST FACTS

**Surface gravity (Earth = 1):** 0.38

**Time to rotate once:** 24.6 hours

**Year:** 687 Earth days

**Moons:** 2

### Crust

The crust is made mostly of volcanic rock, covered in dust. Unlike Earth's crust, which is broken into moving plates, the Martian crust is a solid shell.

### Mantle

Under the crust is Mars's mantle: a deep layer of silicate rock. In the past, the planet's internal heat kept the mantle soft enough to move like molasses, warping the crust and creating volcanoes.

## Moons

Mars has two small, potato-shaped moons: Phobos, named after the Greek god of fear, and Deimos, named after the Greek god of terror. The moons may be asteroids that flew close to Mars and were captured by the planet's gravity.

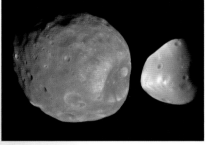

**PHOBOS**          **DEIMOS**

## Orbit and seasons

Mars rotates in just under 25 hours, making its day much the same as Earth's. Its year, though, is longer, lasting 687 days. Because Mars is tilted on its axis, like Earth, it has four seasons—winter, spring, summer, and fall—but they are all freezing cold and bone dry.

### Atmosphere

Mars has a thin atmosphere made mostly of carbon dioxide gas. Strong winds sometimes whip up clouds of dust from the arid ground.

Billions of years ago, vast
**rivers flowed**
on the Martian surface,
carving out giant valleys.

Summer          Winter

**SEASONS IN NORTHERN HEMISPHERE**

Noctis Labyrinthus

Hebes Chasma

Ius Chasma

Ophir Chasma

Capri Chasma

Syria Planum

Sinai Planum

Melas Chasma

Candor Chasma

Coprates Chasma

### Sand dunes

Windblown sand collects on the floor of Valles Marineris, forming huge dunes. In this false-color photo from the Mars Reconnaissance Orbiter, the reddish Martian sand appears blue. The patterns are continually changing as the dunes slowly migrate, blown by the wind.

### Flood channels

In and around Valles Marineris are smaller valleys called outflow channels. These might have formed when ice suddenly melted, triggering floods, or they might have been created by volcanic eruptions.

Syria Planum

Deep trenches called graben formed here as giant slabs of rock dropped away.

Canyon floors are covered with rubble and dust from landslides.

Sinai Planum

Valles Marineris is long enough to stretch from **New York to Los Angeles**.

The canyons contain **one-fifth of all the sand dunes** on Mars.

**35**

# Valles Marineris

**Five times as long and almost four times as deep as Earth's Grand Canyon, the massive Valles Marineris canyon system on Mars is one of the wonders of the solar system.**

Named after the Mariner 9 spacecraft that discovered it in 1972, Valles Marineris is a gigantic crack that first ripped open early in Mars's history as nearby volcanoes made the planet's crust bulge. Today it stretches a fifth of the way around Mars and resembles a vast slash in the planet's face. Over billions of years, floods have gouged out deeper channels and landslides have destroyed valley walls, creating an amazingly varied landscape of canyons, cliffs, and dunes.

### Maze of the night
At its western end, Valles Marineris splits into a maze of steep-walled canyons known as Noctis Labyrinthus, or "maze of the night." The valleys here have more water-related minerals than any other place on Mars. Two billion years ago, when the rest of Mars was dry, they may have been moist enough to harbor life.

A chain of giant volcanoes lies to the west of Valles Marineris.

Some of the canyons in Noctis Labyrinthus are over 16,000 ft (5,000 m) deep.

### Formation
Valles Marineris began to form around 3.5 billion years ago when volcanic activity made a nearby region of the Martian crust bulge and split. Powerful forces pulled the crust apart, causing a central section to drop and form a deep valley. The valley grew wider over time as its walls eroded.

Cliffs collapse in landslides, widening valley

Sediment collects on valley floor

Crust splits and pulls apart

Valley floor sinks

### Size
The immense Valles Marineris is more than 2,500 miles (4,000 km) long and up to 4.3 miles (7 km) deep. It dwarfs the Grand Canyon in Arizona, which is about 500 miles (800 km) long and 1 mile (1.6 km) deep.

Grand Canyon

Valles Marineris

**36** the solar system ○ **EXPLORING MARS**

**150–300** days—the time taken for a spacecraft to reach Mars.

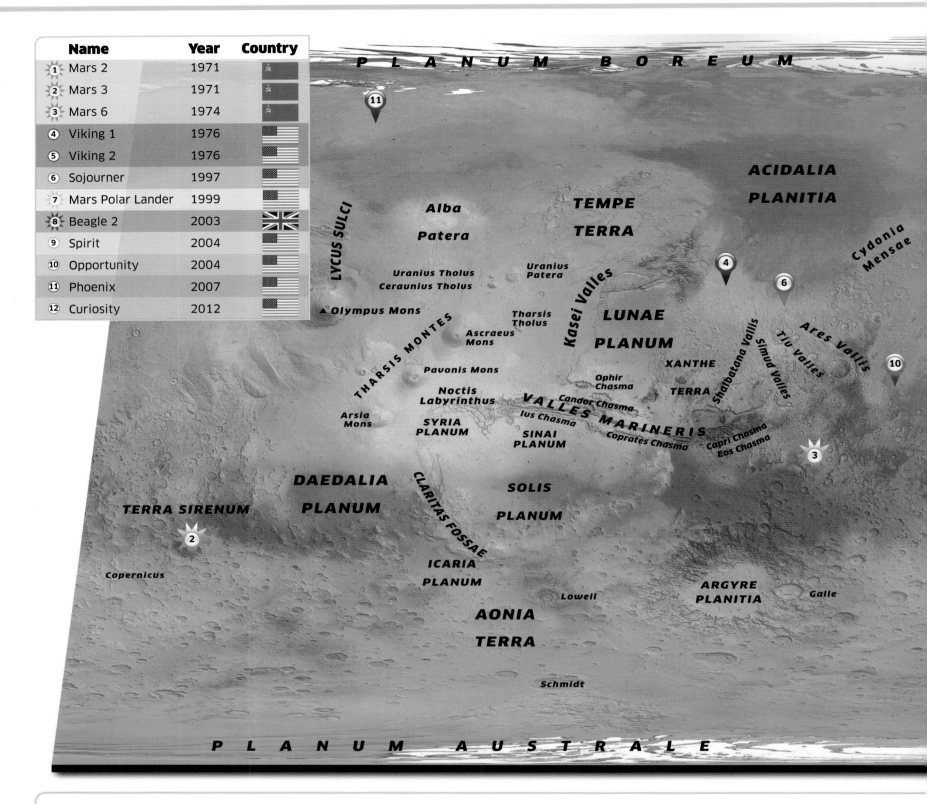

| Name | Year | Country |
|------|------|---------|
| 1 Mars 2 | 1971 | |
| 2 Mars 3 | 1971 | |
| 3 Mars 6 | 1974 | |
| 4 Viking 1 | 1976 | |
| 5 Viking 2 | 1976 | |
| 6 Sojourner | 1997 | |
| 7 Mars Polar Lander | 1999 | |
| 8 Beagle 2 | 2003 | |
| 9 Spirit | 2004 | |
| 10 Opportunity | 2004 | |
| 11 Phoenix | 2007 | |
| 12 Curiosity | 2012 | |

### Viking invaders

In July 1976, Viking 1 became the first spacecraft to land on Mars, followed in September by Viking 2 (above). The landers tested the Martian soil for biological activity but found no evidence of life.

### Bounce-down on Mars

The Pathfinder spacecraft used airbags to land safely on Mars in 1997. It bounced five times before coming to a stop. The airbags then deflated and the spacecraft's side panels folded open like petals to allow a small rover to drive out.

**6** years, 3 months, 22 days—the length of time **Viking 1 continued to work** on Mars.

**330 ft** (100 m)—the distance that the **Sojourner rover traveled** on Mars.

**37**

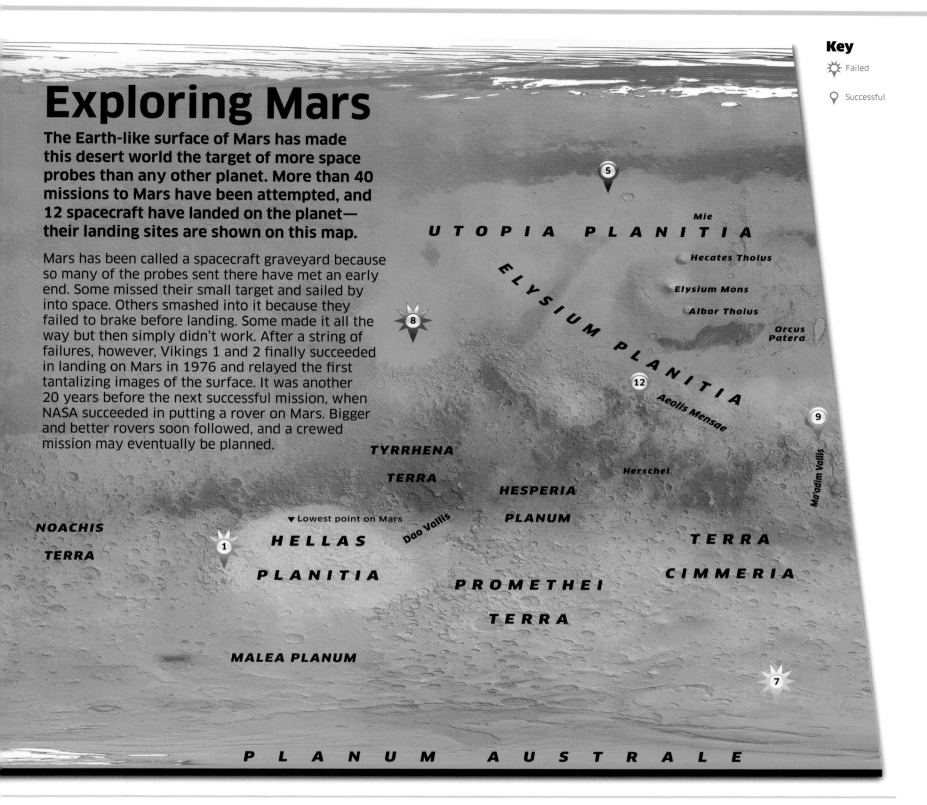

**Key**

☼ Failed

📍 Successful

# Exploring Mars

**The Earth-like surface of Mars has made this desert world the target of more space probes than any other planet. More than 40 missions to Mars have been attempted, and 12 spacecraft have landed on the planet—their landing sites are shown on this map.**

Mars has been called a spacecraft graveyard because so many of the probes sent there have met an early end. Some missed their small target and sailed by into space. Others smashed into it because they failed to brake before landing. Some made it all the way but then simply didn't work. After a string of failures, however, Vikings 1 and 2 finally succeeded in landing on Mars in 1976 and relayed the first tantalizing images of the surface. It was another 20 years before the next successful mission, when NASA succeeded in putting a rover on Mars. Bigger and better rovers soon followed, and a crewed mission may eventually be planned.

UTOPIA PLANITIA

ELYSIUM PLANITIA

Mie

Hecates Tholus

Elysium Mons

Albor Tholus

Orcus Patera

Aeolis Mensae

Ma'adim Vallis

Herschel

TYRRHENA TERRA

HESPERIA PLANUM

Dao Vallis

▼ Lowest point on Mars

NOACHIS TERRA

HELLAS PLANITIA

TERRA CIMMERIA

PROMETHEI TERRA

MALEA PLANUM

PLANUM AUSTRALE

**Missing in action**
In 2003 the Beagle 2 lander from the Mars Express mission began its descent to the Martian surface. Then it went silent. Everyone assumed it had crashed, but in 2014 it was spotted intact on the Mars surface by another probe. It seems that the solar panels simply failed to open.

**Curiosity rover**
The Curiosity rover is the most successful Martian visitor so far and has sent back a huge amount of data. On August 6, 2013, Curiosity marked the anniversary of its landing by playing "Happy Birthday" out loud—the first time music has been played on another planet.

# Red planet

**The rust-colored landscapes of Mars remind us of sandy deserts on Earth, but the temperature here is as cold as Earth's South Pole in midwinter.**

Mars would be deadly to humans without spacesuits, but conditions are ideal for robotic rovers. NASA's car-sized Curiosity rover took this photo of its tracks on February 9, 2014—day 538 of its tour of Mars. The distant hills form part of the rim of a 96-mile- (155-km-) wide crater that Curiosity is searching for signs that Mars may once have been suitable for life.

## Asteroid belt

Most asteroids are in a doughnut-shaped belt between the orbits of Mars and Jupiter, but there are also scattered asteroids among the inner planets and large groups of asteroids in the same orbit as Jupiter, known as Trojans. The belt often looks crowded in illustrations, but in reality the asteroids are so far apart that passengers on a spacecraft flying through the belt probably wouldn't see a single one. The total mass of all the asteroids in the belt is only 4 percent of the Moon's mass.

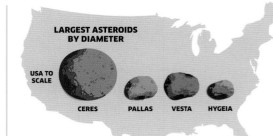

LARGEST ASTEROIDS BY DIAMETER

USA TO SCALE

CERES   PALLAS   VESTA   HYGEIA

## Size

Large asteroids are very rare—only 26 asteroids are known to be more than 125 miles (200 km) wide. However, there are hundreds of thousands of asteroids wider than 0.6 miles (1 km) and millions of smaller ones.

# Asteroids

**Millions of rocks known as asteroids hurtle around the inner solar system, most of them in a belt between the orbits of Mars and Jupiter. They range in size from pebbles to monsters hundreds of miles wide.**

Asteroids are leftovers from the cloud of rubble that gave birth to the planets. Most of the rubble in the inner solar system collected together to become the rocky planets, but the rocks near Jupiter were disturbed by the giant planet's gravity and failed to build up. The asteroid belt is what remains today of that debris. Asteroids follow their own orbits around the Sun, spinning as they go, like planets. They are also called minor planets, and the largest asteroid of all, Ceres, is classed as a dwarf planet. Asteroids occasionally collide, forming craters or even smashing each other. Less often, they crash into moons and planets.

**Head and body**
The shape of Toutatis suggests it might have formed from two asteroids that stuck together, a small asteroid forming the "head" (left) and a larger one forming the "body." Most asteroids have an irregular shape, but the largest ones pull themselves into a sphere through their own gravity.

**2001** The year of the **first soft landing** on an asteroid.

**2069** The year that the asteroid Toutatis will next **pass close to Earth**.

**0** The chance of Toutatis **hitting Earth** in the next **600 years**.

**41**

Because of its potato shape, Toutatis spins around two axes. As a result, it tumbles through space like **a badly thrown football.**

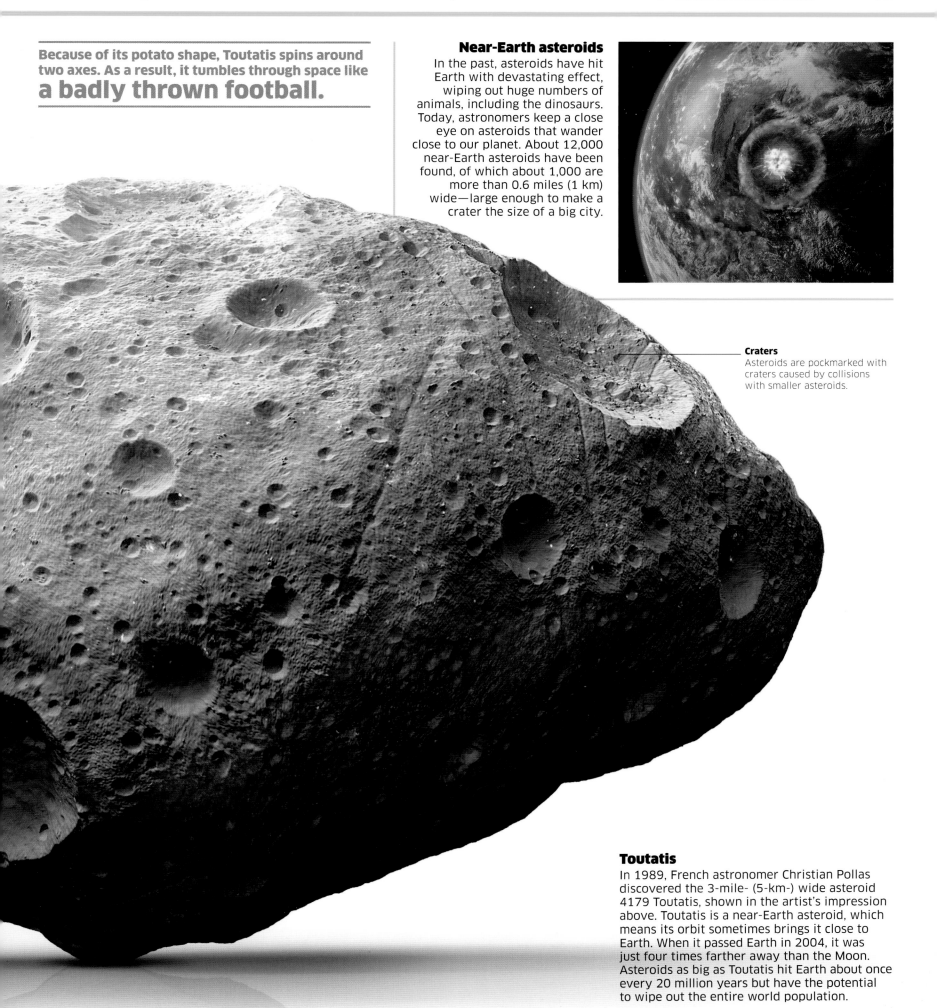

## Near-Earth asteroids

In the past, asteroids have hit Earth with devastating effect, wiping out huge numbers of animals, including the dinosaurs. Today, astronomers keep a close eye on asteroids that wander close to our planet. About 12,000 near-Earth asteroids have been found, of which about 1,000 are more than 0.6 miles (1 km) wide—large enough to make a crater the size of a big city.

**Craters**
Asteroids are pockmarked with craters caused by collisions with smaller asteroids.

## Toutatis

In 1989, French astronomer Christian Pollas discovered the 3-mile- (5-km-) wide asteroid 4179 Toutatis, shown in the artist's impression above. Toutatis is a near-Earth asteroid, which means its orbit sometimes brings it close to Earth. When it passed Earth in 2004, it was just four times farther away than the Moon. Asteroids as big as Toutatis hit Earth about once every 20 million years but have the potential to wipe out the entire world population.

# Shooting stars and meteorites

**The shooting stars we sometimes see streaking across the night sky are not stars at all, but tiny flecks of space rock. Millions of these rock fragments, called meteoroids, hurtle into Earth's atmosphere every year.**

Most meteoroids come from the asteroid belt or from comets, but a few are chipped off the Moon or Mars by meteorite impacts. They are usually no bigger than a grain of sand, but even tiny grains hit the atmosphere so hard and fast—at up to 44 miles (71 km) per second—that they make the air glow brightly as they ram into it, causing the streak of light we call a meteor or shooting star. Most meteoroids burn up entirely in the atmosphere, but a few really big ones survive to crash into the ground as meteorites.

### Incoming meteorite

When a big space rock hits the atmosphere, the effect is dramatic. The air in its path is squeezed violently and heated until it glows brilliantly. As the rock tears through the air, its outer layers are scorched and blasted away, forming trails of vapor and smoke that stream out behind it. A large stony meteoroid can get so hot that it bursts in midair, exploding in a dazzling flash and unleashing a deep roar that carries for miles.

### Rocks in the sky

Meteoroids the size of sand grains become meteors (shooting stars), which are only visible at night. Those as big as basketballs can create brilliant "fireballs" that are visible even by day and may leave a trail of smoke. Some big stony meteoroids hit the atmosphere with such force that they explode in midair. The blast from these "air-burst meteors" can flatten trees. Meteoroids that reach the ground and survive are called meteorites.

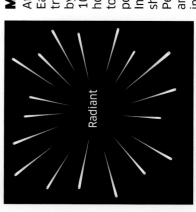

Air-burst meteor
Fireball meteor
Meteor
Meteorite
Meteorite survives impact

### Meteor showers

At certain times of year, Earth passes through the trail of dust left in space by a comet, causing over 100 visible meteors an hour. They all appear to come from the same point, called the radiant. Impressive meteor showers include the Perseids in August and the Geminids in December.

Radiant

### Big hitters

The largest meteorite in North America is the Willamette meteorite in the American Museum of Natural History. This 15-ton lump of iron and nickel is so heavy it has its own foundations to stop it from falling through the museum floor.

**WILLAMETTE METEORITE, 1939**

Every year more than **30,000 meteorites** larger than a strawberry collide with Earth.

In 1908 a **meteor airburst over Siberia** flattened 770 square miles (2,000 square km) of trees.

**4.55** billion years—the **age of most meteoroids**.

**43**

Heat melts or vaporizes the meteoroid's surface as it plows through the atmosphere.

**100** tons of meteors and meteorites collide with Earth every day—about the same weight as 20 elephants.

The glowing colors reveal which chemical elements are present. Iron glows yellow, for instance, while blue-green shows that magnesium is present, and violet indicates calcium.

Ahead of the meteorite, air is compressed with such force that it becomes white-hot and glows.

**Comets and asteroids** have been observed **crashing into Jupiter.**

**−234°F** (−148°C)—the **temperature** of Jupiter's cloud tops.

# Jupiter

**The largest planet of all, Jupiter is more than twice as massive as all the other planets combined. Unlike rocky worlds, such as Earth or Mars, Jupiter is a gas giant—a vast, spinning globe of gas and liquid with no solid surface.**

Jupiter is 1,300 times greater in volume than Earth, and the pull of its gravity is so great that it bends the paths of comets and asteroids flying through the solar system. Despite the planet's great size, it spins quickly, giving it a day less than ten hours long. The rapid rotation makes Jupiter bulge visibly at its equator and whips its colorful clouds into horizontal stripes and swirling storms. The largest storm—the Great Red Spot—is bigger than Earth. Lightning storms flicker through the blackness on Jupiter's night side, and the whole planet is surrounded by belts of lethal radiation that would make a crewed mission extremely dangerous.

Jupiter is 318 times more massive than Earth.

**Core**
At Jupiter's center is a rock core that's hotter than the surface of the Sun. It makes up about 10 percent of the planet's mass.

**Storm spots**
Storms in Jupiter's atmosphere form ovals of different colors. The 7,450-mile- (12,000-km-) wide Great Red Spot has been raging for several hundred years. Its red color is probably caused by sunlight breaking up chemicals in the tops of the highest clouds.

**225** mph (360 km/h)—**typical wind speed** on Jupiter.

**29** miles (46 km) per second—the **speed at which the Galileo probe** entered Jupiter's atmosphere.

Jupiter gives out **1.6 times more energy** than falls on it, due to **internal heating** of the planet.

**45**

Partially opened antenna

## Galileo spacecraft

Although hampered by a partially opened communications dish, this NASA spacecraft made many important discoveries about Jupiter and its moons after its arrival in 1995. It released a probe that dived into Jupiter's clouds and then opened a parachute, allowing it to analyze the chemicals. Galileo orbited Jupiter until 2003.

### Polar lights

Spectacular light displays called auroras (seen here in ultraviolet light) sometimes occur at Jupiter's poles. Like Earth's northern and southern lights, they are caused by charged particles from space that crash into the atmosphere and make the gas atoms glow. The auroras on Jupiter are up to 100 times brighter than those on Earth.

### Liquid metallic layer

Under huge pressure, the hydrogen deep inside Jupiter behaves like a liquid metal. Helium and neon are probably also present in this layer.

### Liquid layer

Above the metallic layer is a vast sea of liquid hydrogen. This sea has no surface; instead, it gradually thins out at the top, merging with the gas in Jupiter's atmosphere.

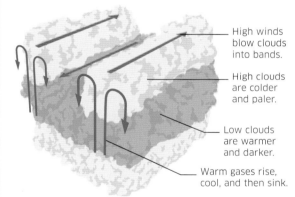

High winds blow clouds into bands.

High clouds are colder and paler.

Low clouds are warmer and darker.

Warm gases rise, cool, and then sink.

## Cloud bands

Jupiter's colorful bands are made up of clouds at different heights. In the paler bands, gases are rising and forming high icy clouds. Gaps between these bands of high clouds allow us to see down to the warmer cloud layers below, which are darker in color.

### Atmosphere

Hydrogen gas makes up 90 percent of Jupiter's atmosphere. The rest is mostly helium, with small amounts of other elements.

Winds blow in opposite directions in neighboring cloud bands, causing swirling patterns at the boundaries.

### Cloud layer

The cloud layer is only 30 miles (50 km) thick. Most of the clouds are thought to consist of frozen ammonia crystals.

**FAST FACTS**

**Surface gravity (Earth = 1):** 2.36

**Time to rotate once:** 9.9 hours

**Year:** 12 Earth years

**Moons:** At least 67

## Tenuous rings

Jupiter's faint rings were first seen in 1979 in images taken by Voyager 1. They have since been detected from Earth by viewing the planet in infrared light. The rings consist mainly of dust from Jupiter's smaller moons.

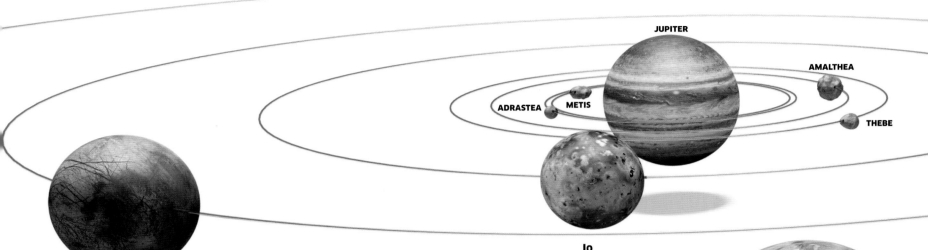

JUPITER

AMALTHEA

ADRASTEA    METIS

THEBE

**Io**
Caught in a tug-of-war between
the gravity of Jupiter and the
other Galilean moons, Io is torn by
powerful forces that have melted its
insides. Molten rock, rich in colorful
sulfur chemicals, erupts all over its
surface from giant volcanoes.

**Europa**
Europa's icy surface is covered in
strange grooves and cracks. Just as
Earth's crust of rock is broken into
colliding fragments, so Europa's crust
of ice is broken into sheets that push
and pull in opposite directions. Water
from a salty ocean deep underground
erupts from the cracks and freezes,
creating new ground.

# Moons of Jupiter

**Jupiter's massive size makes the pull of its
gravity strong. As a result, the giant planet has
trapped nearly 70 known moons in orbit around
it. Some are probably asteroids or comets that
flew too close to Jupiter and were captured by
its gravity. Others are as large as planets.**

Jupiter's four largest moons are called the Galilean
moons because they were discovered by the great
Italian astronomer Galileo Galilei in 1610. These four
worlds are very different. The innermost moon, Io, has
hundreds of active volcanoes. Next is Europa, which is
covered in ice, though a hidden ocean may lie below—
one of the few places in the solar system that might
harbor life. Ganymede is the solar system's largest
moon and the only one with a magnetic field. Callisto
is covered in craters. Its surface is considered the
oldest of any moon or planet in the solar system.

**Ganymede**
This large moon is nearly 10 percent wider
than Mercury and would be called a planet
if it orbited the Sun rather than Jupiter. Its
surface is a jigsaw puzzle of ancient dark
areas with lots of craters, and younger,
paler areas with few craters. Eruptions of
slushy ice from underground have
resurfaced the younger areas.

**Jupiter's moons to scale**

GANYMEDE
CALLISTO
IO
EUROPA
HIMALIA
AMALTHEA
THEBE
ELARA
PASIPHAÉ
CARME
METIS
SINOPE
LYSITHEA
ANANKE
ADRASTEA
LEDA
CALLIRRHOE
THEMISTO
PRAXIDIKE
IOCASTE
TAYGETE
KALYKE
MEGACLITE
S/2000 J11
HELIKE
HARPALYKE
HERMIPPE
THYONE
CHALDENE
AOEDE
EUKELADE
ISONOE
S/2003 J5
AUTONOE
CARPO
EUANTHE
AITNE
ERINOME
EURYDOME
HEGEMONE
ARCHE
EUPORIE
S/2003 J3
S/2003 J18
THELXINOE
ORTHOSIE
S/2003 J16
MNEME
HERSE
KALE
S/2003 J19
S/2003 J15
S/2003 J10
S/2003 J23
KALLICHORE
PASITHEE
S/2010 J1
KORE
CYLLENE
S/2003 J4
SPONDE
S/2003 J2
S/2003 J12
S/2001 J1
S/2010 J2
S/2011 J2
S/2003 J9

Jupiter's moon Io is the **most volcanically active world** in the entire solar system.

Jupiter's moon Ganymede is **larger than the planet Mercury**.

**47**

### Callisto
The solar system's most heavily cratered object, Callisto is peppered with meteorite craters. The large number of craters shows that its surface is very old. Oddly, there are very few small craters on Callisto. Scientists think small craters gradually fade away as the ice in their rims evaporates into space, leaving small hills.

Jupiter

Callisto

## Outer moons
Jupiter's 60 or so outer moons are only a few miles wide and orbit the planet in a messy cloud. The inner moons travel in the same direction as Jupiter's rotation and their circular orbits line up neatly with Jupiter's equator. In contrast, the outer moons orbit in both directions and their orbits are often wildly tilted or oval. This pattern suggests that most of them are captured objects.

Meteorites have blasted holes in Callisto's dark surface, revealing the pale ice below.

No impact craters have been found on Io's surface. Lava and ash quickly hide the scars of any impacts.

**Volcanic crater**
The volcanic crater Tupan Patera, bounded by steep walls, displays a wide range of colors that are caused by lava mixing with materials rich in sulfur.

**Eruption**
In Io's low gravity, eruptions can throw material hundreds of miles into space.

**Lower mantle**
Surrounding Io's core is a partially molten layer of rock around 600 miles (1,000 km) thick.

Though mostly flat, Io has more than 100 mountains, some reaching 11 miles (18 km) in height.

**Core**
Io may have a core of searing hot molten iron or iron sulfide about 930 miles (1,500 km) wide.

**Tidal forces make the ground on Io rise and fall by up to**
**330 ft (100 m),**
**which is five times greater than the highest ocean tides on Earth.**

**2** trillion watts—the **power of the electric current** that flows between Io and Jupiter.

Io is exposed to such **high radiation levels** that an astronaut on the surface would die within hours.

**49**

**Time to orbit Jupiter:** 1.77 Earth days

**Mass (Earth = 1):** 0.015

**Surface temperature:** –262°F (–163°C)

**Diameter:** 2,262 miles (3,643 km)

IO    THE MOON

**Molten upper mantle**
A 30-mile- (50-km-) thick layer of molten rock probably lies under the moon's crust.

**Atmosphere**
Io has a thin atmosphere of sulfur dioxide that freezes onto the ground at night and evaporates by day. Constant strong winds blow from the sunny side of Io to the dark side.

This active volcano, called Pele, has a lava lake in its central crater.

**Crust**
Io has a 25-mile- (40-km-) thick crust of rock covered with solidified lava and sulfur chemicals from eruptions. The varying colors come from different forms of sulfur.

# Io

**The most volcanically active body in the solar system, Jupiter's moon Io is constantly spewing matter into space from its eruptions. Its blotchy, lava-covered face is a world away from the icy terrain of Jupiter's other moons.**

This moon's volcanic eruptions don't just affect Io itself. They pump huge amounts of material into space, forming a vast, doughnut-shaped ring of charged particles around Jupiter, called a plasma torus. The plasma torus allows electric currents to flow through space between Jupiter and Io, triggering lightning storms in Jupiter and causing gases around Io to glow. The existence of Io's volcanoes was predicted by scientists before the Voyager 1 spacecraft had a close encounter with the moon in 1979. The incredible images Voyager took confirmed the scientists' predictions: Io erupts so frequently that the moon is literally turning itself inside out.

## Tidal heating

The cause of Io's volcanic activity is gravity. As it orbits Jupiter, Io is stretched in different directions by the gravitational pull of Jupiter and the other moons. These tidal forces keep changing Io's shape, causing friction that heats up and melts its interior.

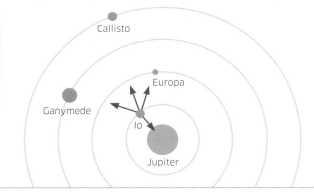

## Changing face

Io's appearance can change quickly because of its frequent eruptions. These two images taken five months apart show how fallout from an eruption blanketed a 250-mile- (400-km-) wide area with black material. The red ring is fallout from another volcano, called Pele.

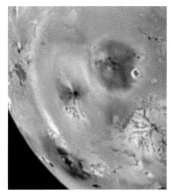

# Saturn

**The spectacular rings around this giant planet make it one of the wonders of our solar system. Saturn is the second-biggest planet after Jupiter, and like Jupiter it has a huge family of moons.**

Saturn is a gas giant—a vast, spinning globe of chemicals that exist as gases on Earth, such as hydrogen. Saturn is 96 percent hydrogen, but only the outer layers are gas. Deep inside the planet, the hydrogen is compressed into a liquid by the weight of the gas above it. Saturn is almost as wide as Jupiter but has less than a third of its mass, making Saturn far less dense. In fact, it is the least dense planet of all. It is also the least spherical: Saturn spins so fast that it bulges at the "waist," making it wider than it is tall. Like Jupiter, it has a stormy outer atmosphere lashed by powerful winds that sweep its clouds into horizontal bands.

Saturn's poles turn blue in winter, an effect caused by sunlight being scattered by relatively cloud-free air.

**Atmosphere**
Saturn's atmosphere is mostly hydrogen and helium, with clouds of ammonia ice and water ice on top. Horizontal winds sweep the creamy-colored clouds into bands like those on Jupiter, but with fewer large eddies and storms.

**Liquid hydrogen layer**
The huge weight of Saturn's atmosphere squeezes the hydrogen underneath into a liquid, forming a vast internal ocean. This sea of liquid hydrogen has no surface—instead, it gradually merges into the gas layer above it.

**Rings**
Saturn's rings are made of fragments of dirty ice orbiting the planet in an almost perfectly flat plane. The ice reflects the Sun's light, often making the rings look very bright.

**FAST FACTS**

**Surface gravity (Earth = 1):** 1.02

**Time to rotate once:** 10.7 hours

**Year:** 29 Earth years

**Moons:** At least 62

Lightning on Saturn is **10,000 times stronger** than lightning on Earth.

Saturn is the only planet in the solar system that is **lighter than water**.

**1979** The year Saturn was first **visited by a spacecraft**.

**51**

**POLAR HEXAGON**

**POLAR HURRICANE**

## Polar hexagon

Around the north pole, clouds form a mysterious hexagonal pattern that has persisted for decades. Each side of the hexagon is wider than Earth. It may be a long-lived wave, but no such pattern is seen at the south pole. In its center is a raging hurricane, shown here in false color, in which wind speeds reach 330 mph (530 km/h)—five times faster than in a hurricane on Earth.

**Core**
At the planet's center there might be a core made of a mixture of rock and the metals iron and nickel.

**Liquid metallic layer**
At great depths, the pressure is so intense that the hydrogen turns into a liquid metal. An additional layer of liquid helium may surround the core.

## Changing view

Saturn is tilted on its axis, so our view of the rings from Earth changes greatly as Saturn orbits the Sun. When the rings are side-on, they are almost invisible. It takes around 15 years for the rings to go from full view to almost invisible and back again.

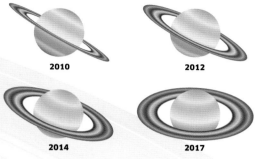

**2010**

**2012**

**2014**

**2017**

## Elongated storm

In 2011 a huge storm broke through Saturn's hazy surface and quickly spread eastward. After a few months, it had spread all the way around the planet, stirring up the clouds into swirls and ripples (shown here in false color).

## Mission to Saturn

In 2004 the nuclear-powered Cassini spacecraft arrived at Saturn, packed with scientific instruments to study the planet and its rings and moons. The data and images it has since sent back have transformed our understanding of Saturn. Cassini released a separate probe, Huygens, that parachuted onto the surface of Saturn's biggest moon, Titan.

Gold-colored space blanket

Radio dish

**CASSINI SPACECRAFT**

# Saturn's rings

**The vast circle of icy debris orbiting Saturn may be the remains of a moon that broke apart in the past. Visible even in small telescopes, Saturn's rings are thousands of miles in diameter but but only a few metres thick.**

Each particle in Saturn's rings is in orbit around the planet, trapped by the gas giant's gravity. The floating chunks of ice also attract each other through gravity, and they are pulled by the gravity of Saturn's moons. All these forces combine to make the material in the rings bunch up at certain distances from Saturn and thin out at others, forming a series of distinct rings and gaps. All the gas giants have ring systems, but those of Jupiter, Uranus, and Neptune are much fainter than Saturn's.

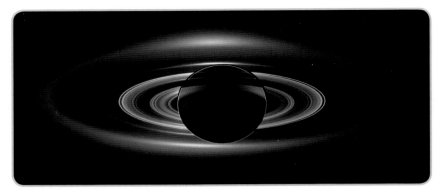

**Through Cassini's eyes**
The Cassini spacecraft has studied the rings in detail since it arrived at Saturn in 2004. In July 2013, Cassini slipped into Saturn's shadow and captured incredible pictures of its rings lit from behind by the Sun. The images reveal hazy, blue outer rings that are not normally visible. The largest of these–the E ring–is a cloud of microscopic ice grains from geysers erupting on Saturn's moon Enceladus.

### Ring system

The main parts of Saturn's rings are given letters, and the gaps within them are named after famous astronomers. The gravitational tug of Saturn's moon Mimas creates the biggest gap, known as the Cassini Division.

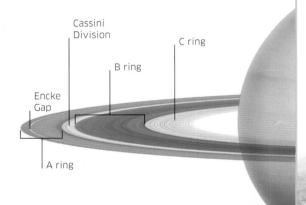

Cassini Division

C ring

B ring

Encke Gap

A ring

### Main rings

The artist's impression below shows the most densely packed part of Saturn's main rings: the B ring. Fragments of ice here occasionally collide and break. The newly exposed icy surfaces capture the sunlight, making Saturn's rings much brighter than the dark, dusty rings of other gas giants.

The icy bodies in the rings range in size from tiny icy grains to boulders as big as houses.

### Shepherd moons

Some of Saturn's moons orbit the planet within the rings. The gravity of these "shepherd moons" sweeps their orbits clear, herding the icy debris elsewhere. Saturn's moon Daphnis (above) also kicks up waves in the rings as it hurtles around the planet.

**174,000** miles (280,000 km)—the **diameter of the main rings**.

**33 ft** (10 m)—the **thickness** of most parts of Saturn's rings.

**4.4** billion years—the likely **age of Saturn's rings**.

53

A comet or asteroid hit Saturn's D ring in 1983, causing wobbles in the ring material that lasted for **over 30 years**.

The rings have their own, very faint atmosphere, mostly made of oxygen.

Most of the ice lies in a very flat plane, but large blocks of ice rise above it, and there are "bumps" up to 2.5 miles (4 km) high.

# Ring world

**Saturn's breathtaking rings are made of billions of sparkling fragments of ice that range in size from snowflakes to icebergs.**

The first person to see the rings was the Italian astronomer Galileo, who called them "ears." Since then, telescopes and spacecraft have revealed ever more detail in the rings, which are made up of thousands of individual ringlets. This image is a mosaic of 126 photos captured by the Cassini spacecraft in 2004. Gravity has pulled the material in the rings into a plane so incredibly thin that a disk of paper made to the same scale would be about 0.9 miles (1.4 km) in diameter.

**56**   the solar system ○ **MOONS OF SATURN**

**150**  The **number of moonlets** so far detected in Saturn's rings.

# Moons of Saturn

**There are so many moons orbiting the planet Saturn that they form what looks like a miniature version of the solar system.**

Saturn has at least 62 known moons, but the true number may be far greater. The innermost moons are part of Saturn's ring system, and some of these have gathered so much dust around their equators that they look like flying saucers. Beyond the rings are Saturn's largest moons, which are hundreds of miles wide and mostly have icy crusts. Largest of all is Titan, which is bigger than the planet Mercury. The inner moons and the large moons all move in the same direction as Saturn's rotation, which suggests they formed at the same time as the planet. Farther out, however, is a chaotic cloud of tiny moons that orbit at wild angles.

Most large moons of Saturn are **tidally locked,** which means they always keep the same side facing Saturn.

**Rhea**
Saturn's second-largest moon has an icy surface with intriguing discolored patches around the equator, which suggest it may once have had rings.

### Orbits of the outer moons

Far from Saturn are dozens of small moons in tilted, noncircular orbits. Many of these orbit in the opposite direction of the main moons. This suggests they formed elsewhere and were captured by Saturn's gravity.

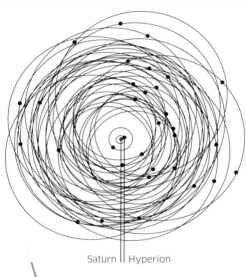

Saturn Hyperion

**Titan**
This is Saturn's largest moon and the second-largest moon in the solar system. It has a thick, hazy atmosphere that hides the surface from view.

**Hyperion**
This peculiar moon has so many deep craters that it looks like a bath sponge. It tumbles as it flies through space, its axis of rotation wobbling due largely to the pull of gravity from Titan. Measurements show that Hyperion is partly empty; large hollows must exist under its surface.

**53** The number of Saturn's moons that have **been named** to date.

Every four years, Saturn's moons Epimetheus and Janus **swap orbits**.

Rhea and Dione both have very thin **oxygen atmospheres**.

**57**

Dione

Prometheus

Atlas

Polydeuces

Daphnis

Telesto

Mimas

Tethys

Pandora

Calypso

Epimetheus

Pan

Janus

Pallene

Enceladus

Methone

### Ice world
Enceladus's icy exterior is the most reflective surface of any body in the solar system. Although the snow-white ground is frozen solid, an ocean of liquid water may lie hidden underneath. Near the south pole, jets of gas and ice grains erupt from ice volcanoes. Much of the ice falls back to the surface, coating Enceladus with volcanic snow.

SATURN

### Saturn's largest 25 moons to scale

TITAN

RHEA

IAPETUS

DIONE

TETHYS

ENCELADUS

MIMAS

HYPERION

PHOEBE

JANUS

EPIMETHEUS

PROMETHEUS

PANDORA

SIARNAQ

HELENE

ALBIORIX

ATLAS

PAN

TELESTO

PAALIAQ

CALYPSO

YMIR

KIVIUQ

TARVOS

IJIRAQ

# Titan

**Saturn's largest moon, Titan, has some tantalizing similarities with Earth. It has nitrogen-rich air, cloudy skies, mountains, rivers, and lakes. However, this chilly world is far too cold for life as we know it.**

In 1980, when the Voyager 1 spacecraft returned the first close-up images of Titan, the scientists back on Earth were disappointed. A thick orange haze covered the moon, hiding its surface from view. However, the haze turned out to be a fascinating mix of the kind of carbon chemicals that existed on Earth billions of years ago, before life began. In the distant future, when the Sun brightens and Titan warms up, conditions on the surface may become just right for life.

## Seeing through the clouds

A layer of haze surrounds Titan, making it impossible to photograph the surface from space. However, the Cassini spacecraft has a radar system that can "see" through the haze by bouncing radio waves off the ground.

**Radar beam**
Each time Cassini flies past Titan, its radar beam can see another strip of the moon's surface, gradually building up to form a complete map.

Cassini

Titan

**Crust**
As hard as solid rock, water ice probably makes up most of Titan's outer crust.

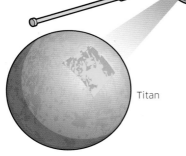

**−5,900 FT (−1,800 M)**          **2,000 FT (600 M)**

## Mapping Titan
Cassini's map of Titan shows the height of the ground in color. The mountain peaks are red. Some of the mountains may be ice volcanoes, from which water rather than lava erupts. As the water flows down the sides, it freezes, making the volcano grow.

## Distant shores

This Cassini radar view has been color-coded to show low-lying, smooth areas as blue, and higher, rougher areas as orange. The colors reveal Titan's lakes and rivers. These contain not water but carbon chemicals such as ethane.

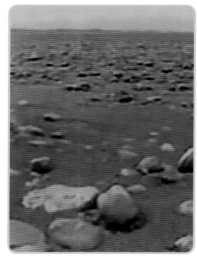

**Surface view**
In January 2005 the European Space Agency's Huygens space probe landed on Titan's surface. Once released from the orbiting Cassini spacecraft, Huygens took three weeks to reach Titan and then parachute down to the surface to return the first images of the hidden world below. This photo shows "rocks" of ice littering the bed of what was once a lake. The smoggy orange sky casts a gloomy light across the whole landscape.

**FAST FACTS**

**Distance from Saturn:** 900 million miles (1.4 billion km)

**Mass (Earth = 1):** 0.002

**Time to rotate once:** 16 Earth days

**Size:** 3,200 miles (5,150 km) wide

**95%** The amount of **nitrogen** in Titan's **atmosphere**.

The **same side** of Titan always faces its parent planet, Saturn.

Titan is the **second-largest moon** in the Solar **System**, after Jupiter's moon Ganymede.

**59**

**Polar lakes**
On Earth, clouds, rain, and lakes are made of water; on Titan, they are made of chemicals called ethane and methane. Both are invisible gases on Earth, but Titan is so cold that there they turn into a liquid. They form droplets in the air that fall as rain, feeding lakes near the north pole, like the one in this artist's impression.

**Atmosphere**
Titan's air is mostly nitrogen, like Earth's air. The nitrogen may have been delivered to Titan by comets crashing into it.

**Core**
Titan's core could be either solid rock or a mixture of ice and rock all the way to the center.

**Mantle**
The top of Titan's mantle might be made of liquid water, forming a hidden ocean. Deeper down, the mantle consists of ice.

The lower part of the mantle is thought to consist of a special kind of ice that forms under high pressure.

## Rocky moons

Uranus's moon Miranda looks as though it was smashed by an impact and then rebuilt, but with the pieces falling in the wrong places. As a result, vast cracks formed as its crust resettled, creating the highest cliff in the solar system: Verona Rupes, which is well over 3 miles (5 km) tall.

ARTIST'S IMPRESSION OF VERONA RUPES

## Uranian moons

Uranus has 27 known moons. The largest, Titania, is 980 miles (1,577 km) wide. The smallest are Trinculo and Cupid, which are only about 11 miles (18 km) wide. All the moons are named after characters from the works of William Shakespeare and the poet Alexander Pope.

- TRINCULO
- CUPID
- FERDINAND
- MARGARET
- FRANCISCO
- MAB
- PERDITA
- STEPHANO
- CORDELIA
- OPHELIA
- SETEBOS
- PROSPERO
- BIANCA
- DESDEMONA
- CALIBAN
- ROSALIND
- CRESSIDA
- BELINDA
- JULIET
- PORTIA
- SYCORAX
- PUCK
- MIRANDA
- ARIEL
- UMBRIEL
- OBERON
- TITANIA

# Uranus

**In 1781 the astronomer William Herschel peered through the telescope in his garden in England and saw what he thought was a comet. It turned out to be something much more exciting: a new planet.**

Uranus is an ice giant much like Neptune, but tipped on its side. For two centuries after Herschel discovered Uranus, very little was learned about it, except that it has moons, rings, and an unusual tilt. Only one spacecraft—Voyager 2—has ever visited the planet, and the pictures it sent back in 1986 revealed a disappointingly boring, pale blue globe with a few faint wisps of cloud. Unlike the other giant planets, Uranus gives off relatively little heat. It does, however, have a strong but lopsided magnetic field.

## Rings

Uranus is surrounded by a set of narrow rings, most of which were discovered in 1977 when they passed in front of a star. More rings, sharing orbits with small moons, were found later.

## Atmosphere

Hydrogen and helium are the main gases in Uranus's atmosphere, but there is also plenty of methane, which gives the planet its pale blue color.

## Mantle

Water, methane, and ammonia combine to form a slushy mixture of ice and liquid in Uranus's mantle. At the base of the mantle there may be a sea of diamond.

## On a roll

Most planets rotate upright like spinning tops, but Uranus's axis of rotation is tipped over on its side. This gives the planet and its moons extreme seasons. In the winter hemisphere, the pole is in constant darkness for 42 years, while the summer pole is in constant sunlight.

Axis

SUN

Summer

Winter

### Core

At the planet's center is a core of possibly molten rock, iron, and nickel, with a temperature of more than 9,000°F (5,000°C).

### Storm clouds

Uranus looked featureless when Voyager visited because its south pole was facing the Sun. When its equator faces the Sun, however, the atmosphere springs to life. Recent images from telescopes reveal horizontal cloud bands like those on Jupiter, violent storms, and giant polar hurricanes.

# Neptune

**The solar system's outermost and coldest planet has a striking blue color like Earth. Similar in size and structure to Uranus, Neptune is an ice giant: a vast ball of gas, liquid, and ice.**

Neptune was the last planet to be discovered and was found thanks to mathematics. Astronomers had noticed that Uranus wandered off its predicted path as though pulled by the gravity of a hidden planet. When they calculated where the mystery world should be and looked through a telescope, they saw Neptune. Just 17 days later, in October 1846, they also saw Neptune's icy moon Triton. Only Voyager 2 has visited Neptune. It flew past the planet in 1989 and sent back pictures of white clouds in Neptune's sky, blown into streaks by furious winds, and faint rings around the gas giant. Triton turned out to be a fascinating world of erupting geysers and frozen nitrogen lakes, surrounded by a thin atmosphere.

A layer of liquid diamond might surround Neptune's core.

**Rings**

Neptune is surrounded by several thin, faint rings made mostly of dust.

### Dust rings

Neptune's rings are made of dark dust that's hard to see, but Voyager 2 took this photo when they were lit from behind by the Sun. The rings have thick and thin sections, making them uneven.

### Neptune's moons

For over a century, Triton was Neptune's only known moon, but 14 others have now been discovered. After Triton, the next largest moon is Proteus, at 260 miles (420 km) wide. Nereid has a highly stretched orbit: it swoops close to Neptune before flying seven times farther out.

TRITON

PROTEUS
NEREID
LARISSA
GALATEA
DESPINA
THALASSA
NAIAD
HALIMEDE
NESO
SAO
LAOMEDEIA
PSAMATHE
S/2004 N1

NEPTUNE

**Geysers on Triton**
Voyager 2 discovered huge geysers on Triton. Jets of nitrogen gas blast icy grains up to 5 miles (8 km) above the surface, shown here in an artist's impression. These are caught by the wind and form dark streaks where they settle back on the ground.

**Mantle**
The mantle is a slushy mixture of liquid and ice made up of water, methane, and ammonia. This layer weighs ten times more than Earth.

**Core**
In the center is a white-hot core of rock and iron that is larger than Earth. The temperature here is over 9,000°F (5,000°C).

**Triton**
Neptune's largest moon is almost as big as Earth's moon. With a surface temperature of –391°F (–235°C), it is one of the coldest places in the solar system. It orbits the "wrong" way, moving in the opposite direction of Neptune's rotation. This suggests Triton was captured by Neptune's gravity.

**Stormy skies**
Raging winds tear across Neptune's sky, blowing at up to 1,300 mph (2,100 km/h)—nearly ten times faster than a hurricane on Earth. Storms come and go. In 1989, Voyager 2 photographed the Great Dark Spot (left), a giant storm that had vanished by the time the Hubble Telescope looked at Neptune in 1994.

**Atmosphere**
Neptune's outer layer is made of hydrogen and helium, with increasing amounts of water, ammonia, and methane at greater depths. Its blue color comes from methane.

The clouds are blown around the planet by winds of up to 1,300 mph (2,100 km/h).

**FAST FACTS**

**Surface gravity (Earth = 1):** 1.12

**Time to rotate once:** 16.1 hours

**Year:** 165 Earth years

**Moons:** At least 14

# Minor planets

**Billions of rocky and icy objects orbit the Sun, some weaving paths between the planets but most orbiting farther out. Called "minor planets," they are leftovers from the solar system's formation, and many are fascinating worlds in their own right.**

There are minor planets scattered throughout the solar system, but most fall into groups that share similar orbits. Closest to the Sun are the asteroids, which are mostly made of rock. Farther out, the minor planets tend to be icy. Some minor planets have their own moons and rings, and the very largest are roundish in shape and classed as dwarf planets. The most famous of these is Pluto, which was once considered a planet.

**Haumea**
The dwarf planet Haumea is egg-shaped rather than round. Its shape is too small to see with a telescope but astronomers figured it out by studying how it reflects different amounts of light as it rotates. Haumea has two moons, Hi'aka and Namaka, shown in this artist's impression.

**Eris**
The dwarf planet Eris was discovered in 2005 and is larger than Pluto. It belongs to the scattered disk—a group of icy objects that travel far north and south of the Kuiper belt disk.

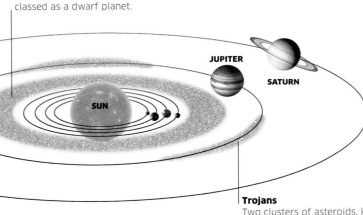

**Asteroid Belt**
Most small rocky bodies orbit the Sun in a belt between the orbits of Mars and Jupiter. The largest known asteroid, Ceres, is classed as a dwarf planet.

**NEPTUNE**

**URANUS**

**JUPITER**

**SATURN**

**SUN**

**Kuiper Belt**
This group of icy bodies forms a belt extending 30–50 times farther from the Sun than Earth. Pluto is the largest known member of the Kuiper belt.

**Trojans**
Two clusters of asteroids, known as trojans and Greeks, share the same orbit as Jupiter.

**Centaurs**
Bodies in the space between the outer planets are called centaurs. They were probably once in the Kuiper belt. Several centaurs behave like large comets.

**1992** The year in which the **first object beyond Pluto** was discovered.

**248** years—the time taken for Pluto to **orbit the Sun once.**

**−382°F** (−230°C)—the **average surface temperature** on Pluto.

**65**

### Pluto's surface

Since Pluto is so far from the Sun, most substances that are gases on Earth are solids on Pluto. The very thin atmosphere on this dwarf planet probably freezes and evaporates with Pluto's changing seasons.

ARTIST'S IMPRESSION OF PLUTO

### Ceres

Ceres, the largest asteroid, is so big that scientists consider it a dwarf planet. This 590-mile- (950-km-) wide body is a battered, rocky world, but it has icy patches on its surface and sometimes releases water vapor into space. In 2015 NASA's Dawn spacecraft became the first one ever to visit Ceres.

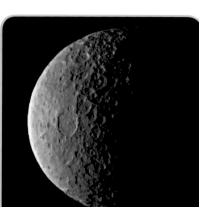

PLUTO

Earth's moon weighs about

## six times more than

the dwarf planet Pluto.

### New Horizons mission

NASA's nuclear-powered New Horizons spacecraft visited the dwarf planet Pluto and its five moons in 2015. After its encounter, the 880-lb (400-kg) craft set off toward other Kuiper belt objects to improve our knowledge of these dim and distant worlds.

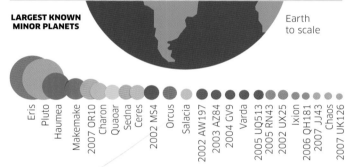

LARGEST KNOWN MINOR PLANETS

Earth to scale

Eris
Pluto
Haumea
Makemake
2007 OR10
Charon
Quaoar
Sedna
Ceres
2002 MS4
Orcus
Salacia
2002 AW197
2003 AZ84
2004 GV9
Varda
2005 UQ513
2005 RN43
2002 UX25
Ixion
2006 QH181
2007 JJ43
Chaos
2007 UK126

### Size

Though small relative to Earth, minor planets rival the solar system's moons in size. Five are recognized as dwarf planets: Eris, Pluto, Haumea, Makemake, and Ceres. However, there may be hundreds of objects beyond Neptune that could qualify as dwarf planets.

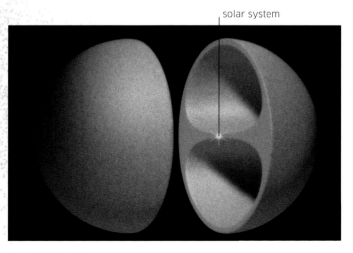

solar system

### Oort cloud

Beyond the Kuiper belt lies a roughly spherical cloud of icy bodies that probably stretches a quarter of the way to the nearest star. Many comets are likely to originate from this planetary deep freeze.

# Comets

**Comets are strange but beautiful sights, like stars with glowing tails. From time to time they swoop into the inner solar system and appear in the night sky, only to shoot back out to space and vanish.**

For thousands of years, people were puzzled by comets or even frightened by them, seeing their unexpected appearance as bad omens. We now know these visitors from the outer solar system are simply ancient lumps of ice and dust—leftovers from the cloud of rubble from which the planets formed, billions of years ago. When comets venture close to the Sun, the ice warms up and releases gas and dust into a gigantic cloud and tails. Comets have changed little since they first formed, which makes them a prime target for space scientists who want to learn more about the early solar system.

## Structure of a comet

The cloud of gas and dust that surrounds the nucleus is called the coma. The coma's largest part, visible in ultraviolet light, is made of hydrogen. Both tails follow the comet's motion around the Sun.

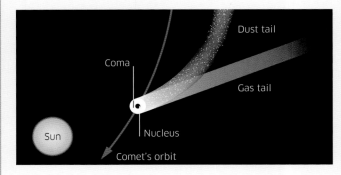

## Around the Sun

The orbits of comets are typically elliptical (oval). Only when comets come close to the Sun do their tails develop. The time taken to make one orbit varies enormously—Comet Encke, a short-period comet, takes only three years to orbit the Sun, but long-period comets can take millions of years.

A TYPICAL COMET ORBIT

SIZE OF COMET 67P RELATIVE TO A CITY

## Comet 67P

The best-studied comet in history is the 3-mile- (5-km-) wide Comet 67P, which was explored by the European spacecraft Rosetta that arrived at it in 2014. Rosetta released a separate probe called Philae to make the first soft landing (as opposed to a violent impact) on a comet nucleus. The harpoon meant to anchor Philae to the comet failed to fire on landing, causing Philae to bounce hundreds of yards into space. It bounced twice before settling.

**Crust**
A crust of jet-black dust makes the surface of the nucleus darker than coal. Comet nuclei are among the darkest objects in the solar system.

**Tall tails**
Comets look as though they are streaking through space with their tails stretched out behind them, but that's just an illusion. In reality, the tails always point away from the Sun, whichever way a comet is traveling. There are two main tails: a gas tail (blue in the photo of Comet Hale–Bopp on left) and a dust tail (white). The gas tail points almost directly away from the Sun, but the dust tail bends back toward the comet's path.

**355** million miles (570 million km)—the longest measured comet gas tail.

Comet dust trails that cross Earth's orbit cause **meteor showers**.

The first comet to have its orbital path calculated was **Comet Halley**.

**67**

**Interior**
The inside of a comet is a jumbled mixture of rocky dust and lumps of ice, all held together loosely by gravity.

**Comet nucleus**
At the heart of a comet is a solid part called the nucleus. Typically only a few miles wide, the nucleus is dwarfed by the cloud of gas and dust that develops around it and the tails that can stretch over millions of miles.

**Jets of gas and dust**
The Sun's warmth makes ice in the comet evaporate to form gas. Jets of gas erupt from the sunward side of the nucleus, carrying dust grains with them.

**Coma**
A vast cloud of dust, gas, and ice particles called a coma builds up around the nucleus as a comet approaches the Sun. The coma can grow larger than the Sun.

# STARS

On a dark night you can see thousands of stars twinkling in the sky, but there are countless trillions more scattered across the fathomless depths of space. Like our Sun, all stars are dazzling balls of hot gas that can shine for billions of years, powered by nuclear fusion.

# How stars work

A star is a brilliant, shining ball of extremely hot gas, mainly hydrogen, that generates fantastic amounts of energy in its core. This energy travels out through the star until it reaches the surface, where it escapes into space as light, heat, and other types of radiation invisible to our eyes. Stars are bright and hot because of the vast quantity of energy they generate.

## PARTS OF A STAR

Stars vary tremendously in their size, but all of them have the same parts. Every star has an extremely hot central region, or core, that produces energy; one or more layers of gas through which this energy travels outward; a very hot surface; and an atmosphere.

SUN

### An average star

Our Sun is an ordinary star that looks huge to us because it's so close. Sun-sized stars have two layers through which energy moves outward from the core: an inner layer where it travels by radiation, and an outer layer that carries it by convection (rising and falling currents). In larger stars, these two layers are the other way around, while some smaller stars have only a convection layer. Like all stars, the Sun has a brilliant surface that emits light and heat.

### How stars shine

The energy produced by a star is released by nuclear fusion in its core. This process involves the nuclei (central parts) of atoms joining together to make more massive nuclei. Fusion can only occur at the extremely high temperatures present in star cores.

Hydrogen nuclei (single protons)

Series of fusion reactions

Helium nucleus

Neutron

Energy

Positrons and neutrinos (tiny subatomic particles)

**NUCLEAR FUSION IN SUN-SIZED STARS**

### Forces in stars

Most stars exist in a stable state through a delicate balance between two forces: gravity, which pushes matter inward; and pressure, generated by energy released from the core, which pushes matter outward.

**Forces in balance**
In a normal star, the inward push of gravity balances the outward pressure.

**Star turns into red giant**
The cores of old stars heat up. The extra heat boosts the outward pressure, so the star swells.

**Collapse to black hole**
When a particularly large star dies, gravity may cause its core to collapse to form a black hole.

## STARLIGHT

As well as visible light, stars emit invisible types of radiation, such as ultraviolet rays and microwaves, all of which travel as waves. The whole range of these different radiations, including light, is called the electromagnetic (EM) spectrum. Stars are too distant for us to visit them to study, but we can tell a lot about them from the light and other radiation they emit.

A    B

These two stars look equally bright in the night sky, but in reality, star A is brighter but farther away.

### Star brightness

A star's brightness, or magnitude, can be stated either as how bright it looks or how bright it really is. These differ, as stars vary in their distance from Earth, which affects how bright they appear. Oddly, a star's brightness is measured on a scale in which a small number denotes a bright star and a large number indicates a dim star.

EARTH    B    A

### The electromagnetic spectrum

Light travels as a wave, and we see light waves of different lengths as colors: red light, for example, has longer waves than blue. Stars produce energy in a huge range of wavelengths, most of which are invisible to our eyes. Many astronomers study stars by using wavelengths we cannot see.

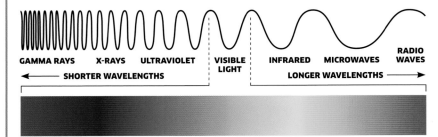

| GAMMA RAYS | X-RAYS | ULTRAVIOLET | VISIBLE LIGHT | INFRARED | MICROWAVES | RADIO WAVES |

← SHORTER WAVELENGTHS            LONGER WAVELENGTHS →

### Studying stars

By studying the spectrum of a star, astronomers can figure out many of the chemical elements it contains. Each chemical element in the star's atmosphere absorbs particular wavelengths in the spectrum of radiation from the hotter gas beneath, producing a unique pattern, like a fingerprint. The dark gaps in the spectrum of light from our Sun (above) are caused by 67 different elements.

### Variable stars

Some stars regularly vary in both size and brightness. These stars are constantly trying to reach an equilibrium between the inward-pulling gravitational force and the outward-pushing pressure. They swell and shrink in regular cycles, varying from a few hours to a few years—being brightest (and hottest) when smallest, and dimmest (and coolest) when biggest.

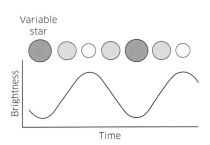

Variable star

Brightness

Time

# HOW FAR ARE THE STARS?

All stars other than the Sun are situated at incredible distances from Earth, which is why they appear as just pinpricks of light in the night sky. They are so far away that a special unit is needed to express their distance. This unit is the light-year, which is the distance light travels in a year. A light-year is about 6 trillion miles (9.5 trillion km).

## Nearby stars

There are 32 stars lying within 12.5 light-years of the Sun, some of which belong to multiple star systems containing two or three stars (binary or trinary systems). Many of these nearby stars are small, dim ones called red dwarfs, but a few are larger, dazzling yellow, orange, and white stars. The diagram below shows their positions in space, relative to the Sun at the center.

## Measuring distance

There are various ways of measuring how far away stars are. One clever technique is to view the same star at two distinct times of year, when Earth is at opposite sides of its orbit around the Sun. If a star is nearby, its position relative to more distant stars appears to shift between these two points of view (an effect known as parallax). The amount of shift can be used to calculate exactly how far away it is. Using this method, astronomers have worked out that Proxima Centauri—the star closest to the Sun—is about 4.2 light-years away.

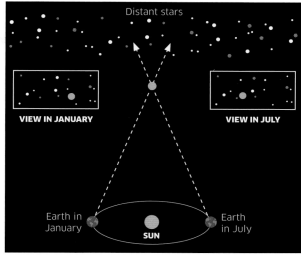

Distant stars

VIEW IN JANUARY          VIEW IN JULY

Earth in January          SUN          Earth in July

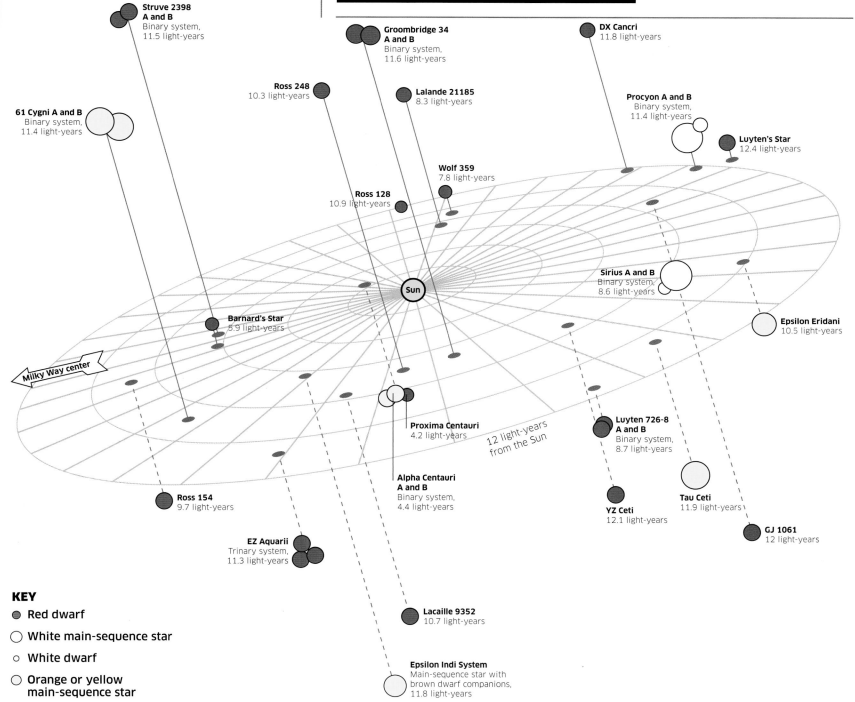

**Struve 2398 A and B**
Binary system, 11.5 light-years

**Groombridge 34 A and B**
Binary system, 11.6 light-years

**DX Cancri**
11.8 light-years

**Ross 248**
10.3 light-years

**Lalande 21185**
8.3 light-years

**Procyon A and B**
Binary system, 11.4 light-years

**61 Cygni A and B**
Binary system, 11.4 light-years

**Luyten's Star**
12.4 light-years

**Wolf 359**
7.8 light-years

**Ross 128**
10.9 light-years

**Sirius A and B**
Binary system, 8.6 light-years

Sun

**Barnard's Star**
5.9 light-years

**Epsilon Eridani**
10.5 light-years

Milky Way center

**Proxima Centauri**
4.2 light-years

12 light-years from the Sun

**Luyten 726-8 A and B**
Binary system, 8.7 light-years

**Ross 154**
9.7 light-years

**Alpha Centauri A and B**
Binary system, 4.4 light-years

**YZ Ceti**
12.1 light-years

**Tau Ceti**
11.9 light-years

**GJ 1061**
12 light-years

**EZ Aquarii**
Trinary system, 11.3 light-years

**Lacaille 9352**
10.7 light-years

**Epsilon Indi System**
Main-sequence star with brown dwarf companions, 11.8 light-years

## KEY

- Red dwarf
- White main-sequence star
- White dwarf
- Orange or yellow main-sequence star

# Types of stars

**In the night sky, all stars look like tiny pinpricks of light. However, stars differ greatly in size, color, brightness, and life span.**

The smallest are tiny dwarf stars less than a thousandth of the Sun's volume. The largest are 8 billion times greater in volume than the Sun. The largest stars are also billions of times brighter than the smallest stars. The characteristics of a star depend mainly on how much matter it contains—its mass. The more massive a star is, the hotter and brighter it will be, but the shorter its life span. This is because big stars burn through their nuclear fuel much faster. Astronomers use the color, size, and brightness of stars to classify them into a number of groups.

## Giant stars

The largest stars are aging stars that have swelled and brightened enormously toward the end of their lives. Giant stars are up to 200 times wider than the Sun and can be thousands of times more luminous. Supergiants and hypergiants are up to 2,000 times wider than the Sun and up to a billion times brighter.

## Dwarf stars

Dwarf stars make up the majority of stars and are relatively small and dim. They include stars about the size of the Sun or somewhat larger and many smaller stars called red dwarfs. They also include white dwarfs—the tiny, dense remnants of giant stars that have lost their outer layers.

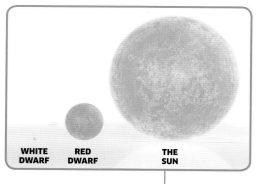

WHITE DWARF   RED DWARF   THE SUN

ORANGE GIANT

RED GIANT

BLUE SUPERGIANT

## Colors

A star's color depends on how hot its surface is. The hottest stars produce a bluish light, while cooler stars are an orangish red. You can see these colors on a clear night by using binoculars to look closely at different stars.

| Color | Temperature |
|---|---|
| Blue | 80,000°F (45,000°C) |
| Bluish white | 55,000°F (30,000°C) |
| White | 22,000°F (12,000°C) |
| Yellowish white | 14,000°F (8,000°C) |
| Yellow | 12,000°F (6,500°C) |
| Orange | 9,000°F (5,000°C) |
| Red | 6,500°F (3,500°C) |

## Star chart

About 100 years ago, two astronomers discovered an ingenious way of classifying stars that also shows the stage each star has reached in its life. The astronomers—Ejnar Hertzsprung and Henry Russell—did this by making a graph of stars with temperature along the bottom and brightness up the side. Most stars, including our Sun, fall into a band on the diagram called the main sequence; these are small to medium stars in a range of colors. The other stars, including giants and dwarfs, form separate groups. These are older stars that would have been in the main sequence millions of years ago.

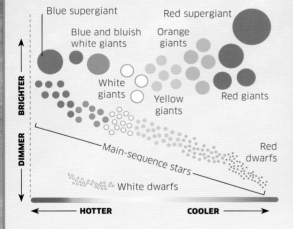

## Seeing stars

Supergiant stars are easy to see if you look for the famous constellation of Orion, the Hunter. Orion's shoulder is a red supergiant called Betelgeuse, which is one of the largest stars in the northern sky. Orion's foot is a blue supergiant, Rigel.

ORION

BLUE HYPERGIANT

RED SUPERGIANT

### Orion Nebula
At a distance of 1,500 light-years from Earth, this colorful gas cloud is the closest star-forming region to Earth. The Orion Nebula contains massive young stars giving off enormous amounts of energy, which makes the surrounding gases glow brightly. You can see the Orion Nebula easily by using binoculars to look at the constellation of Orion, but the colors will be much fainter than shown here.

**Trapezium stars**
In the heart of the Orion Nebula is a cluster of very bright, newly formed stars called the Trapezium. These stars are up to 30 times more massive than our Sun, and their intense energy illuminates much of the surrounding cloud.

This gas cloud is separated from the main part of the nebula by dark dust lanes and is lit up by a young star at its center.

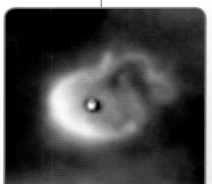

**Star babies**
The youngest stars in the Orion Nebula are still surrounded by dense disks of gas and dust. The Hubble Space Telescope has photographed 30 of these disks, which are also known as proplyds. Planets may eventually form from the gas and dust in them.

# Star birth

**New stars and planets are born in vast clouds of interstellar gas and dust in a process that can take millions of years.**

The gas clouds that give birth to stars are known as molecular clouds and are made of hydrogen gas. While most of the hydrogen is spread out incredibly thinly across space, denser clumps can form if something disturbs the cloud. Once that happens, the clumps of gas may begin to shrink due to gravity and pull in more gas, concentrating it at their centers. Eventually, the core regions become so dense and hot that stars ignite. These brilliant newborn stars may illuminate the clouds in which they formed, creating a dazzling display of light and color.

Nair al Saif is the brightest star in Orion's sword.

**50** million years—how long it can take for a
solar system to form inside a gas cloud.

**2,000** The approximate **number of stars** within the Orion Nebula.

**75**

Intense ultraviolet radiation from young stars makes atoms in the gas clouds emit light. Each element emits a characteristic color. Hydrogen, for instance, glows red. The colors in this photograph are enhanced.

Bubble-shaped region containing hot gas

Fierce stellar winds from massive newborn stars create arcs of gas and dust.

Wisps of hydrogen gas and dust

The dark areas are dust clouds that block light.

## How a star forms

Star formation begins when a gas and dust cloud in deep space is subjected to a trigger event, such as a nearby supernova or an encounter with a nearby star. Once the cloud starts to collapse, gravity does the rest of the work to form a star.

**Clumps form**
Pockets of dense gas form in a molecular cloud (a huge cloud of cold, dark gas and dust).

**Clump contracts**
The force of gravity makes a gas clump shrink and pull in more gas from around it.

**Spinning disk**
The clump shrinks to form a hot, dense core surrounded by a spinning disk of matter. Jets of gas shoot out from its poles.

**Star ignites**
When the center is hot enough, nuclear fusion begins and a star is born. A disk of matter still orbits the young star.

**Disk disperses**
The leftover material is either dispersed into space or clumps together to form planets, moons, and other objects.

## Stellar nurseries

Our galaxy contains many starbirth regions. The Horsehead Nebula looks like a silhouette of a horse's head in ordinary light but is pink in the infrared image below. The Carina Nebula, four times larger than the Orion Nebula, is famous for a gargantuan dust-gas pillar known as Mystic Mountain.

**HORSEHEAD NEBULA**

**MYSTIC MOUNTAIN IN THE CARINA NEBULA**

# Exoplanets

**The first exoplanet—a planet outside our solar system orbiting an ordinary star—was discovered in 1995. Since then, astronomers have found more than 1,000 of these alien worlds, some of which are similar to Earth and may even harbor life.**

Until the 1990s, the only planets known to science were the eight planets that orbit our Sun. People suspected that planets might orbit other stars, but such worlds were impossible to detect because of the vast distances separating them from us. However, as telescopes became more advanced, astronomers began to notice faint changes in the color or intensity of light from distant stars, which suggested planets were passing in front of them. Careful studies followed, and the first exoplanet was confirmed in 1995. Hundreds of extrasolar systems have now been discovered, some with as many as seven planets. These range from small, probably rocky worlds like Earth to giants with rings 200 times wider than Saturn's. There may be hundreds of billions of exoplanets in our galaxy.

Astronomers think there could be
## 11 billion Earth-like
habitable exoplanets in our galaxy.

### The Kepler-62 system

In 2013 the Kepler space telescope discovered five exoplanets orbiting the star Kepler-62, which lies 7 million billion miles (11 million billion km) from Earth. The picture below is an artist's impression of the planets, which are too far away to photograph. Two of them orbit in the star's "habitable zone" where the temperature is right for life. Like all newly discovered exoplanets, the planets in Kepler-62 have catalog names but may receive proper names in the future.

Dense clouds may cover Kepler-62d, which is likely to have a thick atmosphere.

**Sun-scorched**
The planet Kepler-62b orbits very close to the star, zipping around it every six days. Its surface temperature is 887°F (475°C)—probably too hot for life.

**Mars-sized**
Kepler-62c is about the size of Mars. It is fiercely hot, with a surface temperature of 572°F (300°C).

**Largest planet**
Kepler-62d's size suggests it has enough gravity to hold on to a thick atmosphere. Its surface is hotter than boiling water.

The **largest** known exoplanet is about **30 times bigger** than Jupiter.

**Fomalhaut,** in the constellation Piscis Austrinus, is the **brightest known star with an exoplanet.**

**77**

KEPLER-62 SYSTEM

HABITABLE ZONE

Kepler-62

62c    62b

62e

62d

62f

## Habitable zone

Two of the planets in the Kepler-62 system orbit in an area known as the habitable zone (or "Goldilocks zone"), where temperatures are just right for water to exist as a liquid on a planet's surface. Many scientists think liquid water is essential for life to flourish.

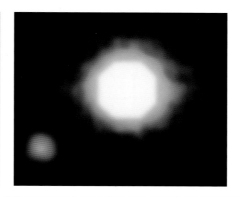

## First photo of an exoplanet

This blurry image, taken in 2004, is the first photo of an exoplanet, which appears as a brown blob next to its brighter parent star. The planet is a type known as a "hot Jupiter"—a boiling-hot gas giant. It lies about 1 million billion miles (2 million billion km) from Earth.

## Worlds beyond

This artist's impression shows how the Kepler-62 system might look from the planet 62f. Planet 62e looms in the sky nearby, while the other three planets and the Kepler-62 star are visible in the background.

Kepler-62e is likely to be a rocky planet with a thick atmosphere and possibly oceans or ice on its surface.

## Earth-like

Kepler-62e is one of the most Earth-like planets known. Its surface temperature is 32°F (0°C), which means it may have liquid water, a cloudy atmosphere, and even life.

## Cold Earth

Kepler-62f is similar to 62e but colder. It may have surface water and ice. Its year is 267 days long, and its surface gravity is probably stronger than Earth's.

The atmosphere contains
significant amounts
of water vapor.

## Orange star

The orange dwarf star HD 189733 A has only
one known exoplanet—the hot Jupiter HD
189733 b, which orbits its parent star every
2.2 days. The planet was detected from a
slight dimming it causes in the star's light each
time it passes between the star and Earth.

The temperature of the planet's atmosphere is over 1,800°F (1,000°C), making the planet inhospitable to life as we know it.

### Blue planet

This artist's impression shows one of the nearest hot Jupiters: HD 189733 b, which is 63 light-years from Earth. Its deep blue color is due to vast numbers of silicate particles—glass rain— in its atmosphere.

Every second, several million pounds of hydrogen boil away from the surface of HD 189733 b.

# Hot Jupiters

**Many of the planets that have been detected outside our own solar system are of a type called "hot Jupiters"—weird, exotic gas giants that are about the size of Jupiter or larger, but much hotter because they orbit close to their stars.**

Hot Jupiters orbit at a distance of 1–46 million miles (2–75 million km) from their stars—much closer than Jupiter, which orbits hundreds of millions of miles from the Sun. These star-snuggling worlds are scorched by their stars, producing extreme weather conditions in their atmospheres, including howling winds, temperatures high enough to melt steel, and molten-glass rain. Scientists think that hot Jupiters must have originated farther away from their stars and then migrated toward them, since there would not have been enough material so close to a star for such huge planets to form there.

### Death of hot Jupiters

Hot Jupiters often have violent deaths. Some spiral in toward their parent star and are consumed. Others boil away into space, leaving behind just a rocky or metallic core.

 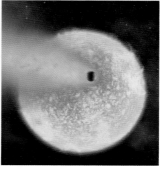

**Pulled in by gravity**
The hot Jupiter WASP-12 orbits so close to its star that gravity is distorting it and ripping off its atmosphere.

**Loss of atmosphere**
The atmosphere of HD 209458 b is boiling away into space at a rate of thousands of tons per second, forming a long tail of hydrogen.

### How hot are hot Jupiters?

The temperatures of some hot Jupiters discovered by the Kepler space observatory—such as Kepler–5b and 7b—are compared here to the surface temperatures of four solar system planets. Some hot Jupiters are hotter than molten lava or even liquid iron.

### Wild orbits

Upsilon Andromedae b was one of the first hot Jupiters to be detected. It is one of four planets orbiting a star 44 light-years away. Shown here are three of the planets' orbits, which are tilted at wildly different angles.

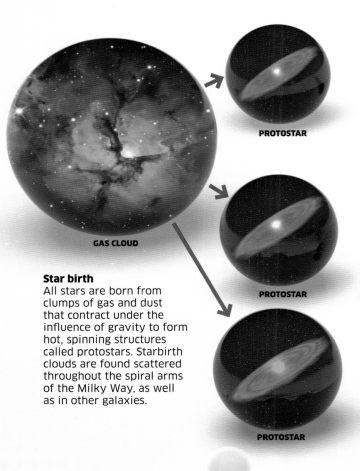

GAS CLOUD

PROTOSTAR

PROTOSTAR

PROTOSTAR

RED DWARF

### Star birth
All stars are born from clumps of gas and dust that contract under the influence of gravity to form hot, spinning structures called protostars. Starbirth clouds are found scattered throughout the spiral arms of the Milky Way, as well as in other galaxies.

### Small stars
The smallest stars (with masses up to a quarter of our Sun's) are relatively cool and dim and are known as red dwarfs. These can shine for hundreds of billions of years. As they age, their surface temperature increases and they eventually become blue dwarfs. Then they cool to white dwarfs, and finally to cold, dead black dwarfs.

### Medium stars
Stars about the same mass as the Sun last for billions to tens of billions of years. They swell into red giant stars at the end of their lives. A red giant undergoes a peaceful death, shedding its outer layers to form a ghostly cloud of wreckage called a planetary nebula.

### Massive stars
Stars with the highest mass—more than eight times the mass of the Sun—have the shortest lives, measured in millions to hundreds of millions of years. Usually white to blue in color for most of their lives, they redden as they age and die in the most spectacular and violent way possible.

The red supergiant **Betelgeuse** is expected to explode as a supernova any day in the next 100,000 years.

# Lives and deaths of stars

**Stars shine as long as they can maintain the delicate balance between the inward pull of their own gravity and the outward pressure of energy from the core. How long this lasts depends on how much matter a star starts off with.**

Massive stars have relatively short lives because they quickly use up their hydrogen fuel in nuclear reactions. The most massive stars die in stupendous explosions called supernovas. Small stars have less fuel but they use it slowly and can last for hundreds of billions of years before they gradually fade away. Medium-mass stars, like the Sun, evolve along an intermediate path and end up as beautiful objects called planetary nebulas when they die.

**Red supergiant**
When a massive star has fused all the hydrogen fuel in its core, it starts producing energy by fusing together helium atoms. Eventually the core runs out of helium, but it continues to force together atoms to form heavier and heavier elements until iron atoms are formed. At the same time, the star swells into a red supergiant. When the core turns into iron, it can no longer produce enough energy to withstand the inward pull of the star's gravity and the star collapses violently and then explodes in a supernova.

The very largest stars may have life spans as short as **3 million years**.

Our Sun will **become a red giant** in 5 billion years and may grow large enough to **swallow Earth**.

**81**

Star's light begins to dim

BLUE DWARF

BLACK DWARF

## Life stories

Contrasted here are the life stories of the three main types of stars: low-mass stars (top row); medium-mass stars like the Sun (middle row); and massive stars (bottom row). Small stars have the longest lives. In fact, they live for so long that no red dwarf in the universe has yet evolved to the blue dwarf or black dwarf stage.

### White dwarf
Left at the heart of a planetary nebula is all that remains of the red giant's core: a small, brilliant star called a white dwarf. This causes the surrounding cloud to shine. Over a long period of time it cools to a black dwarf.

BLACK DWARF

### Red giant
A red giant forms when a medium-mass star runs out of hydrogen in its core. The core begins to use helium as a fuel, while hydrogen is "burned" as a fuel in a shell surrounding the core. At the same time, the star expands to a giant size.

When all its fuel is used up, the outer layers of a red giant are shed.

### Planetary nebula
A planetary nebula is a glowing cloud of material shed by a red giant, often with a beautiful and complex shape. Planetary nebulas last for only a few tens of thousands of years.

### Supernova
When it can produce no more energy by nuclear fusion reactions, a red supergiant disintegrates in a supernova explosion. The star's outer layers dissipate into space while its core continues to collapse on itself. Depending on its mass, the core of the star implodes to form either a neutron star or a black hole.

### Neutron star
If the remaining core has between 1.4 and 3 times as much mass as our Sun, it collapses to about the size of a city and becomes a neutron star—an incredibly compact object made of neutrons that spins at a furious rate. Neutron stars are so dense that a single teaspoonful of their matter has a mass of about 10 million tons.

### Black hole
If the remaining core is more than three times more massive than the Sun, it shrinks until it is infinitely smaller than an atom and forms a black hole—a region of space from which nothing (not even light) can escape.

### Supernova remnant
Supernovas leave behind clouds of wreckage that slowly disperse into space. The material in the cloud may eventually form new stars, repeating the cycle of star birth and death.

# Butterfly Nebula

**When stars like our Sun die, they cast off their outer layers as glowing clouds of wreckage. These ghostly remains are known as planetary nebulas.**

Planetary nebulas were so named because the first to be noticed were round in shape, like planets. Others, however, fling their gas in two directions to form wings or a figure-eight shape. The Butterfly Nebula, captured here by the Hubble Space Telescope, is about 500 times wider than our solar system, and the gas in its wings is hurtling through space at 590,000 mph (950,000 km/h). Hidden in its heart is all that remains of the original star's core—a tiny, feeble star called a white dwarf.

# Red supergiants

**The largest stars in the universe are red supergiants. These are massive stars that have swollen to a vast size as they grow old.**

All stars produce energy by the process of nuclear fusion. Inside the star's core, the temperature and pressure are so high that hydrogen atoms are forced together, fusing them into helium atoms—a process that releases colossal amounts of energy. Massive stars use up the fuel in the core quickly and then begin to balloon in size as nuclear fusion spreads out from the core. The outer layers of the most massive stars expand into an immense sphere of glowing gas, forming a red supergiant. Eventually, the star disintegrates in a sudden and violent explosion called a supernova, leaving behind either a tiny neutron star or a black hole.

**Hydrogen-fusing shell**

**Convective layer**
Pockets of hot gas rise within the convective layer, before cooling and sinking back down. This process of rising and falling is called convection.

**Structure**
This model reveals the inner structure of a red supergiant in the last moment of its life, before a supernova explosion destroys it. The size of the core, which is minuscule relative to the supergiant's full extent, is exaggerated in our model. After hydrogen runs out, the core fuses a succession of heavier elements, forming a series of shells in the star's center. The heaviest element a star can fuse is silicon, which powers the star for about a day, causing iron to build up. When the star attempts to fuse iron, it explodes.

**Helium-fusing shell**

**Our local red supergiant**
The red supergiant closest to Earth is a star called Antares, which is 880 times wider than our Sun. Although 550 light-years away, Antares is easily visible in the night sky. It could explode in a supernova at any point in the next million years or so, but it poses no threat to Earth.

**Outer layers**
The outer part of the star consists of thinly spread hydrogen gas. There is no distinct surface. Instead, the gas fades gradually into the emptiness of space.

**SIZE OF THE SUN FOR COMPARISON**

A supernova explosion can **outshine an entire galaxy.**

The red supergiant **Antares is over 57,000 times brighter** than the Sun.

**85**

**Core**
Nuclear fusion takes place only in the core, where elements such as hydrogen are fused to make heavier elements.

Iron core

Silicon-fusing shell

Oxygen-fusing shell

Neon-fusing shell

Carbon-fusing shell

**Warm color**
The outer layer of a red supergiant has a temperature of about 6,900°F (3,800°C), which is much lower than the surface temperature of a Sun-like star. The cooler surface gives the star its reddish color.

## Life and death of a supergiant

Two powerful forces govern the life of a star: gravity, which pulls matter in the star inward, and pressure, which pushes matter outward. Normally balanced, these forces can become unbalanced at the end of a star's life.

**1 HYDROGEN BURNING**
For most of a star's life, its core turns hydrogen into helium by nuclear fusion. The energy this releases maintains pressure that pushes the star's matter outward, balancing the inward pull of gravity.

**2 HELIUM BURNING**
When hydrogen in the core runs out, massive stars begin to fuse helium. Hydrogen burning spreads to a shell outside the inner core, causing the star's outer layers to expand.

**3 MULTILAYER CORE**
When helium in the core runs out, the star starts to fuse carbon to form neon. Next it fuses neon into oxygen. A series of shells forms in the core region, fusing different elements.

**4 COLLAPSE**
When the core finally tries to fuse iron, disaster ensues. Iron fusion cannot maintain outward pressure, so gravity overwhelms the core. It collapses to the size of a city in a split second, rushing inward at a quarter of the speed of light.

**5 EXPLOSION**
As temperatures in the core soar, a flood of particles called neutrinos is released. The star's collapsing outer layers rebound off this flood, causing a catastrophic explosion brighter than a billion Suns: a supernova.

## Supersize stars

If a typical red supergiant were placed in the center of our solar system, it would extend out to between the orbits of Mars and Jupiter. In contrast, a large red giant would reach out only to about Earth's orbit.

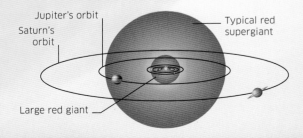

Jupiter's orbit

Saturn's orbit

Typical red supergiant

Large red giant

# Neutron stars

**When a huge star self-destructs in a supernova explosion, one of two things may happen. The core of a particularly massive star, crushed by its own stupendous gravity, shrinks until it is tinier than an atom and becomes a black hole. The core of a smaller star, however, shrinks to the size of a city to become a neutron star.**

Neutron stars are the tiniest, densest stars known and can pack the mass of the whole Sun into an area smaller than Boston. They are so compact that a mere pinhead of matter has more than twice the mass of the largest supertanker on Earth. All neutron stars spin at a furious rate, some rotating as fast as 700 times per second. We know this because neutron stars send out beams of radiation that sweep around the sky as they spin, making them appear to flash on and off if they sweep across Earth. Neutron stars that flash like this are called pulsars.

**Neutron star**
Gravity is so powerful in a neutron star that the solid surface is pulled into an almost perfectly smooth sphere. The surface temperature is about 1,000,000°F (600,000°C).

The field lines curve from the neutron star's magnetic north pole to its south pole.

**A neutron star's gravity is so great than an object dropped from 3 ft (1 m) above its surface would accelerate to 4 million mph (7 million km/h) by the time it landed.**

**100** million—the estimated **number of neutron stars** in our galaxy.

A neutron star's solid surface is **a million times stronger** than steel.

The **highest "mountains"** on a neutron star are **less than 0.19 in (5 mm) tall.**

**87**

## Pulsars

Astronomers have discovered around 2,000 pulsars (flashing neutron stars) since the first one was spotted in 1967. These neutron stars have powerful magnetic fields and produce beams of radio waves from their magnetic poles. As the star spins on its axis of rotation, the two radio beams sweep out cone shapes across the sky, causing them to pulse where they sweep across Earth. The slowest pulsars send out about five pulses of radio waves per second. The fastest send out 716 pulses per second.

**Radiation beam**
A neutron star emits beams of radiation from its magnetic poles. The radiation may take the form of radio waves, X-rays, gamma rays, or even visible light.

**Magnetic field**
The magnetic field of a neutron star can be a quadrillion times more powerful than Earth's magnetic field. It rotates at the same speed as the star.

## Inside a neutron star

Most stars are made of gas, but a neutron star has a crust of solid iron about half a mile (1 km) thick. Beneath this is a sea of subatomic particles called neutrons, crammed together by powerful gravity, forming a kind of liquid that doesn't exist on Earth.

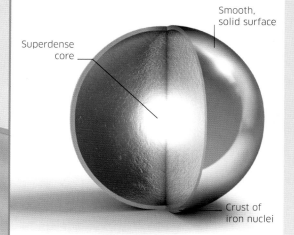

Superdense core

Smooth, solid surface

Crust of iron nuclei

## Size

At 9–15 miles (15–25 km) wide, neutron stars are about as big as a city. Compared to other stars, however, they are tiny. Their density produces incredibly powerful gravity at the surface—an average human on a neutron star would weigh about 7 billion tons.

NEUTRON STAR COMPARED TO VANCOUVER, CANADA

## Density

The material that makes up a neutron star is so dense that a single teaspoonful brought to Earth would weigh more than the entire world population. A soccer ball made from neutron star matter would weigh 5 trillion tons—about the same as Mount Everest.

= **5 TRILLION** TONS

# Black holes

**Black holes are among the strangest objects in the universe. The pull of their gravity is so great that nothing can escape from them—not even light.**

Most black holes form when massive stars run out of fuel and die in an explosion. The dead star's core—unable to resist the crushing force of its own gravity—collapses, shrinking in milliseconds until it is infinitely smaller than an atom. The core becomes what scientists call a singularity: an object so impossibly small that it has zero size but infinite density. Anything straying within a certain distance of the singularity is doomed to be pulled in by gravity and disappear forever. The point of no return forms a spherical boundary around the singularity called an event horizon, which marks how close you can safely get.

**Event horizon**
Anything that crosses this boundary from the outside can never escape.

### Types of black hole

Two main types of black holes exist: stellar and supermassive. Stellar black holes form when enormous stars explode as supernovas at the ends of their lives. Supermassive black holes are bigger and are found at the centers of galaxies, often surrounded by a whirlpool of intensely hot, glowing matter.

## Lensing
Black holes bend light. In this artist's impression, light from the accretion disk is bent to form a glowing halo around the black hole.

## Singularity
Hidden in the black hole's center is a singularity, where matter has been squeezed into a point of infinite density.

## Accretion disk
Gas, dust, and disintegrated stars spiral around some black holes in a disk. The material in the disk is not doomed—it may stay in orbit, just as planets orbit stars.

## Spaghettification
The gravitational pull of a black hole rises so steeply nearby that an astronaut falling into one would be stretched like spaghetti and torn apart.

Black hole

Gravity strongest on legs, stretching them first

## Bending light and stretching time
Black holes have such powerful gravity that they bend light like giant lenses. If Earth orbited a black hole, an observer would see a highly distorted image of the planet, like the one above. According to Albert Einstein's theory of relativity, black holes also slow down time. If an astronaut spent only an hour or so near a black hole, he might return to Earth to find that many years had passed.

## Wormholes
Einstein's theory of relativity says that massive objects bend the four combined dimensions of space and time (space-time). Some experts have speculated that black holes might warp space-time so much that they could create shortcuts, called wormholes, between different parts of the universe or different times. There is no direct evidence that wormholes exist.

WORMHOLE

The pole star, **Polaris**, is actually a **triple star system**.

Some star pairs take **millions of years** to orbit each other.

## Star clusters

Large groups of stars are called clusters. These can contain anything from a few dozen to several million stars. There are two main types of star clusters: globular and open. The Milky Way galaxy contains many examples of both.

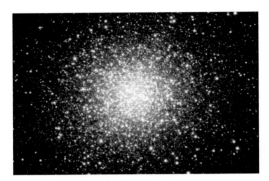

**Globular cluster**
These are roughly spherical collections of up to several million ancient stars that formed at the same time. The example above is the Great Globular Cluster in Hercules.

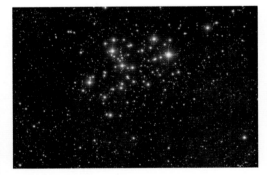

**Open cluster**
Open clusters are loosely bound collections of young stars that formed around the same time from the same cloud of gas. The example here is the Butterfly Cluster in the constellation Scorpius.

# Multiple stars

**Unlike many other stars, our Sun is a loner with no companions. Most of the stars we can see in the night sky belong to multiple star systems—that is, two or more stars orbiting each other, held together by gravity.**

Pairs of stars that simply orbit each other are called binary systems, but there are also systems of three, four, or more stars, with complicated orbital patterns. Some pairs of stars are so close together that material flows between them. These stars are called interacting binaries. As the stars age, the system can develop in a variety of dramatic ways. For example, in an X-ray binary, material flows from a normal or giant star to an extremely dense companion—a neutron star or a black hole—and gives off powerful X-rays as it spirals inward. Alternatively, material spilling from a normal or giant star onto a white dwarf may cause the dwarf to produce occasional brilliant blasts of light called novas.

One side of the donor star becomes distorted as gas is pulled toward the white dwarf by gravity.

The gas forms a funnel shape as it is pulled off the giant star.

**Accretion disk**
Gravity causes the material in this disk to spiral in toward the star at the center. As it does so, vast amounts of energy are released as heat and radiation.

**White dwarf**
A white dwarf star is the remains of a previous giant star that lost its outer layers. It is extremely dense: one teaspoon of white dwarf material weighs about 15 tons.

## Interacting binary

Here, gas flows from a red giant to a nearby white dwarf, forming a swirling disk as it spirals in toward the dwarf star. The white dwarf becomes unstable as its mass increases, causing nuclear explosions at its surface. From Earth, these outbursts of light look like new stars appearing, which is why they are called novae, from the Latin word *nova*, meaning new.

**Donor star**
In an interacting binary, the star that is losing material to its companion is called the donor. It is usually the larger star in a pair—in this case, a red giant.

Relatively cool, low-density hydrogen gas

## Type 1a supernova

The transfer of gas onto a white dwarf star can lead not just to nova outbursts but eventually, scientists think, to a cataclysmic explosion called a Type 1a supernova. This happens because the mass lost by the white dwarf during each nova blast is less than the mass it gains between outbursts, so it slowly grows. Finally, it becomes so massive that it is totally destabilized, triggering a supernova.

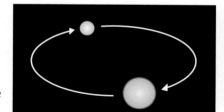

**1 PAIR OF ORBITING STARS**
Two interacting binary stars are orbiting relatively close to each other. One is a yellow star like our own Sun. Its smaller, denser companion is a white dwarf star.

**2 MATTER TRANSFER**
As the Sun-like star ages, it swells to become a red giant. Some of its gas spills onto the smaller white dwarf star. This can lead to a series of surface outbursts, or novas.

**3 WHITE DWARF EXPLODES**
The white dwarf's mass increases until it becomes unstable and explodes as a Type 1a supernova. The explosion may cause the red giant star to be blown away.

# Star cloud

**Every single tiny dot in this image of our galaxy's center is a star, possibly with a family of planets.**

Our eyes can make out about 6,000 stars in the whole night sky, but that's only a ten-millionth of the total number of stars in our galaxy. Most are hidden behind clouds of dust, but the telescope that created this image used infrared light to see them. The image shows an area of sky about the size of your fist held at arm's length. The bright patch is the center of the Milky Way, where a supermassive black hole lies hidden.

# GALAXIES

Our Sun is just one of perhaps 200 billion stars that are held together in space by gravity to form a galaxy—a vast, swirling collection of stars, dust, gas, and invisible matter. There are billions of galaxies in the universe, stretching as far as we can see in every direction.

# The cosmos

The cosmos, or universe, is everything that exists—not just on Earth or in the solar system, but also across the mind-bogglingly vast expanses of space. The cosmos includes the galaxy of stars to which our Sun belongs, countless billions of other galaxies, and unfathomable stretches of emptiness between the galaxies. Scientists who study the cosmos are called cosmologists. While astronomers study the stars and galaxies, cosmologists try to find out how and when the universe began, why it has changed over time, and what its eventual fate will be.

## WHAT'S THE UNIVERSE MADE OF?

The universe is made of matter and energy. Matter includes visible objects such as stars, but also a mysterious invisible substance called dark matter, which we can only detect through its gravity. Energy includes radiation, such as light, and dark energy. Almost nothing is known of dark energy, except that it is causing the universe to expand faster and faster.

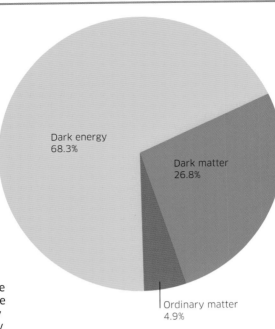

Dark energy
68.3%

Dark matter
26.8%

Ordinary matter
4.9%

### Mass–energy

Scientists have found that matter and energy are interchangeable forms of the same thing, called mass–energy. This pie chart shows how the total mass–energy of the universe divides up into ordinary matter, dark matter, and dark energy.

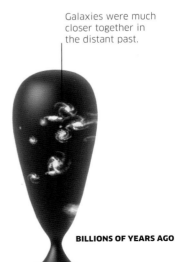

**EARTH**

**THE SUN**
8 light-minutes

**NEAREST STAR TO SUN (PROXIMA CENTAURI)**
4.2 light-years

**NEAREST RED SUPERGIANT STAR (ANTARES)**
550 light-years

**CENTER OF THE MILKY WAY**
27,000 light-years

**NEAREST SPIRAL GALAXY (ANDROMEDA)**
2.5 million light-years

**FURTHEST VISIBLE GALAXIES**
Tens of billions of light-years

## COSMIC DISTANCES

Outside the solar system, distances in space are so huge that we need special units to measure them. One light-year is the distance that light, moving at around 670 million mph (1 billion km/h), travels in a whole year—about 6 million million miles (9.5 million million km). The most distant objects we can see mark the limit of the observable universe, but the whole universe extends much farther.

## THE EXPANDING UNIVERSE

About 90 years ago, astronomers discovered that distant galaxies are rushing away from us at great speed. This isn't just because they are flying through space—it's because space itself is expanding, making the farthest galaxies rush away the fastest. The discovery meant that the universe must once have been much smaller and perhaps began with a sudden, dramatic expansion from a single point. This idea, known as the Big Bang theory, is the best explanation for how the universe began. More recently, scientists have discovered that the expansion is getting faster.

### Expanding space

Although the universe is expanding, it isn't expanding *into* anything. Instead, space itself is expanding. One way to visualize this tricky idea is to imagine a two-dimensional universe on the surface of a balloon. As the balloon inflates, the galaxies get farther apart.

The space between the galaxies expands, though the galaxies remain the same size.

Galaxies were much closer together in the distant past.

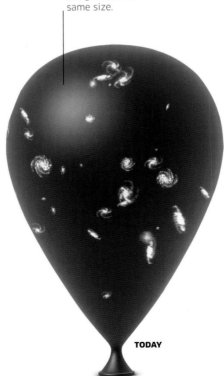

**BILLIONS OF YEARS AGO**

**TODAY**

## Ordinary matter

Everything we can see or touch—from own bodies to Earth, the planets, and stars—is made up of what astronomers call ordinary matter. Ordinary matter is made of atoms, and most of the ordinary matter in the universe is concentrated in galaxies, such as those dotted throughout the Hubble Space Telescope image above.

## Dark matter

Most of the matter in the universe is not ordinary matter but dark matter, which is impossible to see and isn't made up of atoms. Dark matter can only be detected by the gravity it exerts. In the picture above, which shows a cluster of many galaxies, the area colored blue shows where astronomers think dark matter lies, based on their calculations.

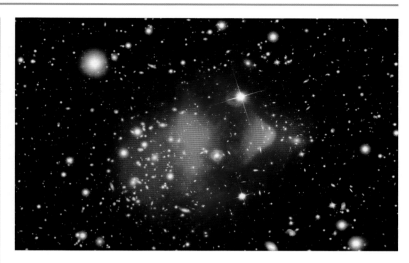

## ⊙ GRAVITY

The force of gravity is the most important force at large scales in the universe. It is gravity that holds planets together in the solar system, keeps stars together in galaxies, and groups galaxies together into galaxy clusters.

### Law of gravity

The English scientist Isaac Newton discovered how gravity works more than 300 years ago. He was the first person to realize that the force of gravity keeps the Moon in orbit around Earth and keeps the planets in orbit around the Sun.

**MODEL OF INNER SOLAR SYSTEM**

### Space-time

Newton's law of gravity allowed scientists to predict the motion of planets with great accuracy, but it wasn't perfect. In 1915, German scientist Albert Einstein published an even more accurate theory. Einstein said that gravity happens because massive objects bend the fabric of space and time, a bit like a heavy ball in a rubber sheet. A star, for instance, creates a kind of dent in space-time that causes planets to circle around it.

One day, galaxies will be so far apart that they will be impossible to see.

**BILLIONS OF YEARS IN THE FUTURE**

# Milky Way

**Seen from the southern hemisphere in winter, the Milky Way's central area forms a spectacular band of light stretching across the night sky.**

Although the Milky Way is a spiral galaxy, we see its disk as a plane because we are inside it. The bright cloud on the right marks the star-packed heart of the galaxy. The dark lanes are vast interstellar dust clouds that block the light of the stars behind them. Here, photographers on Castlepoint Beach in New Zealand try to capture the galaxy in all its midwinter glory.

**1923** The year in which **astronomers** first realized that there are galaxies beyond our own.

**12–13** billion years—the **age of the Milky Way** galaxy.

# Galaxies

**Like nearly all stars, the Sun belongs to a huge collection of stars held together by gravity: a galaxy. Our galaxy is just one of hundreds of billions of galaxies floating in the vastness of the universe.**

On very clear, dark nights you can sometimes see a band of milky light across the sky. The light comes from stars in the main part of our own galaxy, the Milky Way. The Milky Way is disk-shaped, but because we are inside it, we see its light as a band. It is so huge that its size defies imagination. It would take 150 billion years to cross the Milky Way at the speed of an airliner, and even the nearest star would take 6 million years to reach. Almost everything the naked eye can see in the sky belongs to the Milky Way. Beyond it, countless other galaxies stretch in all directions as far as telescopes can see.

## Milky Way

The Milky Way is shaped like two fried eggs back-to-back. In the center is a bulge containing most of the galaxy's stars, and around this is a flat disk. The disk is made up of spiral arms that curve out from the center. There are two major spiral arms and several minor ones. In the heart of the central bulge is a black hole 4 million times more massive than the Sun.

**The Milky Way contains about 200 billion stars.**

**Scutum–Centaurus Arm**
This is one of the two main spiral arms of the galaxy. The area where it joins the central bar is rich in star-forming clouds.

Dark lane formed by dust

**Barred spiral**
The Milky Way is classed as a barred spiral galaxy because the central bulge is bar-shaped.

Norma Arm

**1**

**Eagle Nebula**
Glowing clouds of gas and dust occur throughout our galaxy. The dark pillars in this image of the Eagle Nebula are clouds of dust and hydrogen thousands of times larger than the solar system. Inside these clouds, new stars are forming.

**2**

**Galactic center**
The bright white region seen here marks the center of our galaxy. This is an extremely active place. At its heart, matter spirals into a gigantic black hole. The reddish areas next to the center are large arcs of glowing gas.

**3**

**Solar system**
Our solar system orbits the galactic center once every 225 million years, traveling at about 120 miles (200 km) per second. So far, it has completed only 23 orbits.

**120,000** light-years—the **width of the Milky Way** galaxy.

**95%** of the mass in our galaxy is **dark matter**.

**200** billion—the **estimated number of galaxies in the observable universe**. **101**

**Orion Arm**
Our solar system is located close to the inner edge of this small arm, which is about 10,000 light-years long. Many of the brightest stars in the night sky can be found in this arm.

**Carina–Sagittarius Arm**
Situated inside the Orion Arm, this minor spiral arm is rich in bright nebulas and star clusters.

Nebula

Outer Arm

**Perseus Arm**
A major arm of the Milky Way, this is around 100,000 light-years long and curves around the outside of the Orion Arm, which includes our solar system. Numerous star clusters and nebulas dot the Perseus Arm.

## Galaxy shapes

Galaxies come in various shapes and sizes, from fuzzy clouds with no clear shape to beautiful spirals with graceful, curving arms. The main types of galaxy shapes are shown below. Whatever their shape, all galaxies spin—though their individual stars do not all orbit the center at the same speed. As the stars in a galaxy orbit, they may pass in and out of crowded areas, like cars passing through traffic jams. These crowded areas appear to us as spiral arms.

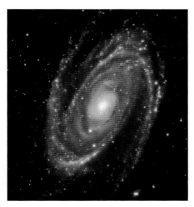

**Spiral**
These galaxies consist of a central hub of stars surrounded by a flat rotating disk containing stars, gas, and dust. The material in the disk is concentrated into two or more spiral arms, which curve outward. The spiral galaxy here, known as Bode's Galaxy, is relatively close to our own, at 12 million light-years away.

**Barred spiral**
This type is similar to a spiral except that a straight bar of stars, dust, and gas runs across the center, connecting curved or spiral arms. Our own galaxy, the Milky Way, is a barred spiral, as is NGC 1365 (left). At 200,000 light-years across, NGC 1365 is one of the largest galaxies known.

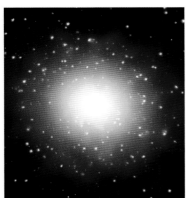

**Elliptical**
These galaxies can be spherical, football shaped, or even cigar-shaped, with no clear internal structure. They contain mostly very old red stars, which give the galaxy an orange or reddish hue, but little gas and dust. Their stars follow a variety of orbits. M60, shown here, is quite a large elliptical galaxy.

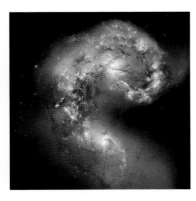

**Irregular**
Galaxies of this type have no particular shape or symmetry. Some are made by collisions between two galaxies. For example, the Antennae Galaxies (left) were separate spirals until 1.2 billion years ago, when they started merging.

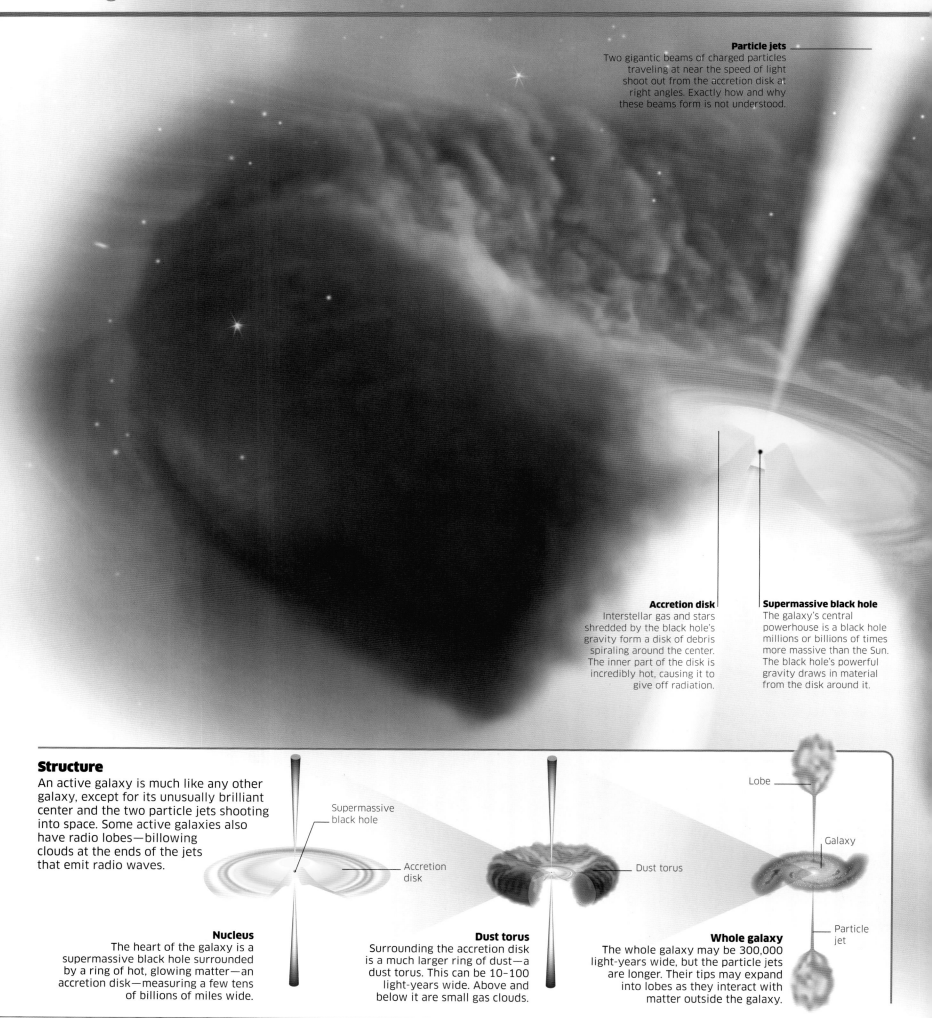

**Particle jets**
Two gigantic beams of charged particles traveling at near the speed of light shoot out from the accretion disk at right angles. Exactly how and why these beams form is not understood.

**Accretion disk**
Interstellar gas and stars shredded by the black hole's gravity form a disk of debris spiraling around the center. The inner part of the disk is incredibly hot, causing it to give off radiation.

**Supermassive black hole**
The galaxy's central powerhouse is a black hole millions or billions of times more massive than the Sun. The black hole's powerful gravity draws in material from the disk around it.

## Structure

An active galaxy is much like any other galaxy, except for its unusually brilliant center and the two particle jets shooting into space. Some active galaxies also have radio lobes—billowing clouds at the ends of the jets that emit radio waves.

Supermassive black hole

Accretion disk

Dust torus

Lobe

Galaxy

Particle jet

**Nucleus**
The heart of the galaxy is a supermassive black hole surrounded by a ring of hot, glowing matter—an accretion disk—measuring a few tens of billions of miles wide.

**Dust torus**
Surrounding the accretion disk is a much larger ring of dust—a dust torus. This can be 10–100 light-years wide. Above and below it are small gas clouds.

**Whole galaxy**
The whole galaxy may be 300,000 light-years wide, but the particle jets are longer. Their tips may expand into lobes as they interact with matter outside the galaxy.

Light from the farthest **quasars** has taken over **12 billion years** to reach us.

A **quasar** can emit **10,000 times more light** than our own galaxy.

**103**

# Active galaxies

**Galaxies glow in the darkness of space thanks to the light from their stars. A few galaxies, however, also blast out vast amounts of light and other types of radiation from their cores. These are active galaxies.**

The center, or nucleus, of an active galaxy emits a staggeringly large amount of electromagnetic radiation. This energy floods out into space not only as visible light but also as radio waves, X-rays, ultraviolet radiation, and gamma rays. The radiation comes from an intensely hot and dense disk of matter spiraling around and into a black hole perhaps a billion times the mass of the Sun—a supermassive black hole. Active galaxies also fling out jets of particles that penetrate deep into intergalactic space. These strange galaxies include some of the most distant objects we can see, such as quasars—objects so astonishingly far away that their light has taken billions of years to reach us, meaning they probably no longer exist.

**Dust torus**
In some active galaxies, a ring (torus) of gas and dust blocks our view of the central black hole and accretion disk.

Beyond the dust torus are the stars and clouds of gas and dust that make up the bulk of the galaxy.

## Types of active galaxies

Active galaxies seen from different angles or distances can look very different. As a result, astronomers have distinct names for what look like different objects but are actually part of the same family.

**Radio galaxies**
When seen with a radio telescope, radio galaxies are flanked by gigantic, billowing clouds called lobes. Those of Hercules A (above) are nearly ten times longer than our Milky Way galaxy.

**Seyfert galaxies**
These galaxies have much brighter centers than normal galaxies. Most, such as NGC 1566 above, are spiral in shape.

**Quasars**
The brightest objects in the universe are quasars, which are active galactic nuclei billions of light-years away. Studying them allows astronomers to look back in time billions of years.

**Blazars**
When the particle jet of an active galaxy points directly toward Earth, we see a blazar. These are active galactic nuclei, usually in elliptical galaxies.

# Colliding galaxies

**Neighboring galaxies sometimes drift close enough for the force of gravity to make them collide. Flying into each other at millions of miles per hour, they crash in a blaze of fireworks as colliding gas clouds give birth to thousands of new stars.**

Because the stars in a galaxy are so far apart, galaxies can collide without any of their stars crashing into one another. In fact, during a collision, two galaxies can pass right through each other. Nevertheless, the gravitational tug-of-war wreaks havoc on galaxies' shapes, tearing spiral arms apart and flinging billions of stars into space. Often the collision slows down the movement of the galaxies so much that a second or third pass-through happens. In time, the two galaxies may merge to form one larger galaxy.

The Whirlpool Galaxy has two very clear spiral arms. It was the first galaxy to be described as a spiral.

The dark stripes are "lanes" of dust that block the light from the stars behind them.

The Whirlpool Galaxy has a very bright center because it is what astronomers call an active galaxy—one in which huge amounts of light are being released by gas and dust spiraling into a central black hole.

Clusters of hundreds of thousands of hot, newborn stars blaze with a bluish light.

## Whirlpool Galaxy

About 300 million years ago, the Whirlpool Galaxy was struck by a dwarf galaxy that now appears to dangle from one of the larger galaxy's spiral arms. The dwarf galaxy, called NGC 5195, may already have passed through the Whirlpool Galaxy twice. The gravity of the dwarf galaxy has stirred up gas clouds inside the Whirlpool, triggering a burst of star formation. On a dark night, you can see this galactic collision through a small telescope in the constellation Canes Venatici.

**4** billion years—time left until the **Milky Way and Andromeda galaxies collide**.

The galaxy that will form when the **Milky Way and Andromeda merge** has already been given a name: **Milkdromeda**.

**105**

One arm of the Whirlpool seems to have been tugged out by gravity toward the dwarf galaxy, which lies behind it.

This dark lane is a bridge of dust joining the two galaxies. It blocks the light from the stars behind, which tells us that the dwarf galaxy must be farther away than the Whirlpool Galaxy.

The shape of the dwarf galaxy has been distorted by the collision. Any spiral arms it may once have had are no longer visible.

The bright pink areas are clouds of gas and dust that have been stirred up by the collision, causing millions of new stars to form.

## Oddball galaxies

The universe contains many strange-looking galaxies that do not seem to fit into the usual galaxy classification system. Astronomers think many of these oddities are the result of collisions, mergers, or other interactions between two or more galaxies.

### Cartwheel Galaxy
This bizarre object formed when a spiral galaxy bumped into a smaller companion 200 million years ago. The shock wave it produced rearranged the galaxies into a bluish ring and a central bright portion.

### The Porpoise
Here, what was once a spiral galaxy is being reshaped by the gravity of a galaxy below it. The end result looks like a porpoise leaping over a fuzzy oval ball. A burst of newly formed blue stars forms the porpoise's nose.

### Antennae Galaxies
These intertwined spiral galaxies are going through a "starburst" phase. Clouds of dust and gas are compressing each other, causing stars to form rapidly. The areas of star formation glow with brilliant pinks and blues.

## Future galactic merger
Our own galaxy—the Milky Way—is hurtling toward the neighboring Andromeda Galaxy at 250,000 mph (400,000 km/h). Billions of years from now, they will collide and eventually merge. Above is an artist's idea of how the collision might look from Earth around the time it starts, with the Andromeda Galaxy (left) grown to an enormous size in the night sky.

## Nearby clusters

Spread out in many directions from the Local Group are other galaxy clusters, a few of which are shown below. Clusters are grouped into even bigger structures called superclusters.

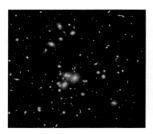

**Abell 1689**
This buzzing hive of galaxies is one of the biggest clusters known.

**Virgo cluster**
Two elliptical galaxies resembling eyes lie near the center of this cluster.

**Leo cluster**
The Leo cluster is part of a huge sheet of galaxies known as the Great Wall.

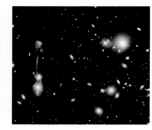

**Abell 1185**
This cluster contains an odd-looking galaxy called the Guitar (left).

## Gravitational lensing

Galaxy clusters contain so much matter that their gravity can bend light rays passing close by. As a result, they act like giant lenses in space and can distort the shapes of more distant galaxies as viewed from Earth. This effect is known as gravitational lensing.

Actual galaxy

Galaxy cluster acting as lens

The distorted image we see from Earth

Light bent by lens

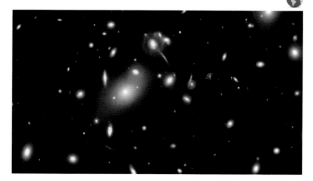

**Space bananas**
The banana-shaped arcs in the lower left of this image of galaxy cluster Abell 2218 are galaxies beyond the cluster. Their appearance has been warped by gravitational lensing.

## Local Group

Our home galaxy belongs to a cluster called the Local Group. The Local Group has three large spiral or barred spiral galaxies—the Milky Way, Andromeda, and Triangulum—and more than 50 smaller dwarf and irregular galaxies. They are spread out over a region roughly 10 million light-years across. Many of the smaller galaxies are clustered around the two largest spirals.

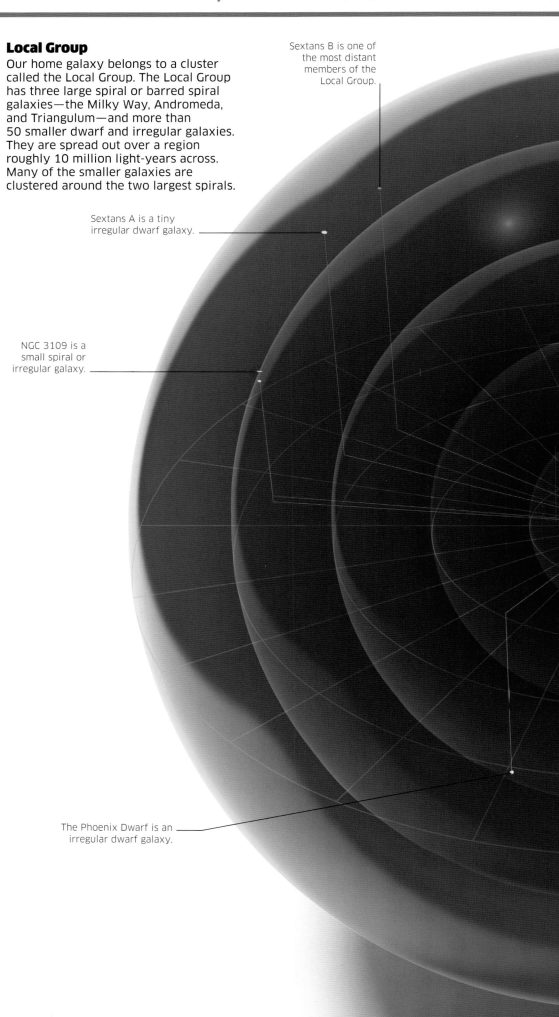

Sextans B is one of the most distant members of the Local Group.

Sextans A is a tiny irregular dwarf galaxy.

NGC 3109 is a small spiral or irregular galaxy.

The Phoenix Dwarf is an irregular dwarf galaxy.

**90%** of the mass in galaxy clusters is **dark matter**.

The **Triangulum Galaxy** is the **most distant object** visible to the naked eye.

There are **billions** of galaxy clusters in the universe.

**107**

# Galaxy clusters

**Galaxies are held together in clusters by gravity, sometimes orbiting each other and often colliding. These clusters typically measure a few million light-years across.**

Some galaxy clusters are quite sparse and contain only a few galaxies. The cluster that our own Milky Way galaxy belongs to is one of these. Other clusters are much denser and contain hundreds or thousands of galaxies, often arranged chaotically but sometimes forming a neat, spherical pattern. A giant elliptical galaxy usually lies at the center of these dense clusters. Galaxy clusters don't just contain galaxies. They also contain large amounts of thin, hot gas and mysterious dark matter, which we can't see.

**Milky Way**
Our home galaxy is a barred spiral and is the second-largest galaxy in the Local Group (after Andromeda). A swarm of small galaxies surrounds it.

IC10 is flying toward the Milky Way at 217 miles (350 km) per second.

M110 is a dwarf elliptical galaxy.

The Wolf-Lundmark-Melotte galaxy lies on the edge of the Local Group.

**Andromeda Galaxy**
The largest galaxy in our cluster is Andromeda—a beautiful barred spiral some 140,000 light-years wide that has about a trillion stars. On a dark night with no light pollution, it can be seen quite easily through binoculars or even with the naked eye as a gray smudge. We see the galaxy nearly edge-on.

**Triangulum Galaxy**
Sometimes called the Pinwheel Galaxy or M33, Triangulum is a spiral galaxy. It is the third-largest galaxy in the Local Group. About 50,000 light-years wide, from Earth it appears almost face-on. It is visible through binoculars or, less easily, with the naked eye on a very dark night.

## The shape of space

The three dimensions of space are "bent" by the gravitational pull of all the matter in the universe into a fourth dimension, which we cannot see. Since this is hard to visualize, scientists use the metaphor of a two-dimensional rubber sheet to explain the idea. Scientists used to think that the rubber sheet might be bent in any of three ways, depending on how densely packed with matter the universe is. We now know that the observable universe has a "flat" shape.

**Closed**
A dense universe would bend itself into a closed shape. In such a universe, traveling in a straight line would eventually bring you back to your starting point.

**Open**
If the universe is of low density, it might extend into an "open" shape. In this case, it would be infinite in size and have no outer edge.

**Flat**
Our universe appears to have just the right concentration of matter to have a "flat" shape. This suggests it will keep expanding forever, and like an open universe it might be infinite in size.

**① Earth**
Our home world is a small, rocky planet floating in the enormous emptiness of space. Our nearest neighboring planet, Venus, is about a 15-minute journey away at the speed of light.

**② Solar system**
Earth belongs to a family of planets and other objects that orbit the Sun. The farthest planet, Neptune, is 4.5 hours away at the speed of light, but the whole solar system is over 3 light-years wide.

**③ Local stars**
The closest star to the Sun is about 4 light-years away. Within 16 light-years of the Sun, there are 43 star systems containing 60 stars. Some of these star systems may have families of planets too.

**④ Milky Way**
The Sun and its neighboring stars occupy a tiny fraction of the Milky Way galaxy—a vast, swirling disk containing 200 billion stars and enormous clouds of gas and dust. It is over 100,000 light-years wide.

**100** billion trillion—the estimated **number of stars** in the observable universe.

**109**

# The universe

**Everything in the universe is a part of something bigger. Earth is part of the solar system, which lies in the Milky Way galaxy, which is just a tiny bit of the whole universe.**

The scale of the universe defies imagination. Astronomers use light as a yardstick to measure distance because nothing can cross the vast expanses of interstellar space faster. Yet even one light-year—the distance light travels in a whole year, or 6 trillion miles (10 trillion km)—is dwarfed by the largest structures observed in the known universe. Only a fraction of the universe is visible to us: the part of the universe from which light has had time to reach Earth since the Big Bang. The true extent of the universe is unknown—it may even be infinite in size.

Edge of observable universe

Orion arm of the Milky Way

**5 Virgo supercluster**
Our galaxy is just one of tens of thousands of galaxies that are clustered together in a group called the Virgo supercluster. This vast array of galaxies is more than 100 million light-years across.

**6 Supercluster filaments**
Superclusters form a web of massive, threadlike structures called filaments, which occupy about 5 percent of the visible universe. Between these are immense, bubblelike voids.

**7 Observable universe**
The part of the universe we can see is about 93 billion light-years across, with Earth at the center. It contains millions of superclusters, forming a vast, foamlike structure. What lies beyond is unknown.

The Milky Way and nearby galaxies are being drawn toward a mysterious concentration of mass in intergalactic space called the **Great Attractor**.

## Afterglow of the Big Bang

A faint afterglow of the Big Bang exists throughout space. This radiation was released when the universe was about 380,000 years old and still extremely hot. The image on the right is a map of the radiation across the whole sky. The variations in intensity, shown in color, are due to minute variations in density in the early universe. Gravity, working on these tiny variations, created the uneven distribution of matter we can see in the universe today, with clusters of galaxies separated by immense voids.

One millionth of a trillionth of a trillionth of a second after the Big Bang

One millionth of a second after the Big Bang

350,000 years after the Big Bang

400,000 years after the Big Bang

500 million years after the Big Bang

3 billion years after the Big Bang

Energy turns into particles

Atoms form

The universe becomes transparent as light begins to pass freely through space.

# The Big Bang

**About 14 billion years ago, the universe suddenly appeared from nowhere as a tiny concentration of pure energy. It then expanded trillions of trillions of times in an instant—an event known as the Big Bang.**

In the first millisecond of existence, the intense energy of the newborn universe produced a vast number of subatomic particles (particles smaller than atoms). Some of these joined together to form the nuclei (centers) of atoms—the building blocks of all the matter we see in the universe today. But it wasn't until the universe was about 380,000 years old that actual atoms formed, and it wasn't until hundreds of millions of years later that galaxies and stars appeared. As well as producing energy and matter, the Big Bang also gave rise to four basic forces that govern the way everything in the universe works, from the force of gravity to the forces that hold atoms together. Ever since the Big Bang, the universe has continued to expand and cool down, and it will probably continue doing so forever.

**1** The universe starts as an unimaginably hot point of energy, infinitely smaller than a single atom.

**2** In a tiny fraction of a second, it expands to the size of a city, and the rate of inflation then slows. This is not an explosion of matter into space, but an expansion of space itself.

**3** So far, the universe is just energy. But soon, a seething mass of tiny particles and antiparticles (the same as their corresponding particles, but with the opposite electric charge) form from this energy. Most of these cancel out, turning back into energy, but some are left over.

**4** The leftover matter begins to form protons and neutrons.

By now, the universe is about a millionth of a second old. Within a few minutes, the neutrons and many of the protons join to form atomic nuclei.

**5** About 380,000 years later, the universe has cooled enough for atomic nuclei to combine with electrons to make hydrogen and helium atoms.

**6** The universe is now a vast cloud of hydrogen and helium atoms. Light can pass more easily through space, so the universe becomes transparent. Gravity acts on tiny variations in the gas cloud, pulling the gas into clumps that will eventually become galaxies.

**7** Around 550 million years after the Big Bang, the first stars ignite in the densest parts of these gas clumps. By 600 million years after the Big Bang,

12 billion years
after the Big Bang

7 billion years
after the Big Bang

8

9

10

galaxies have formed. The first
galaxies are small and irregular, with
many bright knots of star formation.
As they evolve and merge, they grow
larger and develop spiral shapes.

**8** Now 5 billion years old, the universe
consists of vast clusters of galaxies
arranged in threads with gigantic voids
between them.

**9** About 8 billion years after the Big
Bang, the expansion of the universe
accelerates. Our solar system forms about
9 billion years after the Big Bang.

**10** The universe is predicted to continue
expanding forever, becoming cold
and dark everywhere.

Solar system
forms

Universe keeps
expanding forever

# EXPLORING SPACE

People have studied the stars and planets for centuries, but it wasn't until 1957 that the first human-made object went into orbit, marking the beginning of the Space Age. Since then, thousands of rockets have been launched, hundreds of people have become astronauts, and 12 men have walked on the Moon.

## SPACE TAXIS

The Space Shuttle is the only reusable spacecraft that has ever been to space. After taking off vertically like a rocket, it landed back on Earth like a plane. Five different shuttles operated between 1981 and the end of the program in 2011. Many of the missions were for building the International Space Station (ISS).

The main part of the Space Shuttle was called the orbiter.

Booster rockets fell back to Earth after launch, to be retrieved and reused.

**ATLANTIS LIFTING OFF FROM KENNEDY SPACE CENTER**

**Soyuz**
Russia's Soyuz craft have been operating since the 1960s and are now used to ferry astronauts to the ISS.

**Orion**
For future trips to the Moon, asteroids, and Mars, Orion will be launched by the US Space Launch System (SLS) rocket.

**Dragon**
Dragon became the first privately built craft to visit the International Space Station (ISS) when it docked in 2012.

**Boeing CST-100**
This future craft, designed to be reused ten times, will ferry crews of up to seven to the International Space Station.

# Space exploration

Space starts a mere 60 miles (100 km) above our heads. It is a short journey away—less than ten minutes by rocket—but it is a dangerous and difficult one. We've been sending spacecraft to explore the solar system for only 60 years or so, but we've been using telescopes to explore the skies for more than 400 years, and our curiosity about the cosmos goes back millennia. The more we discover, the more we want to explore.

## LAUNCH SITES

There are about 30 launch sites on Earth, nine of which are shown below. The best place to launch from is near the equator, where a rocket gets an extra push from Earth's spin. The largest launch site is Baikonur, which sends spacecraft to the International Space Station.

VANDENBERG, US

CAPE CANAVERAL/ KENNEDY SPACE CENTER, US

KOUROU, FRENCH GUIANA

YASNY, RUSSIA

BAIKONUR, KAZAKHSTAN

SRIHARIKOTA, INDIA

JIUQUAN, CHINA

XICHANG, CHINA

TANEGASHIMA, JAPAN

## LAUNCH VEHICLES

Rockets are built not to explore space themselves but to launch other smaller vehicles, such as satellites or planetary spacecraft, into orbit. The smaller vehicle usually travels in the rocket's nose. Built to make the journey only once, rockets are destroyed as they fall back to Earth and burn up. The larger the rocket, the heavier and more complicated the cargo it can carry. Most rockets carrying spacecraft are launched by the US, Russia, and Europe.

- US
- Russia
- China
- Japan
- India

GSLV, MKII, INDIA—161 ft (49 m) tall

PROTON, RUSSIA—174 ft (53 m) tall

H-IIB, JAPAN—186 ft (57 m) tall

ATLAS V, US—191 ft (58 m) tall

LONG MARCH 2F, CHINA—203 ft (62 m) tall

FALCON 9, US—224 ft (68 m) tall

# SPACE EXPLORERS

Over 130 spacecraft have successfully left Earth to explore the solar system. All have been robotic, except for the crewed Apollo craft that went to the Moon. Powered by the Sun or by radioactive chemicals, robotic craft can work for years, peering down onto planets from orbit or landing to explore the surface. They send data and often spectacular images back to Earth.

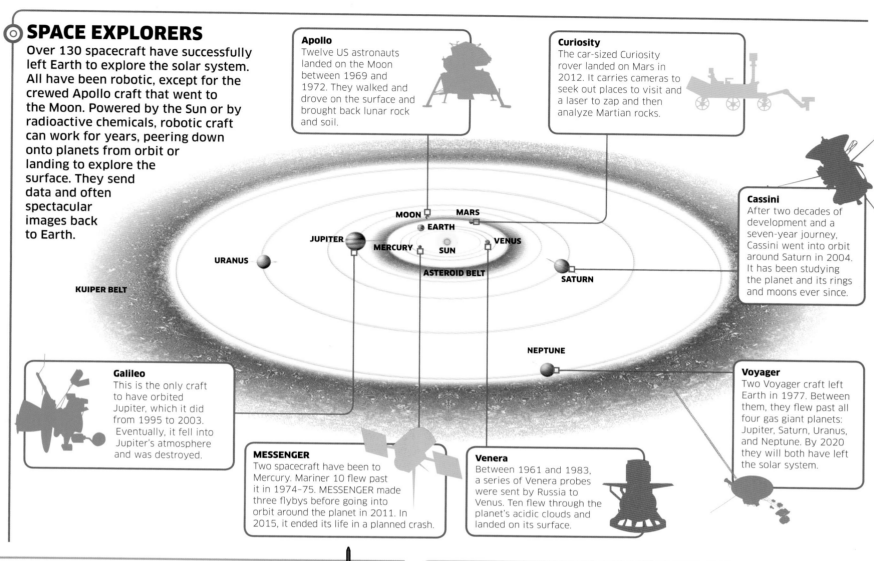

**Apollo**
Twelve US astronauts landed on the Moon between 1969 and 1972. They walked and drove on the surface and brought back lunar rock and soil.

**Curiosity**
The car-sized Curiosity rover landed on Mars in 2012. It carries cameras to seek out places to visit and a laser to zap and then analyze Martian rocks.

**Cassini**
After two decades of development and a seven-year journey, Cassini went into orbit around Saturn in 2004. It has been studying the planet and its rings and moons ever since.

**Galileo**
This is the only craft to have orbited Jupiter, which it did from 1995 to 2003. Eventually, it fell into Jupiter's atmosphere and was destroyed.

**MESSENGER**
Two spacecraft have been to Mercury. Mariner 10 flew past it in 1974–75. MESSENGER made three flybys before going into orbit around the planet in 2011. In 2015, it ended its life in a planned crash.

**Venera**
Between 1961 and 1983, a series of Venera probes were sent by Russia to Venus. Ten flew through the planet's acidic clouds and landed on its surface.

**Voyager**
Two Voyager craft left Earth in 1977. Between them, they flew past all four gas giant planets: Jupiter, Saturn, Uranus, and Neptune. By 2020 they will both have left the solar system.

MOON · MARS · EARTH · JUPITER · MERCURY · VENUS · SUN · URANUS · ASTEROID BELT · SATURN · NEPTUNE · KUIPER BELT

DELTA IV HEAVY, US—236 ft (72 m) tall

N1, RUSSIA—344 ft (105 m) tall

SATURN V, US—364 ft (111 m) tall

SLS, US (LARGE CONFIGURATION)—403 ft (123 m) tall

# SEEING THE INVISIBLE

As well as producing light that our eyes can see, objects in space produce other kinds of radiation that are invisible to us. All types of radiation travel as waves. Astronomers use special telescopes to capture waves of different lengths, from radio waves, which have long wavelengths, to gamma rays, which are very short.

**Infrared telescope**
Star-forming nebulas are easy to see with infrared telescopes, which capture the heat (infrared rays) that the nebulas produce.

**X-ray telescope**
An X-ray telescope can see objects that are releasing huge amounts of energy, such as the area around a black hole.

VISIBLE · ULTRAVIOLET · X-RAY

RADIO · MICROWAVE · INFRARED · GAMMA

**Radio telescope**
Radio waves are the longest. They have revealed galaxies that would otherwise remain unseen.

**Microwave telescope**
Telescopes that capture microwaves allow us to see the afterglow of the Big Bang.

**Optical telescope**
Optical telescopes use visible light but magnify the image, letting us see farther than the naked eye.

**20,000 years ago**
In Africa, people mark pieces of bone with what may be the first record of Moon phases. Farmers follow the cycles of the Sun and Moon to plan their crops.

**5,000–1,000 years ago**
For ancient peoples, astronomy is part of religion. Many sacred monuments, such as Stonehenge in England, are built to align with the Sun or constellations.

# Discovering space

**The history of astronomy and the study of the heavens spans thousands of years, linking ancient religious sites with high-tech 21st-century observatories and spacecraft.**

Since the dawn of history, people have looked into the night sky and wondered what the countless points of light were. It wasn't until fairly recently that we realized the stars are suns like ours, but incredibly far away. Just as early seafarers explored the world in search of new lands, modern explorers have sailed into space on voyages of discovery. Only a few people have visited another world, but scores of robotic probes have ventured to the planets on our behalf.

### 1926: Rocket science
American engineer Robert Goddard successfully fires the first liquid-fueled rocket. It rises 41 ft (12 m) into the air before fizzling out. Over the next 15 years, he launches another 34 rockets, some of which soar to heights of more than 1.2 miles (2 km).

**GODDARD WITH ROCKET**

**FRUIT FLY**

### 1947: First animals in space
The US adapts captured German V2 rockets, used as deadly weapons in World War II, to send the first living creatures into space. The earliest astro-animals are fruit flies, followed by monkeys. The missions aim to see how animals' bodies respond to being in space.

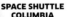

**SPACE SHUTTLE COLUMBIA**

### 1976–77: Mars and beyond
Two American space robots, Viking 1 and 2, land on Mars, carry out soil tests, and send back color images. In 1977, the space probe Voyager 2 blasts off, eventually flying by Jupiter, Saturn, Uranus, and Neptune.

### 1971–73: Living in space
Space stations allow astronauts to spend weeks in orbit. The first, in 1971, is the Russian Salyut 1. The US follows with its own, Skylab, in 1973.

**SKYLAB SPACE STATION**

### 1981: Shuttle launch
The 1980s see missions begin for the Space Shuttle, the first reusable crewed orbiter. Shuttles will remain in service until 2011. In 1986 the Russians start to build the Mir space station.

### 1990: Hubble
The Hubble Space Telescope is placed in orbit. It reveals many distant wonders of space never seen before.

**PILLAR AND JETS IN THE CARINA NEBULA**

### 2009–12: Kepler Observatory
NASA launches the Kepler Observatory, which uses a special light-measuring device to search for planets orbiting distant stars.

**ARTIST'S IMPRESSION OF KEPLER SPACECRAFT**

**Footprints** left by astronauts on the Moon will stay visible for at least **100 million years**.

**18** The number of **astronauts who have died** during spaceflight missions.

**117**

STONEHENGE, ENGLAND

COPERNICUS'S DRAWING OF THE SOLAR SYSTEM

## 1540s: A shocking idea

Polish astronomer Nicolaus Copernicus writes a book about a shocking new idea. He suggests that the Sun, not Earth, is at the center of the solar system.

## 1890s: Science fiction

The first science fiction novels hit the market. Books like *The War of the Worlds* and *The Time Machine*, both written by H.G.Wells, arouse public interest in space exploration and also inspire serious science projects.

ISAAC NEWTON'S TELESCOPE

## 1600s: Telescopes

Italian astronomer Galileo Galilei greatly improves telescope design, and the solar system can now be seen clearly. English scientist Isaac Newton explains how gravity holds the planets in orbit around the Sun.

## 1957: Sputnik

In Russia, rocket scientists achieve two firsts this year. They send up the first artificial satellite, Sputnik 1, and a month later they launch Sputnik 2, which carries Laika, the first dog to go into orbit. As planned, Laika perishes at the end of the mission.

80 мɵ
MONGOLIA·МОНГОЛ ШУУДАН

## 1961: First person in space

Russian cosmonaut Yuri Gagarin becomes the first person in space, orbiting Earth in a flight lasting just over 100 minutes. Later in the decade, the Russians achieve the first human spacewalk (1965) and the first soft landing on the Moon by a spacecraft (1966).

STATUE OF YURI GAGARIN IN MOSCOW, RUSSIA

LUNOKHOD 1

## 1970: First rover

Russians launch the first lunar roving vehicle: Lunokhod 1, a remote-controlled, eight-wheeled buggy. It soft-lands on the Moon and operates for 11 days, sending back pictures and taking soil samples.

## 1969: Men on the Moon

The United States' Apollo 11 craft lands the first people on the Moon: Neil Armstrong and Buzz Aldrin. The astronauts stay for nearly 24 hours, collecting Moon rocks and taking photographs of the lunar surface.

COMET 67P

## 2014: Comet landing

A robotic device detaches from the Rosetta space probe and makes the first soft landing on a comet, called 67P. It returns images and information about the comet's water content.

## Into the future

Over the coming decades, a focus of space research will be the continuing hunt for distant planets that might harbor life. A manned mission to Mars by 2050 may be feasible.

**118** exploring space ○ **TELESCOPES**

**798** The **number of segments** in the main mirror of the European Extremely Large Telescope.

# Telescopes

**The first telescopes were little more than handheld wooden tubes, but they allowed astronomers to discover mountains on the Moon and moons around Jupiter. Today's giant telescopes let us see billions of light-years into the far reaches of space.**

Like eyes, telescopes collect light and focus it to create an image. Unlike our eyes, however, telescopes can train their sights on tiny targets and can add together the light they receive over a long period. The bigger a telescope is, the more light it can collect and the sharper the image. With a large telescope, we can zoom in on distant galaxies or volcanoes on Mars. The first telescopes used glass lenses, but big lenses bend under their own weight, so astronomers switched to mirrors to make telescopes bigger. In the largest telescopes, dozens of mirror segments are arranged together to form one giant, curved mirror. Earth's atmosphere blurs our view of space, so large professional telescopes are built on mountains where the air is dry and still, or launched into space.

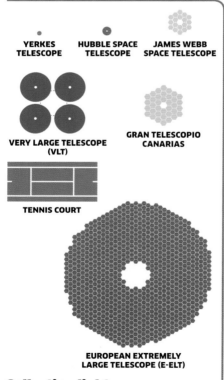

YERKES TELESCOPE

HUBBLE SPACE TELESCOPE

JAMES WEBB SPACE TELESCOPE

VERY LARGE TELESCOPE (VLT)

GRAN TELESCOPIO CANARIAS

TENNIS COURT

EUROPEAN EXTREMELY LARGE TELESCOPE (E-ELT)

## Collecting light

A key part of a telescope is the mirror or lens that collects light. The world's largest telescope lens (in the Yerkes telescope) is only 40 in (1 m) wide. Mirrors made of hexagonal segments in a honeycomb pattern can be far bigger. The E-ELT mirror will be nearly four times larger in area than a tennis court.

The second mirror receives light from the main mirror and reflects it to a third mirror.

The adaptive mirror changes shape to counteract blurring caused by the atmosphere.

The main mirror is made of 798 hexagonal segments, each 5 ft (1.45 m) wide.

The fifth mirror sends light to the instrument platform.

Lasers create artificial stars to help the telescope remove blurring.

The third mirror sends light to the adaptive mirror above.

Springlike devices at the base of the building stop vibrations from distant earthquakes from shaking the telescope.

**10,000** The approximate **number of professional astronomers** in the world.

The largest telescopes can collect **100 million times more light** than the human eye.

**119**

A cradle tilts the telescope.

Cameras are housed on the instrument platform.

The main deck supports the telescope's weight of 2,800 tons and can rotate to turn the telescope around.

## Laser guidance

Moving air in the atmosphere makes stars twinkle, distorting the images telescopes capture. The E-ELT will use an ingenious system to cancel out this twinkling movement. It will shine lasers into the sky to create an artificial star and analyze the star's twinkling motion. A computer-controlled "adaptive mirror" will then change shape 1,000 times per second to counteract the motion, giving the telescope near-perfect vision.

## How simple telescopes work

A telescope uses a lens or a mirror to collect light from distant objects and focus it to create an image. In simple telescopes, the image is viewed through an eyepiece lens that magnifies the image. Telescopes that use lenses to capture light are called refractors. Those that use mirrors are called reflectors.

Light from object

Main lens

Image forms at focal point

### Refractor

A glass lens collects the light and focuses it into an image. A smaller lens inside the eyepiece magnifies the image.

Light from object

Image forms at focal point

Main mirror

Second mirror

### Reflector

A mirror collects the light and reflects it onto a second mirror. The light is then directed to a focus, and the image is viewed through an eyepiece, which may be on the side of the telescope. The mirror is made of glass with a thin coating of aluminum.

## In a different light

Telescopes collect wavelengths of energy other than light. Each wavelength reveals different details in an object. A typical galaxy, such as the Andromeda Galaxy (below), gives off energy in many wavelengths. X-rays, for instance, come from very hot areas, and radio waves come from colder areas.

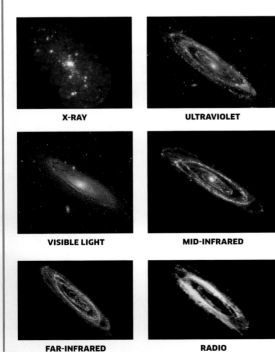

**X-RAY**      **ULTRAVIOLET**

**VISIBLE LIGHT**      **MID-INFRARED**

**FAR-INFRARED**      **RADIO**

## Extremely Large Telescope

The world's largest telescope is currently being built on the Cerro Amazones mountain in Chile, where the sky is clear almost every night and there are excellent views of the southern stars. Called the European Extremely Large Telescope (E-ELT), it will be as tall as a 15-story building, and its enormous mirror will gather more light than all 13 of the world's current largest telescopes combined. A computer-controlled "adaptive mirror" will make the images as sharp as those of a space telescope.

**120**

**43.5** ft (13.2 m)—the length of Hubble, about the size of a **tour bus**.

**40** million—the approximate **number of stars** Gaia looks at every day.

The aperture door closes during repair missions to protect the mirrors.

Radio dish

A very strong carbon-fiber frame keeps Hubble perfectly straight.

Light from object in space

Second mirror

Solar panels

## Hubble telescope

Hubble was launched into orbit by a Space Shuttle in 1990 and orbits Earth at a height of 355 miles (570 km), circling the planet once every 97 minutes. Astronauts have made five trips to service Hubble, the last one in 2009, when they installed a new camera. Eventually Hubble will wear out and be replaced by the James Webb Space Telescope.

# Space telescopes

**The best place to see the stars is from space, where Earth's atmosphere doesn't get in the way. Space telescopes work much like ground telescopes but give a pin-sharp view of distant objects and keep working all day and night, all year round.**

Dozens of telescopes have been launched into space. They orbit Earth as satellites or orbit the Sun, staying close to Earth. They collect not just visible light but other types of radiation that our eyes can't see or that can't get through the atmosphere, such as X-rays or ultraviolet radiation. Each space telescope is designed for a specific job. The Kepler telescope is searching for exoplanets, for example, and Gaia is making a 3-D map of stars around the Sun. Telescopes in space wear out just like the ones on Earth, but the repair person can't visit if things go wrong. Only the Hubble Space Telescope was designed to be serviced in space by astronauts.

**1** billion—the approximate number of pixels in Gaia's camera—the **largest camera in space**.

**120** gigabytes—the **amount of data** Hubble sends to Earth each week.

The James Webb's mirror will collect **seven times** more light than Hubble's mirror.

**121**

**Main mirror**
The 8-ft- (2.4-m-) wide main mirror in the Hubble Space Telescope collects light and reflects it onto a second mirror. The second mirror reflects the beam back through a hole in the middle of the main mirror to a suite of cameras and scientific instruments. Hubble's main mirror is almost perfectly smooth. If it were scaled up to the size of Earth, the biggest bump on its surface would be just 15 cm (6 in) high.

Guidance cameras aim the telescope at a target and keep it pointing in the right direction.

Wide Field Camera 3 takes photographs using visible light.

A spectrograph can tell which elements are in stars and galaxies by studying the color of their light.

A "soft capture mechanism" was attached to Hubble in 2009 to make it easy for spacecraft to grab hold of.

## Looking deep
When we look into space, we are looking back in time. Since its launch, Hubble has let us see deeper and deeper into space, revealing young galaxies in the early universe. The James Webb Space Telescope will look even deeper to see newborn galaxies.

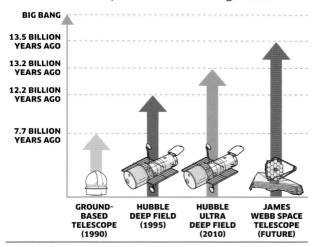

BIG BANG

13.5 BILLION YEARS AGO

13.2 BILLION YEARS AGO

12.2 BILLION YEARS AGO

7.7 BILLION YEARS AGO

GROUND-BASED TELESCOPE (1990)

HUBBLE DEEP FIELD (1995)

HUBBLE ULTRA DEEP FIELD (2010)

JAMES WEBB SPACE TELESCOPE (FUTURE)

## Hubble hits
Astronomers have processed the data from Hubble to create many beautiful images, including galaxies, starbirth regions such as the Eagle Nebula, and dying stars such as the Cat's Eye Nebula.

**SOMBRERO GALAXY**

**CAT'S EYE NEBULA**

**EAGLE NEBULA**

# Rockets

It takes a staggering amount of energy to break free from Earth's gravitational pull and fly into space. The only vehicles capable of doing this are rockets, which harness the explosive power of burning fuel to lift cargo such as satellites and spacecraft into orbit. **Most of a rocket's weight is fuel, and nearly all of it is consumed in the first few minutes, burning at a rate of up to 15 tons every second.**

People used rockets as weapons for hundreds of years before they became safe and powerful enough to reach space. Since the first spaceflight in 1944, rockets have gotten larger and more complicated. A modern rocket is really several rockets in one, with separate "stages" stacked together. When the lowest stage runs out of fuel, it drops off, making the remaining vehicle lighter. The stage above then ignites. The cargo is usually in the uppermost stage, under the rocket's nose. Most rockets are built to fly to space only once and are destroyed as their parts fall back to Earth.

### Launch pad
The SLS's space journey will start at the Kennedy Space Center in Florida. Launch pad 39B was once used by the Apollo Moon missions and the Space Shuttle.

### Space Launch System
Standing taller than the Statue of Liberty, the Space Launch System (SLS) is a giant new rocket being built by NASA for spaceflights in the 2020s. When complete, it could launch crewed spacecraft to the Moon, near-Earth asteroids, and Mars. The configuration shown here has one main rocket stage and two booster rockets on the side. Inside the rocket's nose is the Orion spacecraft, with its own rocket engine. Taller configurations with an extra stage will allow the SLS to launch heavier cargo.

### How rockets work
Most of the body of a rocket is taken up by huge tanks containing fuel and an oxidizer (a chemical needed to make fuel burn). Once ignited, these two chemicals react explosively to make hot gases, which rush out of the rear nozzle. The rush of hot gases creates the force of thrust that pushes the rocket forward.

Liquid oxygen

Fuel

Pumps

Combustion chamber

Nozzle

Exhaust gases

THRUST

**Escape rocket**
The nose cone is a small rocket designed to carry the crew module away safely during an emergency.

Steering engines for escape rocket

**Crew module**
This is the only part of the Orion spacecraft that will return to Earth, using a parachute to splash down in the ocean.

### Onward to Mars
Powered by its own rocket engine, the Orion spacecraft will be able to carry astronauts farther into space than ever before. The crew will live inside the conical section at the front, which is based on the command module used by astronauts during the Apollo Moon missions.

**2,500** tons—the weight of the SLS rocket, equivalent to **7.5 jet airliners**.

**44** million horsepower—the combined power of the SLS's two **booster rockets**.

**2** The average number of **rocket launches** from Earth every week.

**123**

## Cargo weight

The heavier a rocket's cargo, the more fuel is needed to lift it, which adds further to the weight. The Saturn V rocket used for the Apollo Moon missions carried a cargo as heavy as 20 elephants, but the whole rocket weighed as much as 400 elephants.

**CARGO WEIGHT**

**SLS MAXIMUM CARGO** 130 tons

**SATURN V** 118 tons

**SLS WITH ORION (SMALL CONFIGURATION)** 70 tons

**SPACE SHUTTLE** 29 tons

## Thrust

The force that pushes a rocket is called thrust. To reach low Earth orbit, a rocket must generate enough thrust to reach a speed of 18,000 mph (29,000 km/h)—nine times faster than a bullet.

**MAXIMUM TOTAL THRUST**

**SLS** 37 million Newtons (8.4 million pounds)

**SPACE SHUTTLE** 35 million Newtons (7.8 million pounds)

**SATURN V** 34 million Newtons (7.6 million pounds)

### Main engines
At the base of the rocket are four RS-25 engines—the same kind of engine that was used to power the Space Shuttles. Working together, the SLS's main engines and boosters produce as much power as 13,400 train engines.

### Service module
The central section of the Orion spacecraft carries fuel and other supplies.

### Spacecraft engine
Orion's engine will be able to propel the craft to Mars in three to four months.

### Boosters
Two booster rockets provide most of the thrust needed for liftoff. They produce enough power in two minutes to supply 92,000 homes for a whole day.

124 exploring space ∘ **FIRST PERSON IN SPACE**

**6** The **number of crewed spaceflights** made in the Vostok spacecraft.

# First person in space

**In 1961, Russian pilot Yuri Gagarin became the first person in space when he made a daredevil two-hour trip around Earth in a tiny spacecraft called Vostok 1. Since then, more than 500 people have been to space.**

The race to put the first person in space began in October 1957, when Russia's unmanned Sputnik 1 became the first spacecraft to orbit the planet. Sputnik 2 followed later that year, carrying a dog called Laika—a stray from the streets of Moscow. The craft was not designed to return to Earth, so Laika died during the mission. About three years later, Yuri Gagarin made his historic trip, and within six weeks of his return the US pledged to put men on the Moon. The first space travelers were jet pilots who were used to dangerous, physically grueling flights and had been trained to use ejector seats and parachutes. But even for experienced pilots, space travel could be deadly. Of the 100 or so uncrewed missions before Gagarin's flight, half ended in failure. And prior to Vostok 1, no one was certain that a human could travel to space and return alive to Earth.

The descent module was covered by a heat shield material to protect it from temperatures of about 5,400°F (3,000°C) as it reentered the atmosphere.

The walls were insulated to reduce noise and vibration.

Air tanks for cabin

**SERVICE MODULE**

Radio antenna

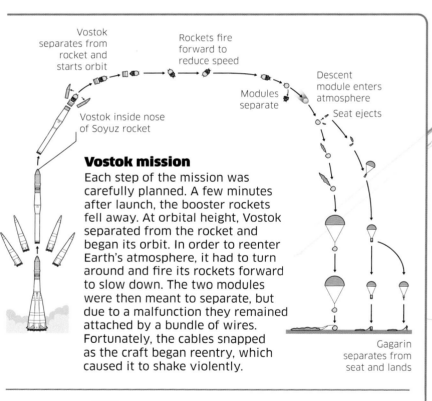

Vostok separates from rocket and starts orbit

Rockets fire forward to reduce speed

Vostok inside nose of Soyuz rocket

Modules separate

Descent module enters atmosphere

Seat ejects

Gagarin separates from seat and lands

### Vostok mission

Each step of the mission was carefully planned. A few minutes after launch, the booster rockets fell away. At orbital height, Vostok separated from the rocket and began its orbit. In order to reenter Earth's atmosphere, it had to turn around and fire its rockets forward to slow down. The two modules were then meant to separate, but due to a malfunction they remained attached by a bundle of wires. Fortunately, the cables snapped as the craft began reentry, which caused it to shake violently.

### Around the world

Gagarin took off from the Baikonur Cosmodrome (space center) in Kazakhstan and traveled east around the planet, taking 108 minutes to complete a single orbit. Vostok's modules separated when he was over Africa, and Gagarin landed shortly afterward in a grassy field near the Russian town of Engels.

# 1963 The year of the **first spaceflight by a woman** (Russian engineer Valentina Tereshkova).

**125**

TV camera

Instrument panel

## Vostok

The Vostok spacecraft consisted of two sections that separated before Gagarin headed for home. He traveled in the ball-shaped descent module—the part of the craft designed to return to Earth. Only 7.5 ft (2.3 m) wide, it housed little besides Gagarin, his ejector seat, and an instrument panel. The other section was the service module, which carried air tanks, fuel, and a small rocket to turn the craft around in space. In 1961, nobody knew whether Gagarin would be able to operate controls when he was weightless, so Vostok was flown by remote control.

**DESCENT MODULE**

Radio antenna for communication with Earth

### Russian hero

Yuri Gagarin was a pilot in the Soviet air force before he trained to be a cosmonaut (Russian astronaut). He was only 27 when he flew in Vostok and was a Russian hero for the rest of his life, with huge crowds gathering wherever he went. He never returned to space and was killed piloting a jet in 1968. Today, a 130-ft- (40-m-) tall titanium statue of him stands in Moscow, and his home town has been renamed Gagarin in his honor.

In case of emergency, Yuri Gagarin was given a **ten-day supply** of food and water and instructions on how to override the control systems.

Ejection rockets

### Ejector seat

The ejector seat had two purposes. If the rocket launch went wrong, the seat would throw Gagarin like a human cannonball into a safety net. Its main job, however, was to eject him from the descent module about 4 miles (7 km) above the ground. The hatch of the descent module blew off first. Exactly two seconds later, small rockets fixed to the base of the seat ignited to fire it out of the descent module.

Entry hatch

**126** exploring space ○ **SPACE PROBES**

**6** The number of Saturn's **moons discovered** by Cassini.

## Types of spacecraft

Most spacecraft simply fly past or orbit their target, but some attempt to land. Landers may stay put on the surface or rove around. Probes such as Huygens are released by an orbiter to enter a planet's or moon's atmosphere. All types have power, communication systems, and scientific instruments onboard.

**DEEP IMPACT**

### Flyby and impactor
As Deep Impact flew by the comet Tempel 1 in July 2005, it released an impactor that "bombed" the comet's surface, releasing gas and dust.

**CURIOSITY**

### Rover
Four rovers have traveled across Mars, the most recent arrival being Curiosity in August 2012. Its task is to investigate whether Mars is, or was, suitable for life.

**GALILEO**

### Orbiter and probe
From 1995 to 2003, Galileo orbited Jupiter and flew close to its larger moons. It released a probe to study the top 100 miles (160 km) of Jupiter's atmosphere.

**PHILAE**

### Lander
Released by the Rosetta spacecraft, this refrigerator-sized lander touched down on the nucleus of a comet in late 2014. Philae took the first images from a comet.

**VOYAGER 2**

### Flyby
Voyager 2, launched in 1977, flew past Jupiter, Saturn, Uranus, and Neptune. The only craft to have visited the outer two planets, it is now heading out into deep space.

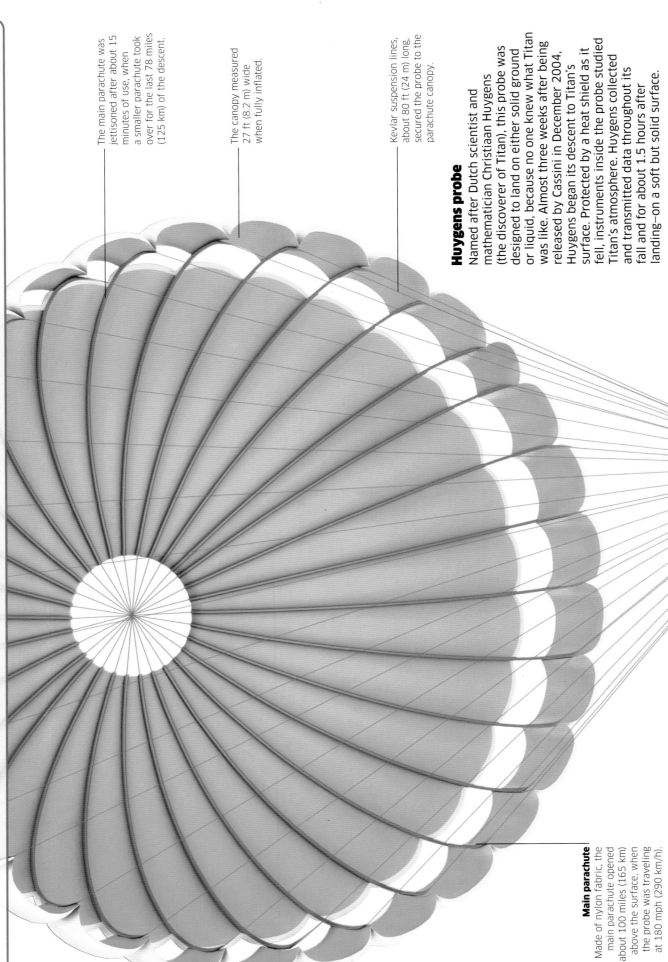

The main parachute was jettisoned after about 15 minutes of use, when a smaller parachute took over for the last 78 miles (125 km) of the descent.

The canopy measured 27 ft (8.2 m) wide when fully inflated.

Kevlar suspension lines, about 80 ft (24 m) long, secured the probe to the parachute canopy.

## Huygens probe
Named after Dutch scientist and mathematician Christiaan Huygens (the discoverer of Titan), this probe was designed to land on either solid ground or liquid, because no one knew what Titan was like. Almost three weeks after being released by Cassini in December 2004, Huygens began its descent to Titan's surface. Protected by a heat shield as it fell, instruments inside the probe studied Titan's atmosphere. Huygens collected and transmitted data throughout its fall and for about 1.5 hours after landing—on a soft but solid surface.

**Main parachute**
Made of nylon fabric, the main parachute opened about 100 miles (165 km) above the surface, when the probe was traveling at 180 mph (290 km/h).

**Voyager 1** is the **most distant spacecraft** from Earth and has left the solar system forever.

**12** The **number of asteroids** visited by spacecraft.

**3** billion miles (5 billion km) and 9.5 years—**New Horizon's journey to Pluto.**

**127**

## Space probes

**Robotic spacecraft can work for years at a time in remote locations and in harsh conditions that humans could never endure.**

Each craft is designed for a specific mission. It could be orbiting Mars, which is what Mars Express does, or traveling with a comet as it flies around the Sun, like Rosetta. Once these craft have reached their destinations, their onboard instruments test and record conditions on these faraway worlds. Some craft, such as Cassini-Huygens, are two in one. Cassini, the bigger of the two, left Earth for Saturn in 1997 with Huygens attached to its side. After a seven-year journey, the pair arrived at the planet. Then Huygens started its own mission, parachuting down onto Titan, the largest of Saturn's many moons.

### Inside Huygens
Under Huygens's covers was a platform of instruments. Attached to the lower side of this platform were instruments that analyzed the gases in Titan's air and the materials on the ground. Another instrument measured the probe's landing speed and determined what the landing site was like.

Upper casing

Instrument platform

Gas analysed here

Cover

Batteries

### Bridle
The three-legged bridle allowed Huygens to fall steadily, even in gusty winds. It also helped the probe to rotate slowly, so that its camera could scan Titan's surface and clouds.

### Probe
Instruments inside the probe started to work once the main chute opened and the heat shield was released.

Four radar antennae on the probe measured the height above ground.

Atmospheric gases entered the probe through holes in the cover.

### Heat shield
A shield covered in heat-resistant tiles protected Huygens when it slammed into Titan's atmosphere and began to slow down. After doing its job, the shield dropped off.

### Getting there
On its way to Saturn, Cassini-Huygens got help from Venus twice, and Earth and Jupiter once each. Too heavy to fly direct, it flew by these planets and was boosted by their gravity, gaining enough speed needed to reach Saturn.

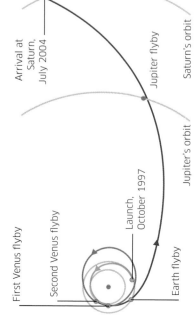

First Venus flyby

Second Venus flyby

Launch, October 1997

Earth flyby

Jupiter's orbit

Saturn's orbit

Jupiter flyby

Arrival at Saturn, July 2004

### Cassini spacecraft
Cassini is the fourth craft to visit Saturn and the first to orbit it. About the size of a small bus, it has 12 instruments to study the planet, its rings, and its moons. It is so far away that messages between Cassini and Earth take over an hour.

Radio dish

Cameras

Fuel tank

Radioactive power source

Main rocket engines

# Rovers

**Most spacecraft that touch down on other worlds have to stay where they land. Rovers, however, are built to explore. These sophisticated robots are sent commands by radio signal from Earth but are programmed to find their own way around.**

The smallest rovers are the size of a microwave oven; the largest are as big as a car. Solar panels provide power, and an internal computer serves as a rover's "brain." Rovers are packed with scientific instruments, from special cameras to onboard chemical laboratories. They use radio antennae to send their data and discoveries back to a control center on Earth.

A radio antenna communicates with Earth.

### Spirit rover
The rover Spirit, shown here, was one of a pair of identical rovers that landed on opposite sides of Mars in 2004. Spirit lost power in 2010, but its twin, Opportunity, is still working. It receives commands from Earth in the morning and sends back data in the afternoon, once it has finished traveling, taking pictures, and testing rock.

An extendable "arm" with an elbow, a wrist, and a handful of tools can reach out to touch objects.

### Rock drill
Opportunity uses a drill to grind the surface off rocks so it can obtain deeper samples for chemical analysis. The rock shown here, nicknamed "Marquette Island," is about the size of a basketball and is unlike any of the rocks around it. It may have been thrown out of an impact crater some distance away.

### Wheels
The four corner-wheels have motors that make them swivel, allowing the rover to turn. It can turn fully around in place.

**20** minutes—the time taken for a **message from a Mars rover** to reach Earth.

**7.5** months—the approximate length of the **journey from Earth to Mars.**

**100** watts—**Opportunity's power consumption,** about the same as a **household light bulb.**

**129**

### Panoramic camera
Four cameras held on a mast at head height serve as the rover's eyes. Two "pancams" take color photos of the Martian landscape, helping scientists choose places to visit. Two "navcams" take 3-D images of the ground, helping the rover plan its route.

### Finding the way
Rovers are given destinations, but they find their own way there, using their cameras and onboard computers to calculate the safest path. They travel only an inch or two per second and stop every few seconds to reassess the route. Opportunity's top speed is 0.11 mph (0.18 km/h) but its average speed is a fifth of this.

**TRACKS LEFT BY OPPORTUNITY**

### Rover records
Opportunity holds the record for the greatest distance traveled by a rover. The first rover to visit another world was Russia's Lunokhod 1, which landed on the Moon in 1970. The "lunar roving vehicles" that explored the Moon during NASA's Apollo missions were not robotic rovers but crewed vehicles designed to carry astronauts and equipment.

**OPPORTUNITY 2004–15**
**25.7 MILES (41.4 KM)**

**LUNOKHOD 2 1973**
**24.2 MILES (39 KM)**

**APOLLO 17 LUNAR ROVING VEHICLE (LRV) 1972**
**22.2 MILES (35.74 KM)**

**APOLLO 15 LRV 1971**
**17.3 MILES (27.8 KM)**

**APOLLO 16 LRV 1972**
**16.8 MILES (27.1 KM)**

**LUNOKHOD 1 1970–71**
**6.5 MILES (10.5 KM)**

**CURIOSITY 2012–15**
**5.5 MILES (8.8 KM)**

**SPIRIT 2004–10**
**4.8 MILES (7.7 KM)**

**SOJOURNER 1997**
**0.06 MILES (0.1 KM)**                 — **ON MARS**

**YUTU 2013–14**
**0.06 MILES (0.1 KM)**                 — **ON THE MOON**

When fully illuminated, the solar panels generate about 140 watts of power for up to four hours each day.

### Hazcams
Four "hazcams"—hazard-avoidance cameras—take 3-D pictures of nearby obstacles, such as large rocks, that the rover has to steer around.

The aluminum wheels help calculate the distance traveled—four turns equal 3 ft 3 in (1 m).

### Balancing act
The wheels are attached to the body by an arrangement called a rocker-bogie suspension. This clever system of levers allows the wheels to ride over bumpy ground while the rover's body stays level.

**130** exploring space ○ **CREWED SPACECRAFT**

**1** month—the length of time life-support systems on Soyuz can **keep the crew alive**.

Explosive bolts push the modules apart for descent.

## Back to Earth

Only the Descent Module returns to Earth—the other two modules are jettisoned and burn up in Earth's atmosphere. The Descent Module's thrusters control its return before it is slowed by a series of parachutes. Three-and-a-half hours after leaving the International Space Station, it lands in open country in Kazakhstan. The crew are helped out and flown away by helicopter.

## Descent Module

The astronauts are here for the launch and return to Earth. The module's helmet shape stabilizes it during the parachute descent and keeps it at the right angle as it touches down at 3.4 mph (5.4 km/h).

This antenna transmits pulses to calculate the craft's position when docking with the International Space Station.

## Orbital Module

The crew lives inside this module during orbit. It has a toilet, communication equipment, and storage.

Seats

Periscope

## Hatch

Astronauts pass through this hatch to enter the International Space Station.

Docking mechanism for joining the International Space Station

## Cockpit

The crew of three sits elbow to elbow for launch and return. In front of them is the control desk with guidance and navigation controls to maneuver the craft. Above the desk is the hatch into the Orbital Module.

**355** The number of people who have **flown in a Space Shuttle**.

**131**

# Crewed spacecraft

**People first went into orbit around Earth in the 1960s. Only 24 have gone farther—to the Moon. Astronauts come from many countries, but they have been launched into space by just three nations.**

Russia and the US have been launching crewed missions for around 50 years; China launched its first crewed spacecraft in 2003. The first vehicles carried one astronaut, then two, and later three—always in cramped conditions. Today's Soyuz is a three-person craft that is used only once. For 30 years, the Space Shuttle was the alternative ride. It carried more crew in greater comfort and returned intact. New reusable spacecraft are now in development, including spacecraft that will ferry paying tourists into space.

**Radio antenna**
for communicating with Earth and space station

**Thrusters**
The thruster jets are used to make small maneuvers in space.

**Solar panels**
Two large solar panels, one attached at either side, are linked to rechargeable batteries.

**Liquid fuel storage**

**Service Module**
This non-crew area contains the engines, fuel, guidance systems, and other instruments.

## Soyuz

Russia's Soyuz spacecraft is the world's safest and cheapest system for taxiing up to three people to and from low Earth orbit, and it is the only vehicle that can take astronauts to the International Space Station (ISS). It has three parts: the Descent and Orbital modules used by the crew, and the Service Module housing engines and equipment.

## Space vehicles

Cargo bay

SpaceShipTwo

White Knight

### Gemini
One of the first US crewed spacecraft was Gemini, which took ten two-man crews into orbit in 1965–1966. There they carried out America's first spacewalk.

### Space Shuttle
The five Space Shuttles flew crews of up to eight into space between 1981 and 2011. In total, the reusable Space Shuttle fleet completed 21,030 orbits of Earth.

### SpaceShipTwo
The privately owned SpaceShipTwo is designed for future space tourism. Released above Earth by the White Knight aircraft, it uses a rocket to climb to the edge of space.

### Dragon V2
This reusable craft, able to make at least ten flights, will carry future crews to the ISS and back. Launched by a Falcon 9 rocket, it will touch down back home on its landing legs.

# Space Shuttle

**The Space Shuttle was the world's first reusable spacecraft, designed to carry a crew of 2–8 astronauts to space and back.**

NASA's fleet of five Shuttles operated for 30 years, launching 135 times and spending a total of 3.6 years in flight. Launched with the aid of two disposable solid-fuel rockets, they reached orbit in only 8 minutes, accelerating from 0 to 16,000 mph (25,000 km/h). The shuttle program ended in 2011, having lasted twice the 15-year life span it was originally designed for.

**9** As the craft approaches Earth, the Service Module is jettisoned. The Command Module turns around so its heat-shielded base faces Earth's atmosphere.

**10** The Command Module enters Earth's atmosphere in a blaze of fire. After it slows down, parachutes open for a gentle splashdown in the Pacific Ocean.

**4** The CSM turns around and then docks with the Lunar Module, forming the complete Apollo spacecraft.

**2** The third Saturn V rocket stage fires for six minutes to send the craft out of Earth's orbit and toward the Moon.

**3** The combined Command and Service Modules (CSM) separate from the rocket. The panels protecting the Lunar Module open like petals.

**1 Launch**
Each Apollo mission was launched from NASA's Kennedy Space Center in Florida. The three stages of the Saturn V rocket burned for about 12 minutes in total to put the spacecraft and the rocket's upper stage into orbit around Earth.

Escape rocket for emergencies

**Command Module**
The crew lived inside this small conical module.

**Service Module**
This module contained the engine, fuel, and other supplies.

Apollo spacecraft

**Lunar Module**
This part of the spacecraft landed on the Moon.

Third stage

Engine

# Apollo program

**The Apollo missions of the 1960s and '70s are the only space missions that have put people on another world. Reaching the Moon required an extraordinary three-part spacecraft and the largest rockets that have ever been launched.**

Between 1969 and 1972, NASA launched six successful Apollo missions and put 12 astronauts on the Moon. Each mission took a crew of three men a total of 950,000 miles (1.5 million km) through space on a looping, figure-eight journey to the Moon and back. Launched by the gigantic Saturn V rocket—which had to be built anew for each trip—the astronauts traveled in an Apollo spacecraft made of three parts that could separate. The spider-like Lunar Module carried two men down to the lunar surface. The remaining crew member stayed in the cone-shaped, silvery Command Module, which also carried the crew home. Attached to this was the cylindrical Service Module, housing the spacecraft's rocket engine, fuel, and supplies.

Second stage

First stage

Engines

**Saturn V**
Standing 364 ft (111 m) high, the Saturn V launch vehicle was taller than the Statue of Liberty. The main body was made of three different rockets, or stages, stacked together. The Apollo spacecraft, tiny by comparison, was on top. The main rockets fired in sequence, each stage propelling the sections above to greater speeds and heights before running out of fuel and falling back to Earth.

**15** tons—the quantity of fuel **burned every second** during launch.

**300** The **total number of hours** Apollo astronauts spent on the Moon.

In 1970, Apollo 13 was **damaged by an explosion** on the way to the Moon and had to return to Earth.

**135**

### Command and Service Modules

The Command and Service Modules flew as a single unit (the CSM) for most of each mission. Astronauts lived in the Command Module—the conical front part—which had five triple-glazed windows for viewing the Moon, Earth, and docking maneuvers. The living quarters were cramped and had very basic facilities, with no toilet. Instead, astronauts used plastic bags or a special hose connected to the vacuum of space.

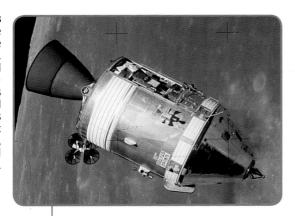

## Mission control

The nerve center of each Apollo mission was the control room at Johnson Space Center in Houston, Texas. Here, scientists and engineers kept a round-the-clock watch over the spacecraft and talked to the crew via radio. The crew remained in continual radio contact with mission control, except when the spacecraft traveled behind the Moon.

**5** The Apollo spacecraft sails to the Moon, a journey of about three days. It slows down to enter lunar orbit.

The Apollo program cost
## $24 billion
and employed 400,000 people at its peak.

**7** The Lunar Module separates from the CSM and lands on the Moon. The CSM stays in orbit with one astronaut on board.

**8** The top half of the Lunar Module returns to orbit and docks with the CSM, allowing the crew to get back on board. The Lunar Module is then abandoned in space, and the CSM sets off for Earth.

**6** Once the craft is safely in lunar orbit, two astronauts go through a hatch into the Lunar Module, ready for their descent to the Moon.

# Lunar lander

**In the greatest adventure that humans have ever been part of, six Apollo spacecraft touched down on the Moon between 1969 and 1972. The 12 men who landed explored the lunar surface and returned with bags of precious rock samples.**

The race to reach the Moon was won on July 20, 1969, when US astronaut Neil Armstrong became the first person to set foot on it. Armstrong flew to the lunar surface with colleague Buzz Aldrin in the Apollo 11 Lunar Module, nicknamed Eagle, while their colleague Michael Collins remained in orbit in the Apollo Command Module. Armstrong had to take manual control of the Eagle in the last minutes of a hair-raising descent after realizing the planned landing site was unsafe. He touched down with only 30 seconds' fuel left and then made his famous announcement to the whole world: "Tranquility Base here. The Eagle has landed."

Radar antenna for distance measuring

Telescope

**Hatch**
The astronauts used an overhead hatch to move between the Lunar Module and the rest of Apollo.

Controls

Exit and entrance hatch for the Moon's surface

Astronauts used this ladder to climb down to the lunar surface.

Engine for descent to the Moon's surface

Wide footpads stopped the Lunar Module from sinking into the dusty ground.

Ascent stage lifts off

Descent stage stays put

**Liftoff**
When it was time to leave, the ascent engine fired. It lifted the ascent stage back into lunar orbit, where the craft docked with the Command and Service Modules. The two lunar astronauts moved back into the Command Module, stowing their rock samples and cameras. The ascent stage was then jettisoned to crash back into the lunar surface.

The **last man to stand on the Moon** was
Gene Cernan, on December 14, 1972.

**80** hours—the total time spent **outside the Lunar
Module** by the 12 astronauts who visited the Moon.

**137**

**SERVICE MODULE**  **COMMAND MODULE**  **LUNAR MODULE**

The Service Module
housed Apollo's main
engine and carried
air, water, and fuel.

Probes detected
the ground just
before landing.

**Thrusters**
Small thruster jets kept
the ascent stage stable
during its flights to and
from the lunar surface.

Foil space blankets protected
fuel containers and other vital
parts from extreme swings
in temperature.

Four adjustable legs made
sure the Lunar Module was
level on the Moon's surface.

## Apollo spacecraft

There were three parts to the Apollo craft. The
crew traveled in the Command Module. Once
at the Moon, two astronauts transferred to the
Lunar Module for the descent to the surface.
The third stayed in the combined Command
and Service Modules, orbiting the Moon while
awaiting their return. The Command Module
was the only part of Apollo to return to Earth.

## More than 500 million

people watched Neil Armstrong on live
TV when he left the Lunar Module and
stepped onto the Moon.

## Lunar Module

Although the Lunar Module's
spiderlike design looks fragile, it
flew only in the vacuum of space
and didn't need a streamlined
shape. Its upper part—the ascent
stage—was home to the astronauts
during their time on the Moon.
They found its cabin tiny, noisy,
dusty, and so brightly lit by the
Sun that sleep was impossible. The
descent stage powered the craft
to the surface. It later acted as a
launch pad for the ascent stage
to return to orbit.

## Lunar gravity

Gravity on the Moon is only one-sixth as
strong as gravity on Earth. Not only do all
things on the Moon weigh one-sixth of their
Earth weight, but lunar hills are also six
times easier to climb. And, as Apollo 16's
commander John Young found out, you can
jump six times higher on the Moon's surface.

## Memento

Apollo craft and equipment, including six
descent stages and three moon buggies, are
still on the Moon. David Scott and James
Irwin of Apollo 15 left other mementos in
the dusty soil: a list of 14 American and
Russian astronauts who lost their lives, and a
small figure representing a fallen astronaut.

Radio antenna for sending TV signals to Earth

A wire-mesh radio dish folded out like an umbrella to focus radio signals.

Radio antenna for transmitting speech and other sounds

A handheld movie camera could be mounted by the driver's seat.

Driver's seat

The color TV camera could be remotely operated from Mission Control. It was used to film the Lunar Module's liftoff from the Moon.

Instrument panel

Aluminum body

Tires of woven steel wire with V-shaped treads gave much better grip than rubber in the lunar dust.

The vehicle was powered by two large batteries inside this compartment.

Fenders were essential to keep dust from flying. When one fender broke off during the Apollo 17 mission, the astronauts made a replacement out of maps.

**56** miles (90 km)—the **total distance traveled** by all three lunar rovers.

**12** mph (19 km/h)—the **top speed** achieved by the LRV on the Moon.

**4.7** miles (7.6 km)—the **greatest distance** a rover traveled from the landing site.

**139**

The tool caddy at the back carried equipment for collecting samples, including brushes, a hammer, a scoop, and a rake.

The seats were made of aluminum tubing with nylon webbing and had Velcro seatbelts.

Handhold

Under-seat storage allowed astronauts to collect up to 60 lb (27 kg) of rock samples.

# Moon buggy

**The first Apollo astronauts had to explore the Moon on foot. On the last three missions, astronauts took a Lunar Roving Vehicle (LRV)—a battery-powered buggy that allowed them to travel for miles.**

Built from the lightest materials possible, the LRV weighed a mere 77 lb (35 kg) in the Moon's low gravity—about twice the weight of a mountain bike on Earth. Four sturdy metal wheels, each equipped with its own motor, steering, and brake, enabled the LRV to ride safely over craters and rocks while maintaining grip in the loose lunar dust. Apollo 11 astronauts could walk only 330 ft (100 m) or so from the landing site in their bulky suits, but with the LRV to carry them, the crew of Apollo 17 traveled a total of 22 miles (36 km) as they explored and collected samples. Three LRVs were sent to the Moon, and all remain there today. Their last job was to use an onboard camera to film their drivers lifting off for the return to Earth.

Instrument panel

Controller for steering

### Controls

The instrument panel showed speed, direction, tilt, battery power, and temperature. The LRV had no steering wheel. Instead, the driver used a T-shaped controller to steer, accelerate, and brake. The LRV also had a map holder and storage space for tools and rock samples.

## Unpacking the LRV

The LRV was designed to fold flat so it could travel to the Moon attached to the side of the Lunar Module. One astronaut had to climb the ladder and undo the clips that held the LRV securely in place so it could be pulled down.

Lunar Module

LRV

**1 LOWERING THE LRV**
Getting the LRV down to the ground required both astronauts to pull on a series of straps in careful sequence. Pulleys took care of the rest.

Rear wheels

**2 CHASSIS UNFOLDS**
Lowering the LRV caused the rear wheels to fold out and lock into place automatically. The rover's seats were now facing upward.

Unfolded rover

**3 LRV DISCONNECTED**
The front wheels also unfolded and locked in place automatically. Finally, the astronauts raised the seats and other parts by hand.

140   exploring space ○ **SPACESUIT**

**25** The **number of times a suit is used** on the International Space Station.

# Spacesuit

**A modern spacesuit is far more than just protective clothing. It serves as a wearable spacecraft, creating a safe, Earth-like environment for the human body.**

In the early days of space travel, a spacesuit was made in one piece, tailored to fit the astronaut who would wear it. Today, astronauts working outside the International Space Station wear a one-size-fits-all suit made of many parts. A semi-rigid top fits onto pants, and a helmet, gloves, boots, and life-support backpack all go on top. Beneath the suit is a comfortable, one-piece garment containing tubes of flowing water to keep the body cool. On the outside of the suit are controls, tethers that attach the astronaut to the space station, and tools for the jobs to be done.

**Life-support backpack**
This contains oxygen, a battery, a two-way radio, water-cooling equipment, and a warning system. It also removes exhaled carbon dioxide.

Cap with earphones and microphone

Ventilation garment keeps astronaut cool

Rigid fiberglass shell

Checklist of jobs

Helmet lights

TV camera

Gold visor blocks out the Sun's glare

Drink bag

Display and control box for life-support backpack

Tool belt

Mirror to read control box dials

Gloves with heated rubber fingertips

**$12** million—the cost of a **single spacesuit**.

A **modern spacesuit** is 280 lb (127 kg) on Earth but is **weightless in space**.

**300** ft (92 m)—the total **length of water tubes** in the ventilation garment worn under a spacesuit.

**141**

**Rescue unit**
If the astronaut becomes separated from the space station, this unit has thruster jets to fly him or her back to safety.

**Underwear**
Spacewalks can last up to eight hours, so astronauts wear a "maximum absorbency garment" under the suit that serves as a diaper.

**Suit construction**
The suit has 11 layers. The inner yellow layer holds in the oxygen and maintains the pressure. Insulation layers keep the inside temperature comfortable for the astronaut. The outer layer is a mix of waterproof, bulletproof, and fire-resistant materials.

Tethers attach the astronaut to the space station

Colored stripes help astronauts identify each other

The boot's heel attaches to the space station's robotic arm to hold the astronaut securely.

Battery-powered drill for tightening and loosening bolts

## Without a spacesuit
to provide oxygen and pressure, an astronaut would become unconscious within 15 seconds, and the body would swell to twice its normal size.

## Spacesuit evolution
Early astronauts went into space but never left their craft. They wore pressure suits like those used by fighter pilots. As the role of astronauts changed to include "spacewalks" outside the craft, their clothing evolved. Today, astronauts wear a flight suit for journeys, casual clothes while in the space station, and a spacesuit for spacewalks.

**Mercury**
America's Mercury astronauts, who flew between 1961 and 1963, wore silver pressure suits with straps and zippers for a snug fit.

Helmet

Aluminum-coated nylon gave the suit a silver color

**Apollo**
The astronauts who went to the Moon in the late 1960s used the same flexible suit for both flying and walking on the lunar surface.

Inner pressure helmet

Inner layers of Apollo suit (outer "white" layers are not shown)

**First shuttle suit**
In 1981 the first shuttle astronauts wore an escape suit based on a US Air Force pressure suit. A bright orange version was later introduced.

Communications cap under helmet

**Today's suit**
The suit currently used for spacewalks on the International Space Station is called the Extravehicular Mobility Unit.

Impact-resistant plastic helmet

White stands out against the blackness of space

# Spacewalk

**The airless vacuum of space is deadly to the human body. Without a suit, an astronaut would die in under a minute.**

Because there's no air pressure in space to keep water in its liquid state, body fluids would boil in seconds if an astronaut didn't wear a pressurized spacesuit. The suit also shields the body from the ferocious heat of the Sun and the extreme cold of shadows. Here, a Russian astronaut works on the International Space Station. Orbiting Earth at 5 miles (8 km) per second, he circles the planet every 92 minutes, plunging into the freezing blackness of night every 46 minutes before reemerging into dazzling daylight.

# Space stations

**Only three people have spent more than a year continuously in space, all of them on board a space station. These giant orbiting spacecraft allow astronauts to spend long periods living and working off the planet.**

A total of ten crewed space stations have orbited Earth since 1971. The first one, Salyut 1, was small enough to be launched in one piece but had room for three people. Larger space stations are built in orbit by joining roomlike parts called modules, which are constructed on Earth and launched separately. Astronauts used this method to build the International Space Station (ISS), putting the first parts together in 1998. It is the largest human-made object ever to orbit Earth and is easily visible to the naked eye, looking like a bright star that sweeps across the sky in just a few minutes. The ISS is used for scientific research, but space stations may one day be used as staging posts for crewed missions to the planets.

## How big is it?

The ISS is about the size of a soccer field, and is more than 50 percent longer than a Boeing 747 (the world's longest passenger aircraft). It weighs about 450 tons, which is about as much as 375 average cars.

**BOEING 747**
233 ft (71 m) long

**INTERNATIONAL SPACE STATION**
357 ft (109 m) long

## Orbit

Traveling at 17,100 mph (27,600 km/h), the ISS circles Earth about every 90 minutes, crossing from southern to northern hemisphere and back again. Because Earth rotates, the ISS passes over a different part of the planet on each pass, tracing out the blue line below.

## International Space Station

Inside, the ISS is as spacious as a six-bedroom house. Most of the space is taken up by work areas such as laboratories. The crew of six works nine hours a day, five days a week, performing experiments and exercising to stay in shape.

**Kibo**
The largest module is this Japanese science laboratory, used for a wide range of science experiments.

**Canadarm2**
This robotic arm with seven motorized joints moves equipment and astronauts.

**Harmony**
This US module has four small wall closets that serve as bedrooms.

**Columbus**
Astronauts use this European laboratory module to study the effect of weightlessness on animals, plants, and the human body.

**In the lab**
Inside the US Destiny laboratory, an astronaut upgrades Robonaut, the first humanoid robot in space. Considered one of the crew, Robonaut does simple and routine tasks inside the station. Eventually, Robonaut will work outside, alongside spacewalking astronauts.

**48** days (1,152 hours) of spacewalks were needed to build the ISS.

**Tranquility**
Inside this US module is a toilet and an exercise machine.

Mating adapters allow spacecraft and modules to dock with the ISS.

**Room with a view**
Astronauts can look outside from the cupola, a dome-shaped module with seven windows that face Earth. They use the cupola to operate the station's robotic arm or to watch spacewalks and visiting craft. When work is done, it's a great place to gaze at our planet far below.

Radiators remove excess heat from the ISS.

Solar panels power the ISS, generating electricity for everyday life and science experiments.

**Quest airlock**
Astronauts use a hatch in this module to go outside the station on spacewalks.

**Leonardo**
Once used to transport cargo, this module is now used for storage.

**Soyuz**
Astronauts travel to and from the ISS in Soyuz spacecraft.

**Zarya**
The Zarya module was the first part of the ISS to go into space.

**Zvezda**
This Russian module includes sleeping quarters for two, a refrigerator, a freezer, an exercise bicycle, and a toilet.

# Future exploration

**Although no humans have left Earth orbit since the last Apollo Moon mission in 1972, many proposals have been made to send astronauts farther afield, with Mars being the most ambitious target.**

The US space agency NASA has no plans to send astronauts back to the Moon, but China and Russia both hope to launch crewed lunar missions in coming decades. NASA hopes to land astronauts on an asteroid by 2025 and on Mars in later decades, but the costs, technical challenges, and risks involved in a human mission to Mars are enormous. In the meantime, robotic spacecraft and rovers are likely to continue exploring the solar system, advancing our knowledge of the planets without the dangers or costs of crewed expeditions.

## Martian base

This artist's impression shows one proposed idea for a Mars base. The main building is constructed from a series of landers that arrive separately and are joined together by robotic rovers already on the ground. The technology needed to build a base of this sophistication may not exist for decades.

Because Mars has a thin atmosphere and a weak magnetic field, dangerous levels of radiation reach the surface. Living quarters would need to be heavily shielded or underground.

Landers bring supplies of air and water.

Martian soil contains ice that could be melted to produce drinkable water and oxygen.

**−85°F** (−65°C)—the **average temperature** on the surface of Mars.

**147**

### Greenhouse

Long-term settlers on Mars would have to produce their own food in greenhouses. The plants would need a large supply of water, which would be difficult to provide, as well as warmth, air, and artificial light. Growing plants outdoors on Mars would be impossible—the temperature is too low and there is no liquid water.

### Living quarters

Because buried dwellings would have no windows, settlers would use screens to see outside and to keep in touch with Earth. However, live conversations with Earth would not be possible because radio signals from Mars take about 40 minutes to get there and back.

### Inflatable homes

Constructing large buildings on Mars would be impossible, so settlers would either have to live inside landers or bring cleverly packaged dwellings that could be erected simply. One solution might be to use inflatable dwellings. Because the air pressure on Mars is very low, any dwellings would need to withstand being filled with pressurized air.

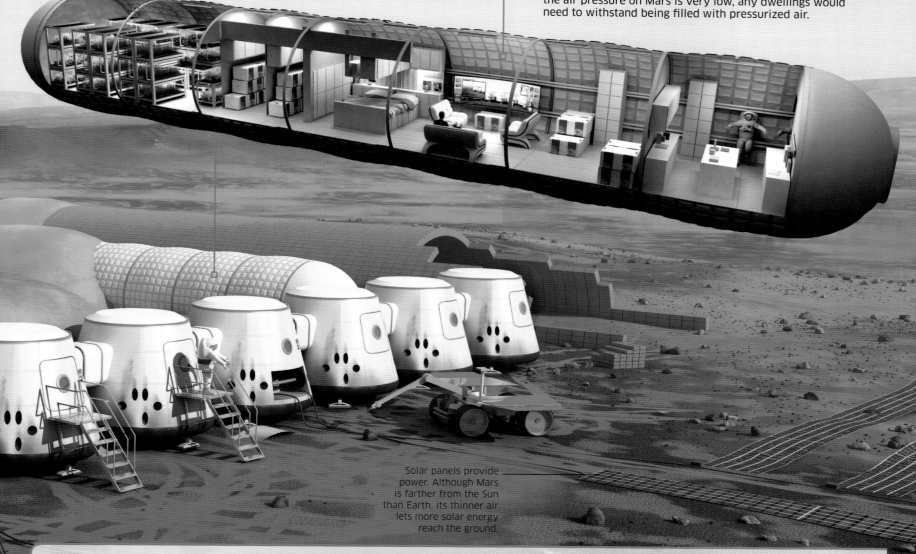

Solar panels provide power. Although Mars is farther from the Sun than Earth, its thinner air lets more solar energy reach the ground.

### Space tourism

Only a handful of people have paid to go into space as tourists, all of them spending time on the International Space Station. One enjoyed his stay so much he went back again. In years to come, private companies may offer new ways for people to visit space as tourists.

### World-view balloon

This high-tech balloon ride will give six tourists a near-space experience. At 20 miles (32 km) above Earth, they'll see dark space above and our blue planet below.

### SpaceShipTwo

A two-and-a-half-hour trip aboard SpaceShipTwo will take tourists just beyond the edge of space. They'll have six minutes to float around the cabin in weightlessness before returning.

# The search for life

**The universe is a huge place. In our home galaxy, there may be as many as 100 billion stars with planets, yet our galaxy is just one of perhaps 200 billion galaxies. It seems unlikely, therefore, that Earth is the only place with life. Large telescopes all over the world are searching space for evidence that life could exist elsewhere. We probably won't come across any little green men—in fact, it may be hard to recognize life if we do find it. An unexplained radio signal, a hint of hidden water, a rock that might contain tiny fossils: these are the sorts of clues scientists are looking for.**

## IS ANYBODY OUT THERE?

In 1961, astronomer Frank Drake devised a method for estimating how many civilizations might be sending out radio signals in our galaxy. Known as the Drake equation, this formula involves seven factors, written as symbols, which have to be multiplied together. The values of some of the factors can only be guessed at, so the equation gives only a very rough idea of our chances of finding extraterrestrials.

## RADIO SIGNALS

If alien civilizations do exist somewhere, it's possible they have discovered how to use radio waves to send signals to each other, just as we do with phones, TV, and radio broadcasts. So one way of finding aliens is simply to search for their radio signals traveling through space. SETI (search for extraterrestrial intelligence) projects do this, using huge radio dishes to scan the skies for distinctive signals. We can also use radio telescopes to send out our own messages, aiming them at likely destinations in our galaxy. So far, neither approach has brought success.

### The Wow! signal

In 1977 a scientist at an American radio observatory noticed that a signal from space was unusually strong. Thrilled that it might be a message from aliens, he wrote "Wow!" on a printout. The Wow! signal was never detected again.

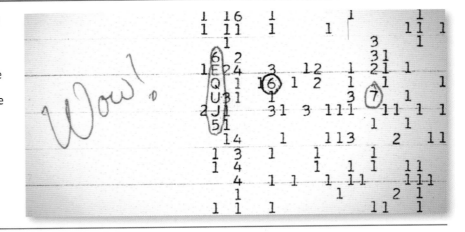

### Searching the skies

The Arecibo radio telescope in Puerto Rico is the largest single-dish radio telescope ever built, measuring more than 1,000 ft (300 m) wide. This telescope sometimes searches for alien radio broadcasts at the same time as making regular astronomical observations.

| Number of alien civilizations that are sending out radio signals | | The rate at which new stars form in our galaxy each year | | The fraction of such stars that have a family of orbiting planets | | For each star, the number of planets that have the right conditions for life | | The fraction of such planets on which life appears | | The fraction of life-supporting planets on which intelligent life develops | | The fraction of civilizations that develop radio technology | | The life span of each civilization, judged by how long it continues to send messages |

$$N = R^* \times f_p \times n_e \times f_l \times f_i \times f_c \times L$$

## The Arecibo message

In 1974, astronomers used the Arecibo radio telescope to send a coded message toward a star cluster 25,000 light-years away. The signal lasted three minutes and consisted of a stream of binary numbers that, when decoded, forms a simple picture telling aliens about life on Earth. Since the signal will take 25,000 years to reach its target—and any reply will take another 25,000 years to come back—the message was symbolic rather than a serious attempt to communicate.

- The numbers 1 to 10
- Atomic numbers for the elements most important to life: hydrogen, carbon, nitrogen, oxygen, and phosphorus
- The chemical components of DNA, the molecule that carries the genetic code of life
- DNA molecule
- Human figure
- The Sun and the planets of the solar system
- The Arecibo radio telescope

# SEARCHING THE SOLAR SYSTEM

Although we have yet to find evidence of life in other parts of our solar system, spacecraft have found evidence of liquid water, which is vital to life on Earth. Hidden oceans exist under the surface of some moons, and water almost certainly once flowed on Mars.

## Mars

Photographs of Mars strongly suggest that water has flowed across its surface in the past, if only for brief periods. Long ago, Mars may have been warmer and wetter, allowing rivers and lakes to exist on the surface. Future Martian landers may try to find out whether there are any buried fossils from Mars's remote past.

**Martian meteorite**
In 1996, scientists amazed the world when they announced the discovery of what looked like fossilized bacteria inside a Martian meteorite found in Antarctica. This evidence of extraterrestrial life seemed so strong that US president Bill Clinton made a televised statement about the discovery. Since then, scientists have argued about the structures inside meteorite ALH84001, which some claim are merely mineral deposits.

## Under the ice

Hidden below the icy surface of Jupiter's moon Europa (left), there likely exists a huge saltwater ocean, warmed by strong tides. Since water and warmth are key to the development of life, Europa is high on scientists' list of solar system locations to search for life. Saturn's moon Enceladus probably also has a liquid-water ocean beneath an ice covering, and this too might be a place that could harbor life.

# THE NIGHT SKY

You don't need to board a rocket to see space—just walk outside on a clear night and look up. The constellations are easy to see with the naked eye, but with binoculars you can see more—from the moons of Jupiter to starbirth nebulas and even whole galaxies.

# The celestial sphere

The celestial sphere is an imaginary sphere around Earth on which any object in the sky can be precisely mapped, just as locations on Earth can be mapped on a globe. Different parts of the sphere are visible from different areas of Earth, and because our planet is continually rotating, different areas of the sphere come into view over the course of a night. Stars and other distant objects stay fixed in more or less the same place on the celestial sphere for long periods of time, but objects in the solar system, such as the Sun, Moon, and planets, are always moving.

## WHAT IS THE CELESTIAL SPHERE?

Think of the celestial sphere as a giant glass ball around Earth with stars pinned to its surface. Because Earth rotates, the celestial sphere also appears to rotate. Like Earth, it has north and south poles and is divided into northern and southern hemispheres by an equator. We can pinpoint any location on Earth with measurements called latitude and longitude. The celestial sphere uses a similar system but the numbers are called declination and right ascension.

Earth's axis

North celestial pole

Lines of declination measure positions north or south of the celestial equator.

MARS

The Sun and planets appear to move around the sky close to a line called the ecliptic.

Sun's motion

SUN

The celestial equator lies directly above Earth's equator.

## THE SPINNING SKY

It's impossible to see the whole celestial sphere at once because Earth gets in the way. However, because Earth rotates and travels around the Sun, different parts of the celestial sphere come into view at different times. How much you can see, and how the stars move, depends on where on Earth you live.

**Key to spheres**
- Observer
- ···· Observer's horizon
- Stars always visible
- Stars visible at some time
- Stars never visible

North celestial pole

Earth

Celestial equator

**View from the North Pole**
From here you can only see the northern half of the celestial sphere—the other half is never visible. As Earth rotates, the stars move in circles around the celestial pole, which is directly overhead.

**View from mid-latitudes**
From mid-latitude regions such as the US and Europe, you can always see the constellations around the celestial pole, but the other constellations change during the night and during the year.

**View from the equator**
From the equator, you can see the whole of the celestial sphere over the course of a year. The north and south celestial poles lie on the horizon, making polar constellations hard to see.

### Through the year

Earth's night-side faces different parts of the celestial sphere over the course of the year as we orbit the Sun. Because of this, different constellations come in and out of view as the months pass. Stars are easiest to see in winter, because the nights are longer and the darkness is much deeper. In summer, nights are shorter and the sky doesn't get so dark, so stars look fainter.

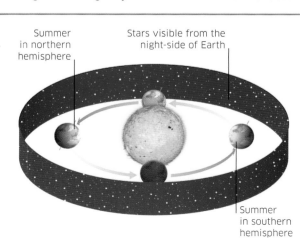

Summer in northern hemisphere

Stars visible from the night-side of Earth

Summer in southern hemisphere

Earth's axis is tilted by 23.4°

Lines of right ascension are used to give east-west positions on the celestial sphere.

The star patterns don't change but the whole sky seems to turn in the opposite direction of Earth's spin.

EARTH'S SPIN

JUPITER

SATURN

EARTH

Equator

VENUS

MERCURY

The south celestial pole is directly above Earth's South Pole.

## ⊚ ORIGINS

In ancient times, people didn't know that Earth rotates, so they naturally thought that the Sun and stars were moving around us. Ancient stargazers thought Earth was the center of the universe, surrounded by a set of glass spheres—one for the stars and separate spheres for the Moon, each planet, and the Sun.

ILLUSTRATION OF THE COPERNICAN SYSTEM, 1661

### Sun in the middle

About 500 years ago, Polish astronomer Nicolaus Copernicus realized he could predict the movements of the planets better by assuming the Sun was in the middle rather than Earth. His revolutionary theory showed that Earth was not the center of creation.

### The zodiac

The Sun's path along the ecliptic takes it through 13 constellations: 12, called the signs of the zodiac, have long been seen as having special significance. The 13th, Ophiuchus, is often overlooked.

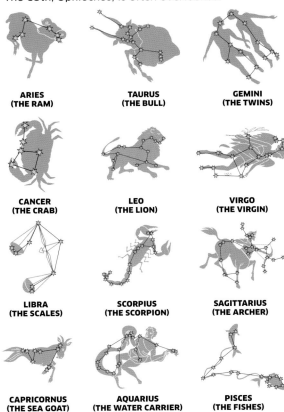

ARIES
(THE RAM)

TAURUS
(THE BULL)

GEMINI
(THE TWINS)

CANCER
(THE CRAB)

LEO
(THE LION)

VIRGO
(THE VIRGIN)

LIBRA
(THE SCALES)

SCORPIUS
(THE SCORPION)

SAGITTARIUS
(THE ARCHER)

CAPRICORNUS
(THE SEA GOAT)

AQUARIUS
(THE WATER CARRIER)

PISCES
(THE FISHES)

# Practical stargazing

One of the things that makes astronomy such a great hobby is that everybody can join in. On a typical dark night, a person with good vision can see up to 3,000 stars, so there are plenty of interesting features to find with the naked eye and learn about. Before getting started, it's best to understand a few basics, such as the way the stars and other objects move across the sky and how astronomers keep track of them. Armed with this essential knowledge, anyone can go out and begin to identify the constellations or learn to spot red giants, starbirth nebulas, or even whole galaxies millions of light-years from Earth.

## BASIC EQUIPMENT

The essentials for a night's stargazing are warm clothes, a star chart of some sort, and a light to see by. If you have a smartphone or tablet, you can download various apps that will show the night sky visible from your location at any time and date. However, many people prefer to use a circular chart called a planisphere.

**Night vision**
It takes about half an hour for your eyes to fully adjust to darkness so that you can see the faintest stars. Avoid bright light or you'll ruin your night vision. If you use a flashlight, a red one is best, since it won't affect your ability to see in the dark.

## SIZING UP THE SKY

Astronomers treat the sky as if it were a huge sphere surrounding Earth. Distances between objects are measured in degrees. There are 360 degrees in a circle, so the distance around the whole sky is 360 degrees. The Moon is about half a degree wide.

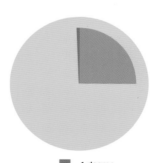

**Handspan**
A hand held at arm's length with fingers spread widely covers an angle of about 22 degrees between the outstretched little finger and thumb.

**Finger joints**
The top part of an index finger is about 3 degrees wide. The middle part is 4 degrees wide, and the bottom part is 6 degrees wide.

**Finger width**
The tip of a finger pointing upward at arm's length is about 1 degree wide and can completely cover a full moon.

- ■ 1 degree
- ■ 90 degrees
- ■ 360 degrees

### Mapping the stars

You can measure the exact position of a star at any moment with two numbers. One is altitude: the star's height above the horizon, measured in degrees. The other is azimuth: the angle from due north, measured in degrees clockwise. The star below, for example, has an altitude of 45 degrees and an azimuth of 25 degrees.

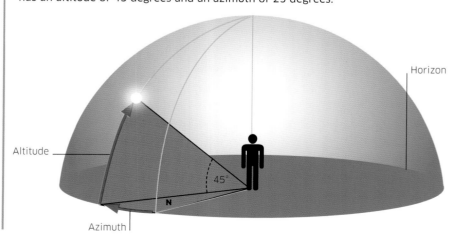

## UNDER DARK SKIES

The key to good stargazing is to find the darkest, clearest skies available. Professional observatories are often located on high mountaintops in remote areas, but the most important thing is simply to get away from city lights and the glow of light pollution. Under a truly dark sky, the Milky Way is an unforgettable sight.

**Planisphere**
This astronomer's tool consists of a circular star chart and an overlay with an oval window. When the time and date marked around the edges of the two layers are correctly aligned, the stars shown in the window will mirror those in the sky above.

## Optical Instruments

Binoculars and telescopes will boost your stargazing. Their big lenses or mirrors collect much more light than a human eye can, revealing very faint objects such as nebulas and galaxies. Their eyepieces, meanwhile, create a magnified image of a small part of the sky, allowing stargazers to separate closely spaced objects, such as double stars, and see more detail on the Moon and planets.

**Binoculars**
Binoculars have two large, light-collecting lenses and use prisms to direct light into magnifying eyepieces. Good binoculars will let you see Jupiter's moons, but you need steady hands to stop the image from shaking.

**Telescopes**
A telescope has either an objective lens or a large primary mirror. It collects much more light than binoculars. The eyepiece gives a highly magnified image of a smaller area of sky. A tripod or other mount is used to steady the telescope and stop it from wobbling.

**Milky Way**
Our home galaxy is visible on clear, moonless nights as a wash of milky light across the sky. The best time to see it is late summer in the northern hemisphere and late winter in the southern hemisphere.

# THE CHANGING SKY

Watch the sky for more than a few minutes and you'll notice that the stars move slowly around the sky, rising in the east and setting in the west. This is an illusion caused by Earth's rotation, and the pattern of movement varies between different parts of the world.

**Motion at the North Pole**
If you watched the sky from Earth's North Pole, no stars would ever rise or set. Instead, they would simply move in circles around the Pole Star, which never moves.

**Motion at mid-latitudes**
From most parts of the world, some stars stay visible throughout the night, traveling in a circle, while other stars rise and set.

**Motion at the equator**
At the equator, all stars rise in the east, cross the sky, and then set in the west. The constellations visible by night change gradually over the course of a year.

## Moving constellations

Earth's orbit around the Sun means that the positions of the constellations in the sky appear to change. You'll notice this if you view the same constellation at the same time over several weeks.

**APRIL 1, 8 PM**

**APRIL 8, 8 PM**

**APRIL 15, 8 PM**

# Northern star-hopping

To the untrained eye, the night sky can look like a bewildering mass of stars. A good way to make sense of it is to look for well-known landmarks and then trace imaginary lines from these to other constellations. This technique is called star-hopping and is easy to do with the naked eye, though you can see more if you have binoculars or a telescope. The chart on this page shows how to star-hop around the north celestial pole, which is visible to people who live in Earth's northern hemisphere.

## FINDING THE WAY

This tour of the northern sky starts with a famous pattern of stars called the Big Dipper. You can use the Big Dipper as a signpost to find the Pole Star and other sights nearby. Some are quite faint, so you will need a clear, dark night to see them all.

**1** **THE FIRST STEP** is to find the Big Dipper and locate the two stars farthest from its "handle," which are known as the Pointers. Draw an imaginary line through the Pointers and extend it to a bright star. This is the Pole Star and it is always due north.

**2** **EXTEND THE LINE** from the Pointers past the Pole Star to reach the faint constellation Cepheus, which looks a bit like a lopsided house. Binoculars will reveal the bright red Garnet Star at the base of the house—the reddest star visible to the naked eye and one of the largest stars known.

**3** **DRAW A LINE** from the third star in the Big Dipper's handle through the Pole Star to find the constellation Cassiopeia, which looks like a flattened "W." If you have binoculars, look for a star cluster just below the central peak of the "W."

**4** **THE LARGE BUT FAINT** and shapeless constellation Draco (the Dragon) is best seen under very dark skies. A line from the fourth star in the Big Dipper's handle cuts across the dragon's body and continues on to its head, a pattern of stars called the Lozenge.

**5** **TRACK DOWN** one of the brightest galaxies in the sky with binoculars: follow a diagonal line across the Big Dipper's rectangle of stars, and continue in the same direction looking for a pair of tiny fuzzy patches. These are the galaxies M81 and its fainter companion M82.

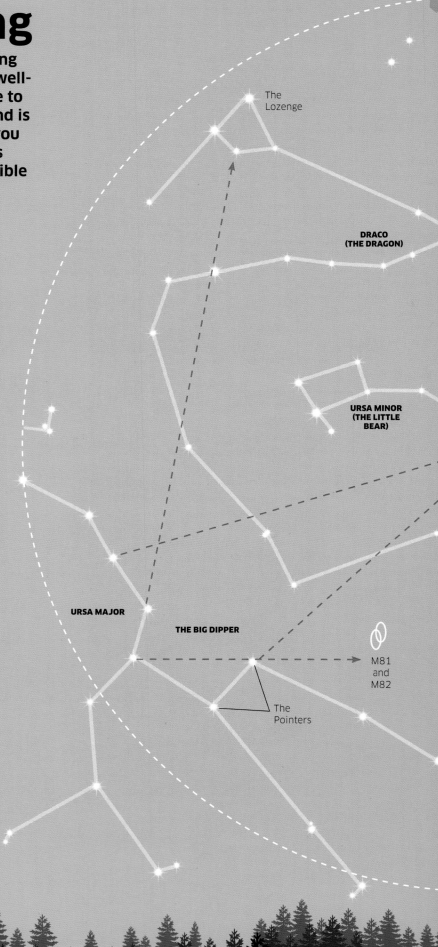

The Lozenge

DRACO
(THE DRAGON)

URSA MINOR
(THE LITTLE
BEAR)

URSA MAJOR

THE BIG DIPPER

M81
and
M82

The
Pointers

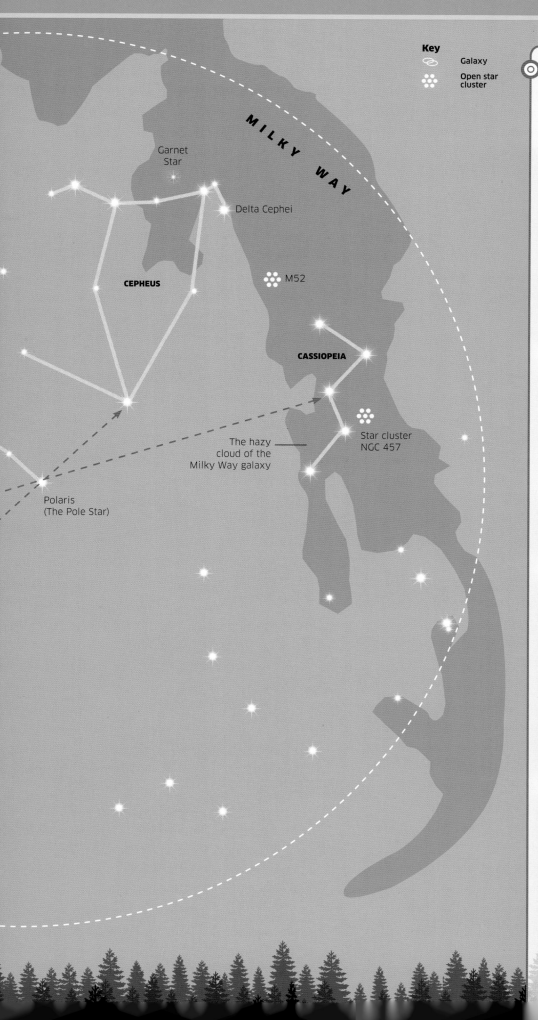

Key

⌾ Galaxy

⚅ Open star cluster

MILKY WAY

Garnet Star

Delta Cephei

CEPHEUS

⚅ M52

CASSIOPEIA

Star cluster NGC 457

The hazy cloud of the Milky Way galaxy

Polaris (The Pole Star)

## ⊚ WHAT TO SEE

Close to the band of the Milky Way, we can see densely packed stars, clusters, and nebulas. Away from it, we can only see a few relatively nearby stars, and some distant galaxies across the gulf of intergalactic space.

**Big and Little bears**
The brightest seven stars of the constellation Ursa Major, the Great Bear, form the familiar pattern known as the Big Dipper. Following the Pointers to the Pole Star reveals a similar pattern of seven stars called Ursa Minor, the Little Bear.

**Pole Star**
Because Earth rotates, stars move across the sky during the night, circling the north celestial pole. However, one star barely moves: the Pole Star, which lies in the tail of the Little Bear (Ursa Minor). Sailors used to use this guiding star to find north on clear nights.

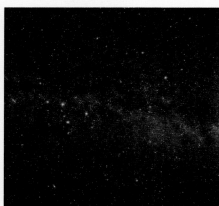

**Cassiopeia and the Milky Way**
The constellation of Cassiopeia lies embedded in the northern reaches of the Milky Way, the pale band of countless distant stars that wraps its way around the sky. This makes Cassiopeia a rich hunting ground for star clusters and other deep-sky objects.

**M81 and M82**
The bright spiral galaxy M81 (top), also called Bode's Galaxy, lies about 12 million light-years from Earth. Nearby in the night sky is M82 (bottom), an irregular cloud of distant stars that is also known as the Cigar Galaxy.

# Southern star-hopping

This chart shows you how to star-hop your way around some of the top sights in the southern night sky, visible to people who live in Earth's southern hemisphere. The southern sky gives stargazers a fantastic view of our Milky Way galaxy and the bright constellations Carina, Centaurus, and the Southern Cross. There are many celestial wonders to spot, from colorful nebulas and star clusters to whole galaxies.

## FINDING THE WAY

Southern stargazers don't have a pole star to guide them, and the constellations closest to the pole are faint and unremarkable. Fortunately, the Milky Way runs close by and is packed with bright stars and other landmarks. The Southern Cross (Crux) and the so-called Southern Pointers make good starting points for finding your way around the sky.

**1** **FIRST IDENTIFY** the Southern Cross (not to be confused with the False Cross) and the Southern Pointer stars Alpha and Beta Centauri. Draw a line from Beta Centauri to the bottom of the Southern Cross and continue on for the same distance again to reach the famous Carina Nebula. This complex mix of a star-forming nebula and a massive star on the brink of explosion is well worth exploring with binoculars.

**2** **TWO BEAUTIFUL STAR CLUSTERS** lie close to the Carina Nebula: NGC 3532 and the Southern Pleiades (IC 2602). This second cluster contains five or six naked-eye stars—see how many you can count (you'll see more by looking slightly to one side of it). Then use binoculars to view many more.

**3** **NEXT FOLLOW A LINE** from the top of the Southern Cross, past the Carina Nebula, and onward by the same distance again. Here you'll find the deceptive pattern of the False Cross, and just beyond it the star cluster IC 2391. This impressive jewel box of stars is best appreciated through binoculars.

**4** **NOW FOLLOW THE** downward (longer) bar of the Southern Cross and cross an empty area of the sky to reach the Small Magellanic Cloud. This small galaxy orbits our own Milky Way galaxy and contains hundreds of millions of stars. Nearby is a impressive globular cluster of stars known as 47 Tucanae.

**5** **FINALLY, RETURN** to the Southern Pointers and follow a line from Alpha Centauri to discover three bright stars that form a triangle shape—the unimaginatively named constellation Triangulum Australe.

Canopus

IC 2391

Large Magellanic Cloud (LMC)

False Cross

CARINA

Carina Nebula

Southern Pleiades

NGC 3532

Acrux

Gamma Crucis

SOUTHERN CROSS (CRUX)

TRIANGULUM AUSTRALE

CENTAURUS

Beta Centauri

Southern Pointers

Alpha Centauri

**Key**

- ⚬⚬ Open star cluster
- ◉ Globular (closed) star cluster
- ▱ Nebula

HYDRUS

Small Magellanic Cloud

47 Tucanae

The hazy cloud of the Milky Way galaxy

## ◎ WHAT TO SEE

The constellations right around the south celestial pole may be faint, but there are many other interesting objects to see a little farther afield. Most of these lie either within the band of the Milky Way or close to it.

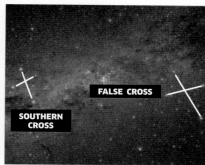

SOUTHERN CROSS

FALSE CROSS

**False Cross**
The False Cross is made of bright stars from the constellations Carina and Vela. It mimics the shape of the true Southern Cross, which is why the two are often confused. However, the False Cross is slightly larger.

**Carina Nebula**
The Carina Nebula is a vast, star-forming gas cloud about 7,500 light-years from Earth. Deep inside it is a massive star nearing the end of its life that will eventually explode in a supernova. Photographs capture the red color of the Carina Nebula, but to the naked eye it appears white.

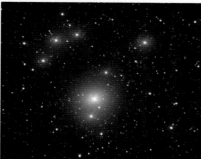

**Southern Pleiades**
The Southern Pleiades cluster (IC 2602) is an open cluster—a group of young stars that formed in the same gas cloud. It is visible to the naked eye, but binoculars will reveal more of the stars within it. There are around 60 stars in total.

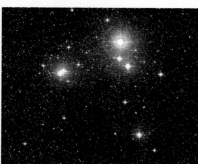

**Open cluster IC 2391**
This bright open cluster likely originated from the same star-forming cloud as the Southern Pleiades, since it has a similar age (about 50 million years) and is a similar distance from Earth (500 light-years).

**Large and Small Magellanic clouds**
These irregular galaxies are satellites of our own galaxy, the Milky Way. In southern skies they look like small, detached clumps of the Milky Way. The large cloud is about 160,000 light-years from Earth, while the small cloud is around 210,000 light-years away.

# Star maps

**From Earth about 6,000 stars are visible to the naked eye, though you can only see about half of these from any location at any one time.**

Over a year you can see all the stars in either the north or south celestial hemisphere, depending on whether you are north or south of the equator, and some of the stars in the other celestial hemisphere too.

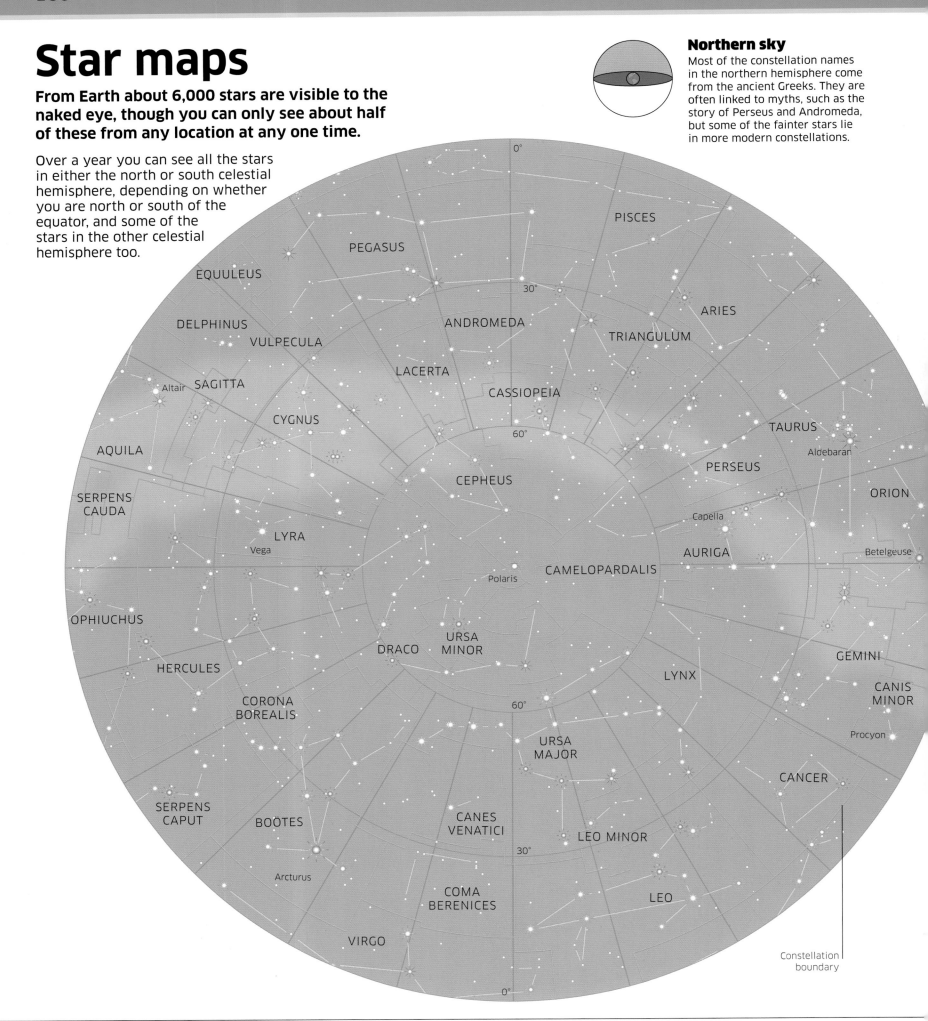

**Northern sky**
Most of the constellation names in the northern hemisphere come from the ancient Greeks. They are often linked to myths, such as the story of Perseus and Andromeda, but some of the fainter stars lie in more modern constellations.

0°

PISCES

PEGASUS

EQUULEUS

30°

ARIES

DELPHINUS

ANDROMEDA

TRIANGULUM

VULPECULA

LACERTA

Altair  SAGITTA

CASSIOPEIA

TAURUS

CYGNUS

Aldebaran

60°

AQUILA

PERSEUS

CEPHEUS

ORION

SERPENS CAUDA

Capella

LYRA

AURIGA

Betelgeuse

Vega

Polaris

CAMELOPARDALIS

OPHIUCHUS

GEMINI

URSA MINOR

DRACO

LYNX

HERCULES

CANIS MINOR

60°

CORONA BOREALIS

Procyon

URSA MAJOR

CANCER

SERPENS CAPUT

BOÖTES

CANES VENATICI

LEO MINOR

30°

Arcturus

LEO

COMA BERENICES

VIRGO

Constellation boundary

0°

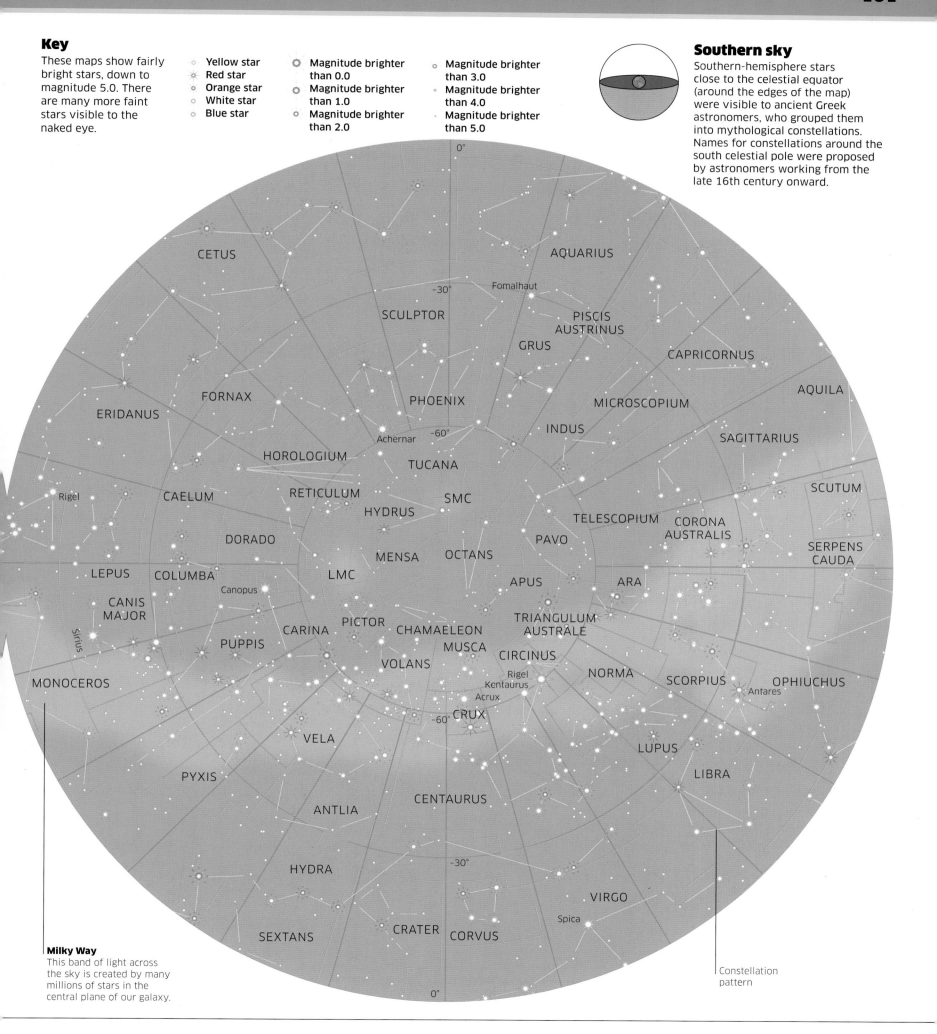

## Key

These maps show fairly bright stars, down to magnitude 5.0. There are many more faint stars visible to the naked eye.

- ◦ Yellow star
- ✳ Red star
- ○ Orange star
- ○ White star
- ○ Blue star

- ◉ Magnitude brighter than 0.0
- ◉ Magnitude brighter than 1.0
- ◉ Magnitude brighter than 2.0
- ○ Magnitude brighter than 3.0
- ◦ Magnitude brighter than 4.0
- · Magnitude brighter than 5.0

## Southern sky

Southern-hemisphere stars close to the celestial equator (around the edges of the map) were visible to ancient Greek astronomers, who grouped them into mythological constellations. Names for constellations around the south celestial pole were proposed by astronomers working from the late 16th century onward.

**Milky Way**
This band of light across the sky is created by many millions of stars in the central plane of our galaxy.

Constellation pattern

### Constellations and labels on the map

CETUS
AQUARIUS
-30°
Fomalhaut
SCULPTOR
PISCIS AUSTRINUS
CAPRICORNUS
GRUS
FORNAX
PHOENIX
MICROSCOPIUM
AQUILA
ERIDANUS
-60°
INDUS
SAGITTARIUS
Achernar
HOROLOGIUM
TUCANA
Rigel
CAELUM
RETICULUM
SMC
TELESCOPIUM
SCUTUM
HYDRUS
CORONA AUSTRALIS
DORADO
PAVO
SERPENS CAUDA
LEPUS
MENSA
OCTANS
COLUMBA
Canopus
LMC
APUS
ARA
CANIS MAJOR
PICTOR
CHAMAELEON
TRIANGULUM AUSTRALE
Sirius
CARINA
MUSCA
CIRCINUS
PUPPIS
VOLANS
Rigel Kentaurus
NORMA
SCORPIUS
OPHIUCHUS
MONOCEROS
Acrux
Antares
-60°
CRUX
LUPUS
VELA
LIBRA
PYXIS
ANTLIA
CENTAURUS
HYDRA
-30°
VIRGO
SEXTANS
CRATER
CORVUS
Spica
0°

# Constellations

Since the earliest times, people have looked for patterns in the stars. The people of ancient Greece knew 48 constellations, named after mythical beings, though the patterns bear little resemblance to the beings they are named after. Today scientists recognize 88 constellations. These modern constellations are not just patterns of stars—they are whole segments of the sky that fit together like a jigsaw puzzle to form a complete sphere.

## KEY

### Deep-sky objects

| Galaxy | Globular cluster | Open cluster | Planetary nebula or supernova remnant | Black hole or X-ray binary | Other deep-sky object |
|---|---|---|---|---|---|

### Star magnitudes

| -1.5-0 | 0-0.9 | 1.0-1.9 | 2.0-2.9 | 3.0-3.9 | 4.0-4.9 | 5.0-5.9 | 6.0-6.9 |
|---|---|---|---|---|---|---|---|

### Constellation widths

Hand symbols are used to indicate a constellation's apparent size in the sky. A spread hand at arm's length spans about 22° of sky, while a closed hand covers about 10°. Combinations of these symbols are used to convey the full width and depth of the constellation.

## CEPHEUS

The constellation Cepheus is named after a mythical king, the husband of Queen Cassiopeia. In Greek mythology, King Cepheus and Queen Cassiopeia were told by an oracle that they must sacrifice their daughter, Princess Andromeda, to a sea monster to stop it from destroying their coastline. In a dramatic rescue, Andromeda was saved from the monster's jaws by the warrior Perseus. All the characters from this myth have constellations named after them. The stars of Cepheus form a shape like a house with a pointed roof. The most famous of its stars is Delta Cephei.

**NORTHERN HEMISPHERE**

NGC 7160

Delta Cephei

Garnet star

IC 1396

**Width:** 

CEPHEUS

## URSA MINOR

This constellation represents a small bear with a long tail. At the tip of its tail lies the Pole Star, called Polaris, which is the brightest star in the constellation. Ursa Minor is sometimes termed the Little Dipper because its main stars form a shape that looks like a smaller version of the Big Dipper in the constellation Ursa Major. It was one of the original constellations known to the ancient Greeks.

**NORTHERN HEMISPHERE**

**URSA MINOR (THE LITTLE BEAR)**

## Things to look for

**Polaris**
Most stars move around the sky, but Polaris stays still and is always due north. Sailors have long used this star to find their way.

Polaris

Kochab

Pherkad

**Width:**

## DRACO

Draco is a constellation representing a dragon. In Greek mythology, this was the dragon slain by the warrior Hercules, who is represented by a neighboring constellation. The dragon's head is formed by four stars near the border with Hercules. The ancient Greeks visualized Hercules with one foot on the dragon's head. From the head, its body curls like a snake across the sky between Ursa Minor and Ursa Major. Draco's brightest star, Etamin, lies in the dragon's head.

**NORTHERN HEMISPHERE**

NGC 6543

Thuban

Etamin

Width: 🖐🖐🤟🤟

**DRACO (THE DRAGON)**

**Cat's Eye Nebula (NGC 6543)**
The fantastic Cat's Eye Nebula in Draco is seen here as pictured by the Hubble Space Telescope. The Cat's Eye is a type of object known as a planetary nebula, consisting of gas thrown off from a dying star. This nebula is also known by its catalog number NGC 6543.

## CASSIOPEIA

A mythical queen from ancient Greece—the wife of King Cepheus and the mother of Princess Andromeda—inspired the name of this constellation. On star maps she is depicted sitting in a chair and combing her hair. In the sky the main stars of Cassiopeia form a W-shape, which is easy to recognize but does not really look much like a person sitting in a chair. Cassiopeia contains several interesting clusters of stars. The brightest of them can be seen with binoculars and small telescopes.

**CASSIOPEIA**

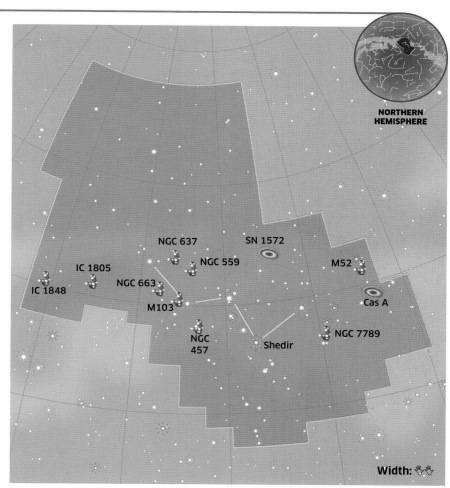

**NORTHERN HEMISPHERE**

NGC 637
SN 1572
IC 1805
NGC 559
M52
IC 1848
NGC 663
Cas A
M103
NGC 457
Shedir
NGC 7789

Width: 🖐🖐

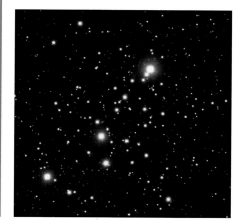

**Star cluster M103**
This star cluster in Cassiopeia is visible through small telescopes. Its three brightest stars form a line across the center. The star at the top right actually lies closer to us than the others, so it is not really a member of the cluster at all.

# CAMELOPARDALIS

Dutch astronomer Petrus Plancius devised this strangely named constellation in 1612. It represents a giraffe. The Greeks called giraffes "camel leopards" because of their long necks and spotted bodies, which is where Camelopardalis gets its name. It is difficult to spot because it contains only faint stars.

**NORTHERN HEMISPHERE**

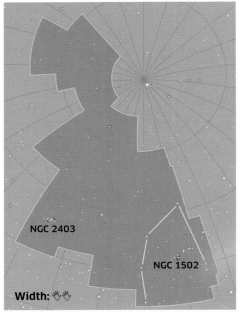

NGC 2403

NGC 1502

Width: 🖐️🖐️

**CAMELOPARDALIS (THE GIRAFFE)**

# LYNX

This is a faint constellation squeezed in between the constellations Ursa Major and Auriga. Polish astronomer Johannes Hevelius created it in 1687. Hevelius had very sharp eyesight, and he named the constellation Lynx because, he said, you would have to be lynx-eyed to see it. It has a number of interesting double and triple stars, which can be studied with a small telescope.

**NORTHERN HEMISPHERE**

LYNX

NGC 2419

Width: 🖐️

# AURIGA

The constellation Auriga is easy to find because it contains the star Capella, one of the brightest stars in the entire sky. To the ancient Greeks, the constellation represented a charioteer carrying a goat and two baby goats on his arm. Capella was the goat and the two fainter stars were the babies. Among the objects of interest in Auriga is a row of three star clusters, M36, M37, and M38, all visible through binoculars. The star that once marked the charioteer's right foot has now been transferred to Taurus, the Bull, which lies to the south.

**AURIGA (THE CHARIOTEER)**

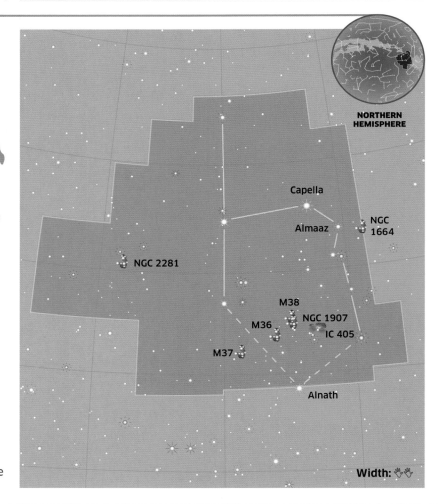

**NORTHERN HEMISPHERE**

Capella

Almaaz

NGC 1664

NGC 2281

M38

NGC 1907

M36

IC 405

M37

Alnath

Width: 🖐️🖐️

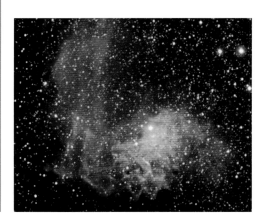

**Flaming Star Nebula**
The Flaming Star Nebula (IC 405) is a giant cloud of gas lit up by a hot star called AE Aurigae. The nebula can only be seen through a large telescope.

# URSA MAJOR

This large constellation's name is Latin for the Great Bear, which it represents. Seven of its brightest stars form a saucepan shape, popularly known as the Big Dipper, which is one of the best-known features in the entire sky. The two stars in the bowl of the saucepan farthest from the handle, called Merak and Dubhe, are known as the Pointers because they point toward the Pole Star, Polaris. The curving handle of the saucepan points toward the bright star Arcturus in the nearby constellation Boötes.

**URSA MAJOR
(THE GREAT BEAR)**

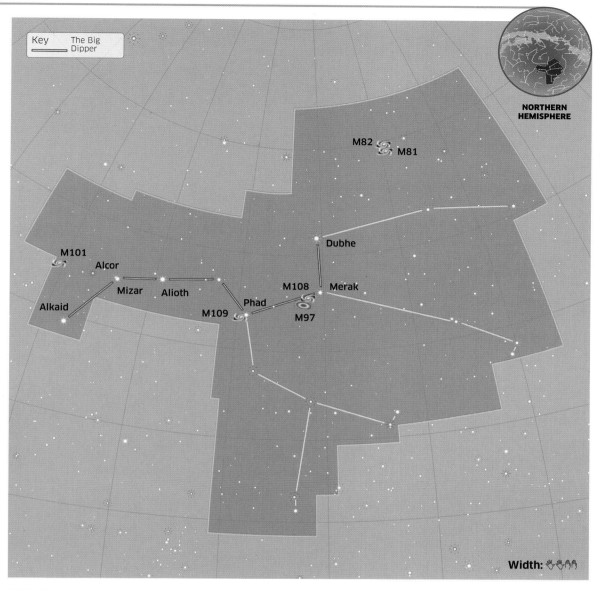

Key — The Big Dipper

**NORTHERN HEMISPHERE**

M82  M81

M101  Dubhe

Alcor

Mizar  Alioth  M108  Merak

Alkaid  Phad

M109  M97

**Width:** 🖐🖐🖐

## Spiral galaxy M81

In the northern part of Ursa Major lie two contrasting galaxies, known by their catalog numbers M81 and M82. M81 is a beautiful spiral, shown in this Hubble Space Telescope image (above). M82 is irregular in shape. It is thought to be undergoing a burst of star formation resulting from an encounter with M81 millions of years ago. M81 and M82 both lie about 12 million light-years away.

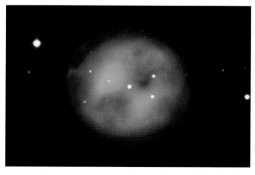

## Owl Nebula

Just under the bowl of the Big Dipper, a glowing cloud of gas called M97 can be seen through a telescope. It is also called the Owl Nebula because of the two dark spots that look like the eyes of an owl. It is a planetary nebula, made of gas thrown off from a dying star.

## Spiral galaxy M101

Near the end of the handle of the Big Dipper lies the spiral galaxy M101. Although it is too faint to see without binoculars or a telescope, its spiral arms show up clearly on photographs. It is sometimes called the Pinwheel Galaxy.

## 🔭 Things to look for

**Mizar** This is the second star in the handle of the Big Dipper. Next to it is a fainter star called Alcor, which can also be seen with the naked eye.

## CANES VENATICI

This constellation was named after a pair of hunting dogs by Polish astronomer Johannes Hevelius in 1687. There are only two stars of any note in the constellation, but it also contains many interesting galaxies. Most famous of these is the Whirlpool Galaxy. This can be seen through binoculars as a faint patch of light, but a large telescope is needed to make out its spiral shape. Another object of note is the globular star cluster M3 near the constellation's southern border.

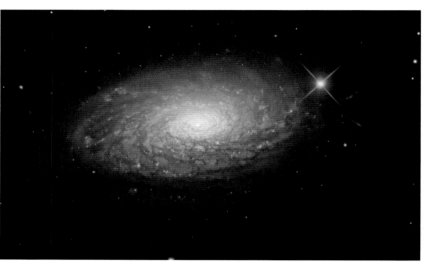

**Sunflower Galaxy**
Another beautiful spiral galaxy in Canes Venatici is the Sunflower Galaxy (M63), seen here through a large telescope. The star on the right is not connected with the galaxy but is much closer to us.

**Whirlpool Galaxy**
Seen here is a Hubble Space Telescope view of the Whirlpool Galaxy (M51), a vast spiral of stars some 30 million light-years away. Behind it, near the end of one of its arms, is a smaller galaxy, which astronomers think will one day merge with it.

NGC 5195

M51

M63

M3

## BOÖTES

Boötes represents a man herding the Great Bear around the pole. He is sometimes referred to as the herdsman or bear driver. This constellation contains Arcturus, the brightest star in the northern half of the sky. It is a giant star and looks pale orange to the eye.

**NORTHERN HEMISPHERE**

Izar

Arcturus

**Width:** 🖐

**BOÖTES
(THE HERDSMAN)**

## HERCULES

This constellation is named after Hercules, the strong man of Greek mythology. In star charts he is often depicted brandishing a club and with one foot on the head of Draco, the dragon, which he killed in a fight. The stars of Hercules are not particularly bright, so the constellation can be difficult to find. Its most noticeable feature is a squashed square of four stars known as the Keystone, which marks the body of Hercules. On one side of the Keystone lies the globular cluster M13.

**HERCULES**

**Star cluster M13**
The globular cluster M13 is a ball of about 300,000 stars some 25,000 light-years away. It can be seen as a hazy patch through binoculars. Telescopes are needed to see the individual stars.

M106

NGC 4449

M94

Cor Caroli

NGC 4631

**Width:** 🤚🖐

**NORTHERN HEMISPHERE**

**CANES VENATICI
(THE HUNTING DOGS)**

**NORTHERN HEMISPHERE**

# ⊚ LYRA

The constellation Lyra represents a small harp, known to the Greeks as a lyre. In mythology, it was the instrument played by the musician Orpheus. Lyra is easy to spot because it contains Vega, the fifth-brightest star in the entire sky, 25 light-years away. Vega forms one corner of the Summer Triangle—a triangle formed by bright stars in three different constellations.

**LYRA (THE LYRE)**

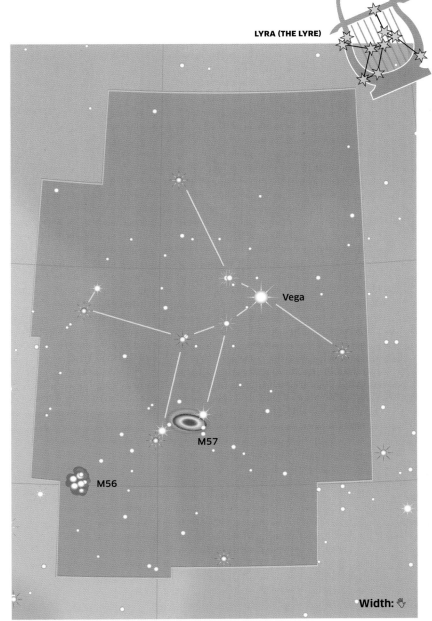

Vega

M57

M56

**Width:** 🖐

Key
—— The Keystone

**NORTHERN HEMISPHERE**

M92

M13

NGC 6210

Cluster
Abell 2151

Rasalgethi

**Width:** 🤚🤚🖐

**Ring Nebula**
The Ring Nebula (M57), seen here through the Hubble Space Telescope, is a shell of glowing gas. At its center is a white dwarf, the remains of the star that lost its outer layers to form the nebula.

# CYGNUS

The ancient Greeks visualized Cygnus as a swan flying along the Milky Way. Its brightest star, Deneb, marks its tail, while the star Albireo is its beak. In mythology, the swan was the disguise used by the god Zeus when he visited Queen Leda of Sparta. The overall shape of the constellation resembles a large cross, so it is sometimes known as the Northern Cross. One of the most exciting objects in Cygnus lies in the swan's neck—a black hole called Cygnus X-1. The black hole itself cannot be seen from Earth, but satellites in space have detected X-rays from hot gas falling into it from a nearby star.

Key
The Northern Cross

NGC 6826

M39

Deneb

NGC 7000

Cyg A

M29

Cyg X-1

Veil Nebula

NGC 6992

Albireo

Width:

NORTHERN HEMISPHERE

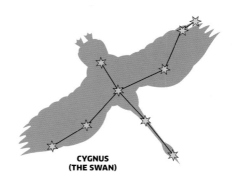

**CYGNUS (THE SWAN)**

## Things to look for

**Albireo** In the head of the swan lies a beautiful colored double star known as Albireo. To the naked eye it appears as a single star, but small telescopes show it as a pair. The brighter star is orange, and the fainter one is blue-green.

**North America Nebula**
Near Deneb lies a cloud of gas popularly known as the North America Nebula (NGC 7000) because of its shape, which resembles the continent of North America. The nebula cannot be seen without a telescope and shows up best in color photographs like the one here.

**Veil Nebula**
In one wing of the swan lie streamers of gas from a star that exploded as a supernova thousands of years ago. The shattered remains of that star are splashed across an area wider than six full moons, forming the Veil Nebula.

# ANDROMEDA

This constellation is named after a princess of Greek mythology who was chained to a rock by her parents, King Cepheus and Queen Cassiopeia, as a sacrifice to a sea monster. Fortunately, she was rescued in the nick of time by the hero Perseus, who lies next to her in the sky. Andromeda's head is marked by the star known as Alpheratz. In ancient times, this star was shared with the constellation Pegasus.

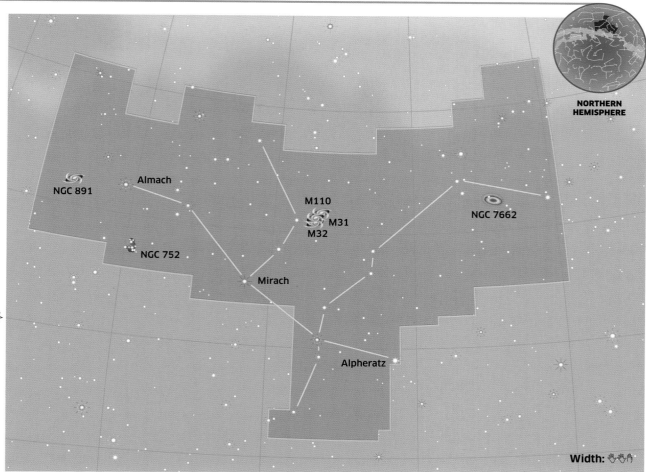

**NORTHERN HEMISPHERE**

NGC 891
Almach
M110
M31
M32
NGC 7662
NGC 752
Mirach
Alpheratz

Width: 🖐🖐🤏

**ANDROMEDA**

# LACERTA

This small figure represents a lizard scuttling between Andromeda and Cygnus. It was devised in 1687 by the Polish astronomer Johannes Hevelius from some faint stars that had not previously been part of any constellation. Of particular note is an object called BL Lacertae. Once thought to be an unusual variable star, it is now known to be the core of an active galaxy.

**NORTHERN HEMISPHERE**

NGC 7243

BL Lacertae

Width: 🖐

**LACERTA (THE LIZARD)**

**NORTHERN HEMISPHERE**

M33

Width: 🤏

# TRIANGULUM

To the ancient Greeks, this small, triangular constellation just south of Andromeda represented either the delta of the Nile River or the island of Sicily. Its main feature is M33, a spiral galaxy faintly visible through binoculars. M33 lies nearly 3 million light-years away and is the third-largest member of our Local Group of galaxies.

**TRIANGULUM (THE TRIANGLE)**

## PERSEUS

The constellation Perseus is named after a hero of Greek mythology who was sent to cut off the head of Medusa, an evil character known as a Gorgon. In the sky Perseus is seen holding his sword aloft in his right hand, with the head of Medusa in his left. The head is marked by the variable star Algol.

NORTHERN HEMISPHERE

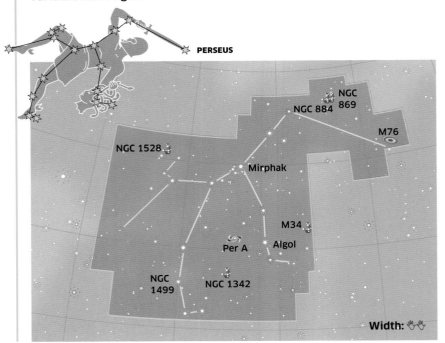

PERSEUS

NGC 869
NGC 884
M76
NGC 1528
Mirphak
M34
Per A
Algol
NGC 1499
NGC 1342

**Width:** 🖐🖐

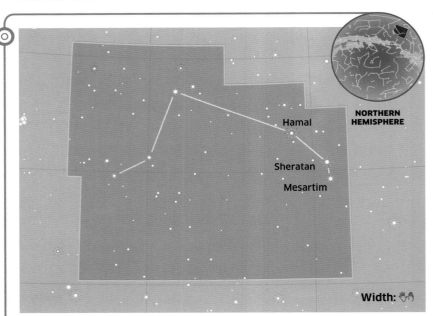

NORTHERN HEMISPHERE

Hamal
Sheratan
Mesartim

**Width:** 🖐👌

## ARIES

Aries represents a ram with a golden fleece in Greek mythology. According to legend, Jason and the Argonauts made an epic voyage from Greece to the Black Sea to find the fleece and bring it back. The constellation's most obvious feature is a crooked line of three stars south of Triangulum. The most southerly (and faintest) of these stars, Mesartim, is a double star that is easily divided by small telescopes.

ARIES (THE RAM)

## CANCER

This constellation represents a crab that had a minor role in Greek mythology. According to the story, when Hercules was fighting the multi-headed Hydra, the crab bit him but was then crushed underfoot. Cancer is the faintest of the 12 constellations of the zodiac. Near its center is a large, hazy star cluster with several alternative names: the Beehive, Praesepe, the Manger, or simply M44.

NORTHERN HEMISPHERE

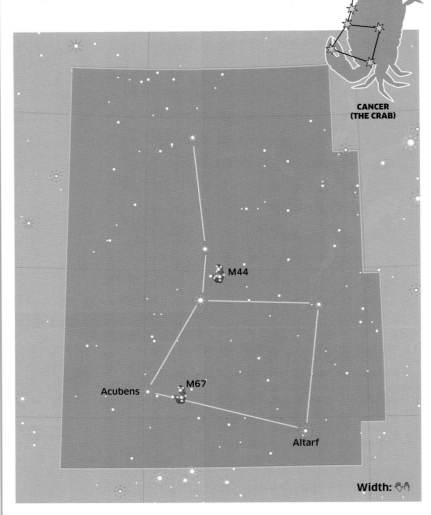

CANCER (THE CRAB)

M44
Acubens
M67
Altarf

**Width:** 🖐👌

**Beehive Cluster**
M44 is an open cluster made of stars that lie about 577 light-years from Earth. While the cluster can be seen by the naked eye, most of its stars are visible only with binoculars or a telescope.

# TAURUS

Taurus, the Bull, is one of the most magnificent and interesting constellations in the sky. In Greek mythology, the god Zeus turned himself into a bull to carry off Princess Europa to the island of Crete. The brightest star in the constellation is Aldebaran, a red giant that marks the glinting eye of the bull. The star at the tip of the bull's right horn, Alnath (or El Nath), was once shared with Auriga to the north.

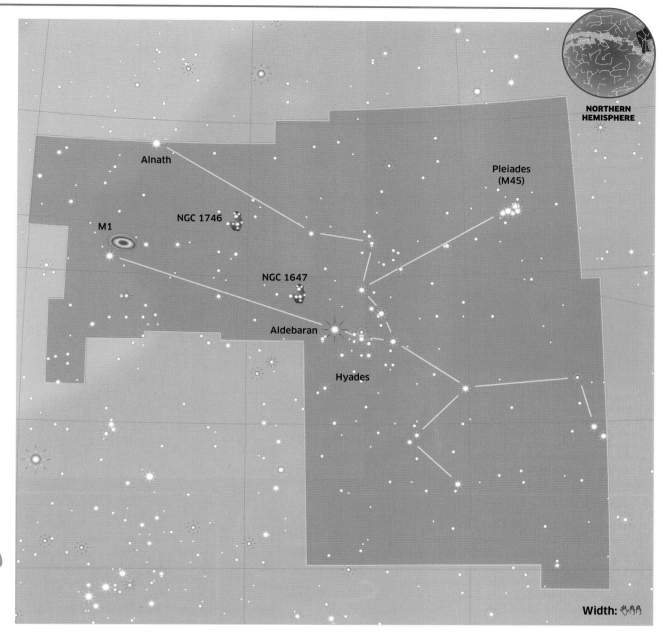

NORTHERN HEMISPHERE

Alnath

NGC 1746

M1

NGC 1647

Aldebaran

Hyades

Pleiades (M45)

Width: ✋👆👆

**TAURUS (THE BULL)**

## Pleiades
The Pleiades Cluster, popularly known as the Seven Sisters, is a beautiful star group. Six or more stars can be seen with the naked eye, and binoculars show dozens. Photographs reveal even more, along with a haze of dust that surrounds them.

## Crab Nebula
In the year 1054, a new star appeared temporarily in Taurus. This was a supernova, the most violent form of stellar explosion. Now only visible through telescopes, the star's shattered remains can be seen as the Crab Nebula (M1). This image was taken with the Hubble Space Telescope.

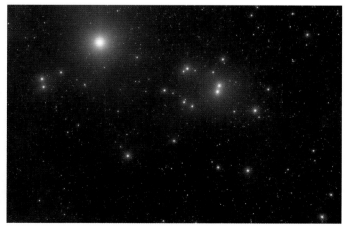

## Hyades
The face of the bull is marked by a V-shaped group of stars called the Hyades, easily visible to the naked eye. The bright star Aldebaran appears to be one of the Hyades but is, in fact, closer to us, and lies in front of the cluster by chance.

## GEMINI

Gemini represents the mythical twins Castor and Pollux. The two brightest stars in the constellation are named after the twins and mark their heads. A small telescope shows that Castor is a double star. These two stars orbit each other every 500 years or so. Larger telescopes show a fainter red dwarf near them. Special instruments have revealed that each of these three stars is itself a close double, making Castor a family of six stars, all linked by gravity.

**Eskimo Nebula**
The Eskimo Nebula (NGC 2392) is a remarkable planetary nebula. It gets its popular name from its resemblance to a face surrounded by a fur-lined hood. Another name for it is the Clown-Faced Nebula.

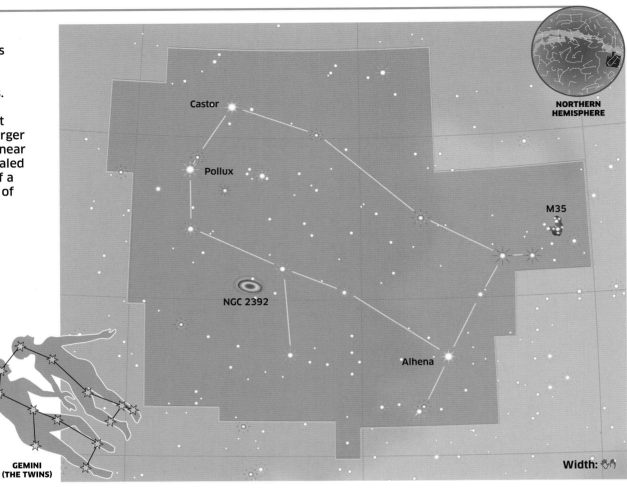

NORTHERN HEMISPHERE

Castor

Pollux

M35

NGC 2392

Alhena

**GEMINI (THE TWINS)**

Width:

## LEO MINOR

This small constellation represents a lion cub. Polish astronomer Johannes Hevelius introduced it in 1687. Leo Minor contains very few objects of interest. The star R Leonis Minoris is a red giant. Its brightness varies at regular intervals—it can be seen with binoculars at its brightest but is not visible even through small telescopes at its dimmest.

NORTHERN HEMISPHERE

**LEO MINOR (THE LITTLE LION)**

R Leonis Minoris

NGC 3344

Width:

## COMA BERENICES

This is a faint but interesting constellation near the tail of Leo, the lion. The ancient Greeks imagined it as the hair of Queen Berenice of Egypt. She cut off her hair to thank the gods after her husband returned safely from fighting a war in Asia. Dozens of faint stars form a wedge-shaped group called the Coma Star Cluster, easily seen in binoculars.

NORTHERN HEMISPHERE

**COMA BERENICES (BERENICE'S HAIR)**

Coma Star Cluster

NGC 4565

M64

M53

M85

M100

M88

M99

M91

M98

Width:

Key
— The Sickle

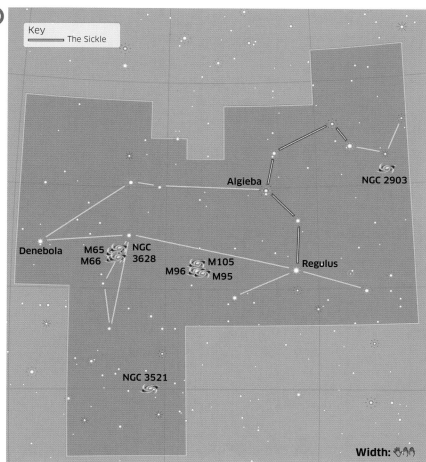

Algieba

NGC 2903

Denebola

M65
M66

NGC
3628

M105
M96
M95

Regulus

NGC 3521

Width: 🖐️🖐️

# LEO

This is one of the few constellations that really looks like what it is supposed to represent—in this case, a crouching lion. In Greek mythology, it was said to be the lion slain by the warrior Hercules as one of his 12 labors. An arc of stars called the Sickle (marked here in purple) forms the lion's head and chest. Leo's brightest star, Regulus, lies at the base of the Sickle. One of the stars in the Sickle, Algieba, can be seen as a double star through small telescopes.

**NORTHERN HEMISPHERE**

**LEO
(THE LION)**

### Spiral galaxy M66
M66 is a beautiful spiral galaxy that lies underneath the hindquarters of Leo, the lion. It forms a pair with another galaxy, M65. They can be glimpsed with small telescopes under good conditions, but large instruments help to see them clearly.

# VIRGO

Virgo is the second-largest constellation. In Greek mythology, it represented both the goddess of justice and the goddess of agriculture. The main stars of Virgo form a lazy "Y" shape. The constellation's brightest star, Spica, is at the base of the Y. The star Porrima, in the middle of the Y, is a double star divisible with a small telescope. In the bowl of the Y is the Virgo Cluster—a cluster of more than 1,000 galaxies about 55 million light-years away.

M90    M88
M89       M84
       M58  M87
M60   M59

**NORTHERN HEMISPHERE**

M49

M61

3C 273

Porrima

Sombrero
Galaxy (M104)

Spica

Width: 🖐️🖐️

### Sombrero Galaxy
The Sombrero Galaxy (M104) is a spiral galaxy seen edge-on that resembles a Mexican sombrero. This view of it was taken by the Hubble Space Telescope. The Sombrero is 30 million light-years away, closer to us than the Virgo Cluster of galaxies.

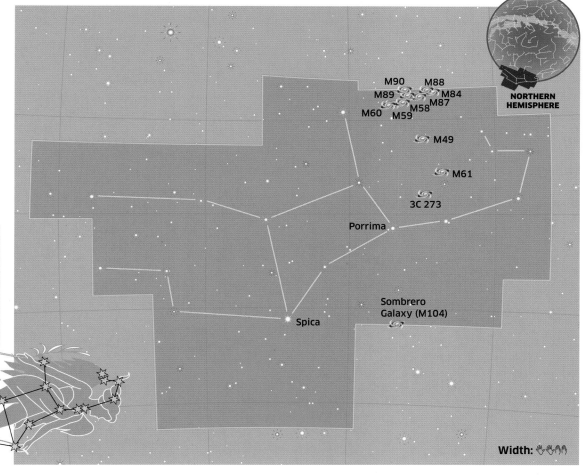

**VIRGO
(THE VIRGIN)**

## LIBRA

The scales of justice are represented by Libra and are held by the goddess of justice, Virgo, who lies next to Libra in the sky. Libra's stars represented the claws of the scorpion, Scorpius, until Roman times.

**SOUTHERN HEMISPHERE**

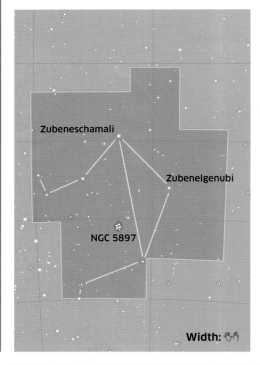

Zubeneschamali

Zubenelgenubi

NGC 5897

**Width:** 🖐️

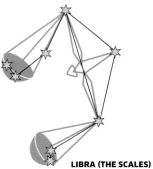

**LIBRA (THE SCALES)**

### 🔭 Things to look for

**Zubenelgenubi** This is a wide double star easily spotted with binoculars or even sharp eyesight. Its strange name comes from the Arabic for "the southern claw."

## SERPENS

The constellation Serpens represents a large snake being held by the man in the constellation Ophiuchus. The head of the snake lies on one side of Ophiuchus, the tail on the other. This is the only example of a constellation being split into two. However, the two halves count as only one constellation. Near the neck of the snake lies M5, one of the best globular clusters in the northern sky, just visible through binoculars. Binoculars will also show an open cluster called IC 4756 near the snake's tail.

IC 4756

M16

**SERPENS (THE SERPENT)**

## CORONA BOREALIS

Shaped like a horseshoe, this constellation represents the jeweled crown worn by Princess Ariadne of Crete when she married the god Dionysus. Within the arc of the crown lies a most unusual variable star, R Coronae Borealis. This is a yellow supergiant that suddenly drops in brightness every few years.

**CORONA BOREALIS (THE NORTHERN CROWN)**

**NORTHERN HEMISPHERE**

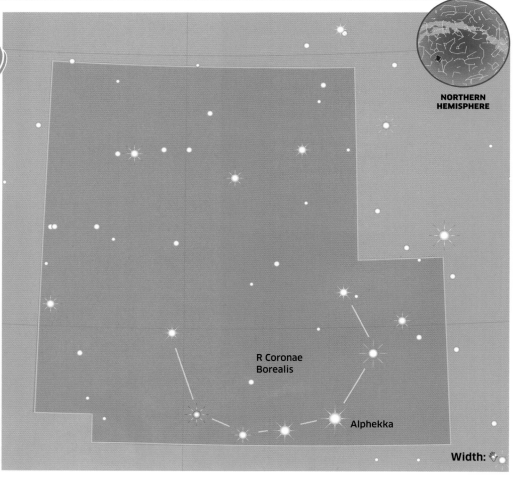

R Coronae Borealis

Alphekka

**Width:** 🖐️

**Jewel in the crown**
Alphekka is the brightest member of the arc of seven stars that makes up the Northern Crown, Corona Borealis. The star is also known as Gemma.

Unukalhai

M5

Width: 🤚🤚

**Eagle Nebula**
In the tail section of Serpens lies a star cluster called M16, visible through binoculars. Surrounding it is a glowing cloud of gas called the Eagle Nebula, seen here through the Hubble Telescope.

SOUTHERN HEMISPHERE

M11

M26

Width: 🤚

SCUTUM
(THE SHIELD)

# SCUTUM

This small constellation represents a shield. It was created in the late 17th century by the Polish astronomer Johannes Hevelius. One of the brightest parts of the Milky Way lies in the northern half of this constellation and is known as the Scutum Star Cloud. Near the border with the constellation Aquila is M11, a star cluster often called the Wild Duck Cluster because its shape resembles a flock of birds in flight.

# OPHIUCHUS

This constellation represents the god of medicine. In the sky he is depicted holding a large snake: the constellation Serpens. Ophiuchus contains several globular clusters that can be seen with binoculars and small telescopes. The brightest of them are M10 and M12.

SOUTHERN HEMISPHERE

M71

NORTHERN HEMISPHERE

Width: 🤚

# SAGITTA

The third-smallest constellation in the sky, Sagitta represents an arrow. It was one of the original constellations known to the ancient Greeks, who said that the arrow was shot either by Hercules, who lies next to it, or by one of the gods. Although its stars are faint, it is quite easy to recognize.

SAGITTA
(THE ARROW)

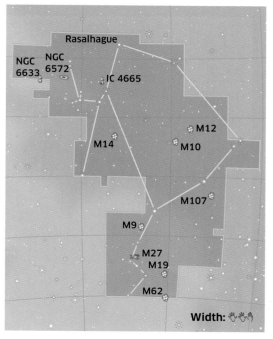

Rasalhague

NGC 6633  NGC 6572

IC 4665

M12
M14  M10

M107

M9

M27
M19

M62

Width: 🤚🤚🤚

OPHIUCHUS
(THE SERPENT HOLDER)

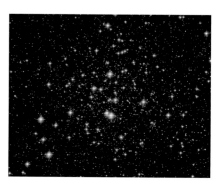

**Globular cluster M71**
Sagitta contains a faint globular cluster, M71, visible through small telescopes. It measures about 27 light-years wide and is thought to be about 10 billion years old.

# AQUILA

Aquila represents a flying eagle, one of the disguises that was said in mythology to have been adopted by the Greek god Zeus. Its main star is Altair, which marks one corner of the Summer Triangle—a famous triangle made of bright stars from different constellations. The other two stars of the triangle are Vega in Lyra and Deneb in Cygnus. The most interesting feature in Aquila is Eta Aquilae, one of the brightest examples of the type of variable star known as a Cepheid.

**NORTHERN HEMISPHERE**

**AQUILA (THE EAGLE)**

Tarazed
Altair
Alshain
NGC 6709
Eta Aquilae

**Width:** 🖐🖐

# VULPECULA

Polish astronomer Johannes Hevelius named this faint constellation in the late 17th century. It represents a fox. An attractive object for binoculars is a group of stars called the Coathanger, shaped like a bar with a hook on top.

**NORTHERN HEMISPHERE**

M27

**Width:** 🖐🖐🖐

**VULPECULA (THE FOX)**

**Dumbbell Nebula**
A famous object in the constellation Vulpecula is the Dumbbell Nebula (M27). This planetary nebula (a shell of gas thrown off from a dying star) can be seen with binoculars on clear nights.

# DELPHINUS

This attractive constellation represents a dolphin. In mythology, this was the dolphin that rescued the Greek musician Arion when he jumped overboard from a ship to escape a band of robbers. The constellation's two brightest stars bear the odd names Sualocin and Rotanev. Read backward, they spell Nicolaus Venator, the name of the Italian astronomer who is thought to have named them after himself.

**NORTHERN HEMISPHERE**

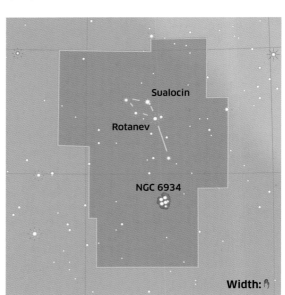

Sualocin
Rotanev
NGC 6934

**Width:** ✋

**DELPHINUS (THE DOLPHIN)**

# EQUULEUS

Equuleus is the second-smallest constellation in the sky, representing the head of a foal. It lies next to the large flying horse Pegasus and was one of the constellations known to the ancient Greeks. There is little of interest in it apart from a double star, Kitalpha, that can easily be divided with binoculars.

**NORTHERN HEMISPHERE**

**EQUULEUS (THE FOAL)**

Kitalpha

**Width:** ✋

# PEGASUS

This large constellation of the northern sky represents a flying horse in Greek mythology. Its most noticeable feature is a pattern called the Great Square, formed by four stars that outline the horse's body. However, only three stars of the Square actually belong to Pegasus—the fourth is over the border in Andromeda (although in the past it was shared by the two constellations). The Square is so large that 30 full moons placed side by side could fit inside it. The horse's nose is marked by the star Enif.

**PEGASUS (THE WINGED HORSE)**

Key — The Great Square of Pegasus

NGC 7331

NORTHERN HEMISPHERE

Scheat

Algenib

Markab

M15

Enif

Width: 🖐🖐🖐

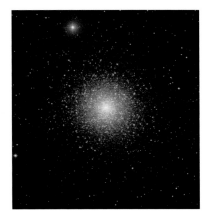

**Globular cluster M15**
Near the star Enif lies M15, one of the finest globular clusters in northern skies. This is easily visible through binoculars as a fuzzy patch. Telescopes reveal it as a vast ball of stars.

# AQUARIUS

The constellation Aquarius represents a young man pouring water from a jar. The jar is represented by a little group of stars around Zeta Aquarii. A string of fainter stars cascading southward represents the flow of water. In the north of the constellation lies the globular cluster M2, visible as a faint patch through binoculars. Two famous planetary nebulas (remains of dying stars) can be found in Aquarius with telescopes.

**AQUARIUS (THE WATER CARRIER)**

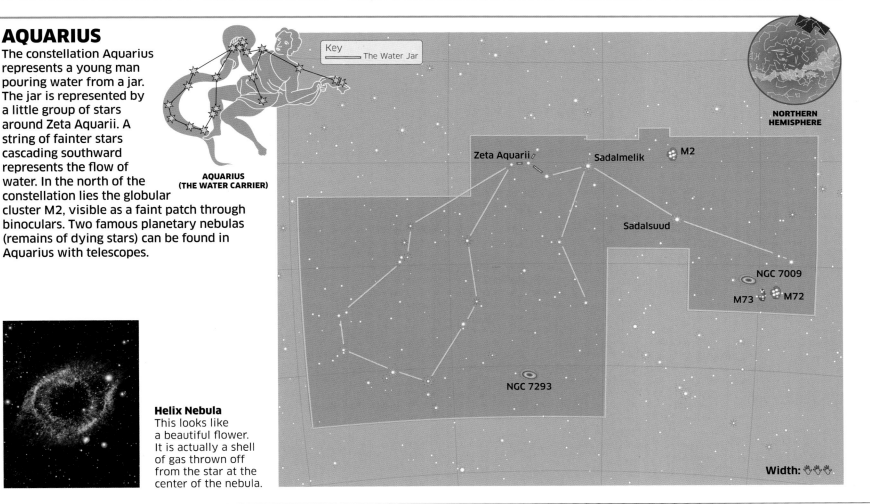

Key — The Water Jar

Zeta Aquarii

Sadalmelik

M2

Sadalsuud

NGC 7009

M73   M72

NGC 7293

NORTHERN HEMISPHERE

Width: 🖐🖐🖐

**Helix Nebula**
This looks like a beautiful flower. It is actually a shell of gas thrown off from the star at the center of the nebula.

## PISCES

Pisces represents two fish with their tails tied together by ribbons. The star Alrescha marks the knot joining the two ribbons. The constellation depicts the Greek myth in which Aphrodite and her son Eros turned themselves into fish to escape from a monster, Typhon. A loop of seven stars called the Circlet marks the body of one of the fish. Pisces includes M74, a beautiful face-on spiral galaxy just visible through small telescopes.

**NORTHERN HEMISPHERE**

PISCES (THE FISHES)

Key
———— The Circlet

M74

Alrescha

Width: 🖐🖐🖐

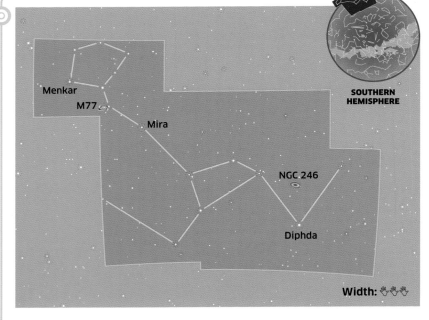

**SOUTHERN HEMISPHERE**

Menkar
M77
Mira
NGC 246
Diphda

Width: 🖐🖐🖐

## CETUS

Cetus, the Sea Monster, is the fourth-largest constellation. In Greek mythology, Andromeda was chained to a rock as a sacrifice to the monster, but Perseus saved her. In the neck of Cetus lies Mira, a famous variable star. When at its brightest, Mira is easily visible to the naked eye, but it fades from view for months at a time.

CETUS (THE SEA MONSTER)

## CANIS MAJOR

The constellation Canis Major and nearby Canis Minor represent the dogs of Orion. Canis Major contains the brightest star in the night sky, Sirius, which lies 8.6 light-years away. South of Sirius is the star cluster M41, which is just visible to the naked eye under clear dark skies and is a beautiful sight through binoculars.

**SOUTHERN HEMISPHERE**

CANIS MAJOR (THE LARGE DOG)

NGC 2360
Sirius
Mirzam
M41
NGC 2362
Adhara

Width: 🖐

## CANIS MINOR

Canis Minor is the smaller of the two dogs of Orion. Its main star, Procyon, is the eighth-brightest in the sky. Procyon forms a large triangle with the other Dog Star (Sirius in Canis Major) and Betelgeuse in Orion. Both Procyon and Sirius are orbited by white dwarf stars, but these companions can be seen only with large telescopes. There is little else of interest in this constellation.

**SOUTHERN HEMISPHERE**

CANIS MINOR (THE LITTLE DOG)

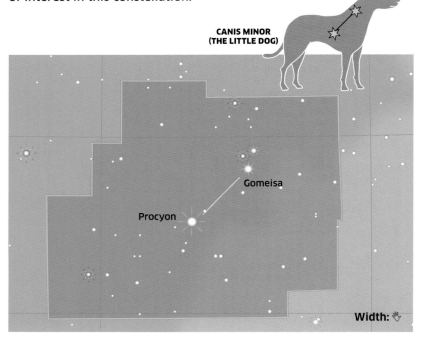

Gomeisa
Procyon

Width: 🖐

# ORION

This constellation represents a giant hunter of Greek mythology. In the sky he is depicted raising his club and shield against Taurus, the Bull, the constellation next to him. The bright star Betelgeuse marks Orion's right shoulder and Rigel is his left foot. Betelgeuse is a red supergiant, which varies slightly in brightness, while Rigel, another supergiant star, is hotter and bluer. One feature that makes Orion easy to identify is the line of three stars that mark his belt. From the belt hangs his sword, which contains one of the treasures of the sky, the Orion Nebula.

**ORION
(THE HUNTER)**

NGC 2175

**NORTHERN
HEMISPHERE**

Betelgeuse

Bellatrix

M78

Mintaka

Alnitak

Alnilam

NGC 2024

Horsehead
Nebula

Orion
Nebula

Rigel

Saiph

**Width:** 🖐🤏

**Trapezium**
At the center of the Orion Nebula lies a group of four stars called the Trapezium, which can be seen through small telescopes. Light from these newborn stars helps make the surrounding gas glow.

**Horsehead Nebula**
Looking like a knight in a celestial chess game, the Horsehead Nebula is a dark cloud of dust, seen here through the Hubble Telescope. The nebula is located just below the star Alnitak in Orion's belt. The background nebula is faint and the Horsehead shows up well only in photographs.

**Orion Nebula**
The Orion Nebula, a large star-forming cloud of gas, looks like a patch of mist in binoculars and small telescopes, but when pictured by the Hubble Space Telescope, its full complexity and color can be seen.

# MONOCEROS

MONOCEROS
(THE UNICORN)

This constellation represents a unicorn, the mythical beast with a single horn. Dutch astronomer and mapmaker Petrus Plancius introduced it in the early 17th century in a gap between Greek constellations. One feature of interest is Beta Monocerotis, which is an excellent triple star for small telescopes. Three attractive star clusters for binoculars or small telescopes are M50, NGC 2244, and NGC 2264.

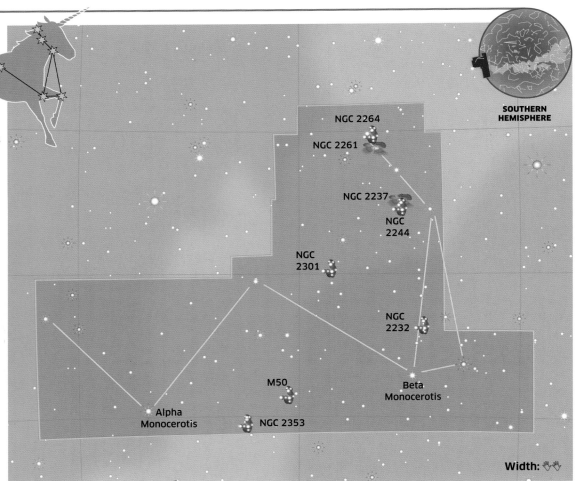

SOUTHERN
HEMISPHERE

NGC 2264
NGC 2261
NGC 2237
NGC 2244
NGC 2301
NGC 2232
M50
Beta Monocerotis
Alpha Monocerotis
NGC 2353

Width: 🖐🖐

### Rosette Nebula
The star cluster NGC 2244 lies within a flowerlike cloud of gas known as the Rosette Nebula. The star cluster can easily be seen with binoculars, but the nebula, glowing like a pink carnation, shows up only on photographs.

# HYDRA

This is the largest constellation of all, stretching more than a quarter of the way around the sky. In Greek mythology, Hydra was a monster with many heads, although in the sky it has only one head, represented by a loop of five stars. Its brightest star is called Alphard, meaning "the solitary one," since it lies in a fairly blank area of sky. M48, near the border with Monoceros, is a star cluster visible through binoculars and small telescopes.

SOUTHERN
HEMISPHERE

HYDRA
(THE WATER SNAKE)

M48
Alphard
NGC 3242
M68
M83

Width: 🖐🖐🖐🖐🖐

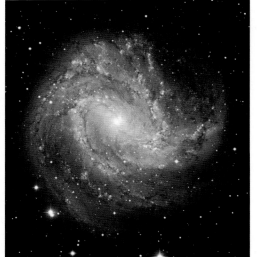

### Spiral galaxy M83
Sometimes known as the Southern Pinwheel, M83 is a beautiful spiral galaxy 15 million light-years away. It can be seen as a faint patch through small telescopes, but larger instruments are needed to bring out the beauty of its spiral arms.

# ANTLIA

This is a small, faint southern constellation invented in the 1750s by the French astronomer Nicolas Louis de Lacaille. Its name, which means "pump," commemorates the invention of a kind of air pump. The constellation's most impressive feature is a spiral galaxy called NGC 2997. This is too faint to see with small telescopes but shows up beautifully in photographs, which reveal clouds of pink gas dotted along its arms.

**SOUTHERN HEMISPHERE**

ANTLIA
(THE AIR PUMP)

NGC 2997

NGC 3132

**Width:** 🖐

# SEXTANS

A faint constellation that was invented in the late 17th century by the Polish astronomer Johannes Hevelius, Sextans represents an instrument called a sextant, which was used for measuring star positions. Sextans contains the Spindle Galaxy (NGC 3115), a galaxy several times larger than our Milky Way.

**SOUTHERN HEMISPHERE**

SEXTANS
(THE SEXTANT)

NGC 3115

**Width:** 🖐

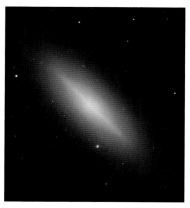

**Spindle Galaxy**
This galaxy appears rod-shaped because we see it edge-on. It is also known by its catalog number NGC 3115.

# CRATER

The word "crater" is Latin for cup, and this constellation represents the cup of the Greek god Apollo. In Greek mythology, Apollo sent a crow to fetch water in the cup. The greedy bird was late because it stopped to eat figs. It blamed the delay on a snake, but Apollo realized what had happened and punished the crow for lying by placing it in the sky, along with the cup and the snake. Crater contains no major objects of interest for users of small telescopes.

**SOUTHERN HEMISPHERE**

**Width:** 🖐

CRATER
(THE CUP)

# CORVUS

Corvus represents a crow that was sent to fetch water in a cup by the god Apollo. It lies next to Crater, which represents the cup. Both lie on the back of Hydra, the water snake. The constellation's most amazing feature is a pair of colliding galaxies called the Antennae—NGC 4038 and 4039. Large telescopes reveal long streamers of gas and stars stretching away from the galaxies like the antennae (feelers) of an insect.

**SOUTHERN HEMISPHERE**

CORVUS
(THE CROW)

Gienah

NGC 4038/9

Alchiba

**Width:** 🖐

# CENTAURUS

Centaurs were mythical creatures of ancient Greece, half man and half horse. This constellation represents a centaur called Chiron, who taught the children of the Greek gods. Small telescopes show that its brightest star, Alpha Centauri, is a double star. There is also a third star: a red dwarf called Proxima Centauri, which is the closest star to the Sun at 4.2 light-years away.

CENTAURUS
(THE CENTAUR)

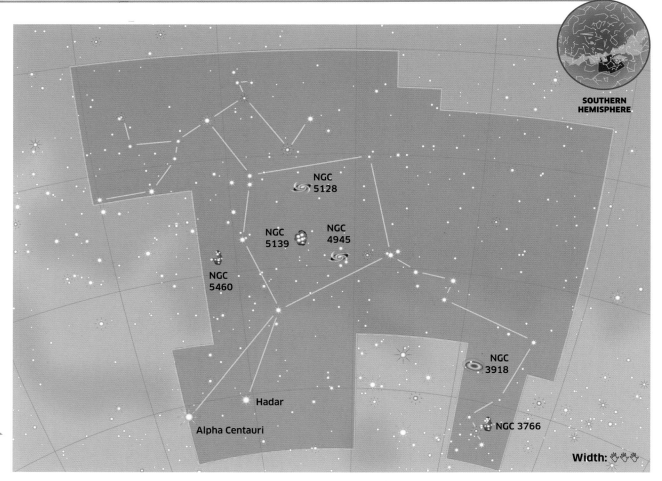

SOUTHERN
HEMISPHERE

NGC
5128

NGC
5139

NGC
4945

NGC
5460

NGC
3918

Hadar

Alpha Centauri

NGC 3766

Width:

# CRUX

Popularly known as the Southern Cross, this is the smallest of all the 88 constellations. Its brightest star, Acrux, is a double star that is easily separated by small telescopes. Near Becrux lies NGC 4755, popularly known as the Jewel Box, a beautiful cluster of stars easily visible through binoculars and small telescopes. A dark cloud of dust called the Coalsack Nebula can be seen against the bright Milky Way background.

SOUTHERN
HEMISPHERE

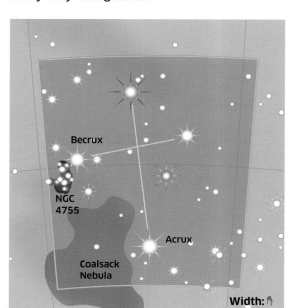

Becrux

NGC
4755

Acrux

Coalsack
Nebula

Width:

CRUX
(THE SOUTHERN CROSS)

# LUPUS

This constellation represents a wolf. Ancient Greek astronomers imagined it as being held on a spear by Centaurus, the centaur. Lupus contains several interesting double stars. In the southern part of the constellation lies a star cluster with the catalog number NGC 5822.

SOUTHERN
HEMISPHERE

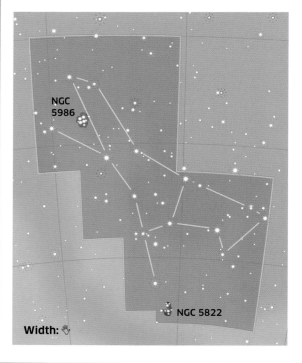

NGC
5986

NGC 5822

Width:

LUPUS
(THE WOLF)

# SAGITTARIUS

This constellation represents an archer drawing his bow and is depicted as a centaur. The eight main stars of Sagittarius form a shape known as the Teapot. Near the lid of the Teapot lies M22, a large globular cluster easily visible through binoculars. There are several fine nebulas in Sagittarius, including the Trifid Nebula (M20).

**SAGITTARIUS (THE ARCHER)**

**Trifid Nebula**
The Trifid Nebula (M20) is a colorful combination of pink gas and blue dust. Its full beauty is revealed in photographs taken with large telescopes, as seen here.

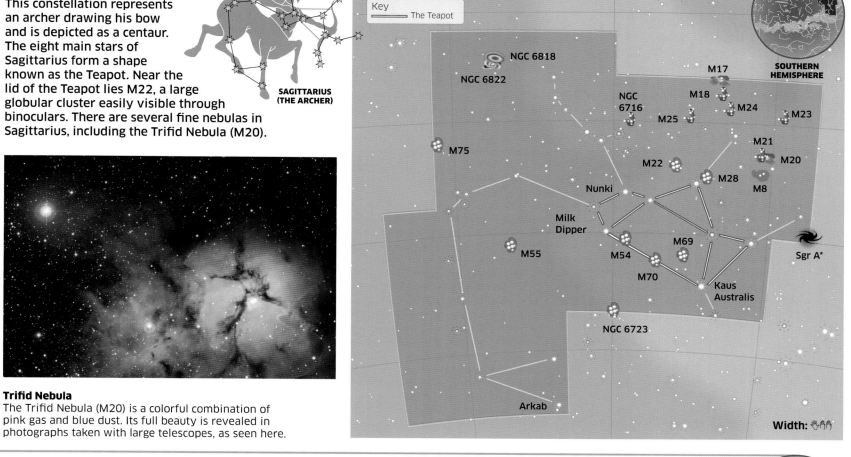

Key
— The Teapot

**SOUTHERN HEMISPHERE**

NGC 6818
NGC 6822
M17
M18
NGC 6716
M24
M23
M25
M21
M75
M20
M22
M28
Nunki
M8
Milk Dipper
M69
M55
M54
Sgr A*
M70
Kaus Australis
NGC 6723
Arkab
**Width:**

# SCORPIUS

This constellation represents the scorpion that stung Orion to death in a story from Greek mythology. At the scorpion's heart lies Antares, a red supergiant hundreds of times larger than the Sun. Next to Antares is M4, a large globular cluster visible through binoculars. At the end of the scorpion's curling tail is a large star cluster, M7, just visible to the naked eye as a brighter spot in the Milky Way. Near it is M6, smaller and best seen through small telescopes. Another beautiful star cluster for binoculars is NGC 6231.

**SOUTHERN HEMISPHERE**

**SCORPIUS (THE SCORPION)**

Sco X-1
M80
Antares
M4
M6
NGC 6383
M7
Shaula
NGC 6322
NGC 6231
NGC 6124
NGC 6388
NGC 6178
**Width:**

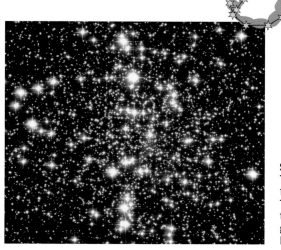

**Star cluster M4**
This sparkling photo from the Hubble Space Telescope shows the heart of the M4 globular cluster, 7,200 light-years from Earth.

## CAPRICORNUS

This constellation is shown as a goat with the tail of a fish. It is said to represent the Greek god Pan, who had the horns and legs of a goat. He grew the fish tail when he jumped into a river to escape from a monster called Typhon. A feature of interest is Algedi, a wide double star, which is easily divided with binoculars or even good eyesight. Dabih is another double, but needs binoculars or a small telescope to divide.

**SOUTHERN HEMISPHERE**

**CAPRICORNUS (THE SEA GOAT)**

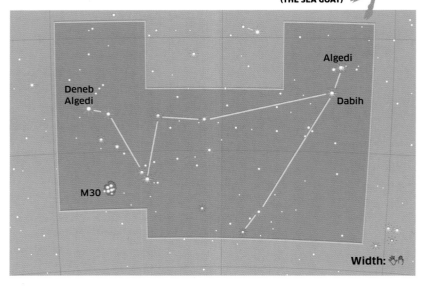

Width: 👐👌

## MICROSCOPIUM

This faint constellation of the southern sky was invented in the 1750s by the French astronomer Nicolas Louis de Lacaille, who studied the southern stars from the Cape of Good Hope in southern Africa. Lacaille invented many new constellations representing scientific instruments—in this case, a microscope.

**SOUTHERN HEMISPHERE**

NGC 6925

**MICROSCOPIUM (THE MICROSCOPE)**

Width: ☝

## PISCIS AUSTRINUS

To the ancient Greeks, this constellation represented a large fish drinking water flowing from a jar held by Aquarius to its north. Its brightest star is Fomalhaut, which lies 25 light-years away. The name Fomalhaut comes from Arabic and means "fish's mouth."

**SOUTHERN HEMISPHERE**

**PISCIS AUSTRINUS (THE SOUTHERN FISH)**

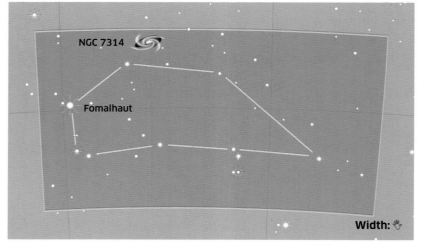

NGC 7314

Fomalhaut

Width: 👌

## SCULPTOR

Invented in the 1750s by the French astronomer Nicolas Louis de Lacaille, this constellation represents a sculptor's studio. Its stars are faint, but it contains a number of interesting galaxies. Most impressive of these is NGC 253, a spiral galaxy 13 million light-years away, seen nearly edge-on and just visible in small telescopes. NGC 55 is another edge-on spiral. Dust clouds and areas of star formation make it look patchy, and it can be seen clearly only with larger telescopes.

**SOUTHERN HEMISPHERE**

**THE SCULPTOR**

NGC 253

NGC 288

NGC 7793

NGC 55

Width: 👌👌

# FORNAX

French astronomer Nicolas Louis de Lacaille came up with this constellation in the 1750s. It represents a furnace used for chemical experiments. On its border lies the Fornax Cluster of galaxies, which is located about 65 million light-years away.

**SOUTHERN HEMISPHERE**

NGC 1097

NGC 1365
NGC 1316

**Width:** 

**FORNAX (THE FURNACE)**

**Barred spiral galaxy NGC 1365**
A prominent member of the Fornax cluster, NGC 1365 is a barred spiral galaxy. Large telescopes are needed to see its full size and shape.

# CAELUM

Caelum is another of the small, faint constellations of the southern sky that were invented in the 1750s by the French astronomer Nicolas Louis de Lacaille. It represents a chisel used by engravers. Caelum is squeezed into the gap between Eridanus and Columba. There is little in the constellation of interest to users of binoculars and small telescopes.

**SOUTHERN HEMISPHERE**

**Width:** 

**CAELUM (THE CHISEL)**

# ERIDANUS

To the ancient Greeks, this large constellation represented a river, either the Nile in Egypt or the Po in Italy. In the sky it meanders from the left foot of Orion deep into the southern sky. Its brightest star is Achernar, at the southern end of the river.

**SOUTHERN HEMISPHERE**

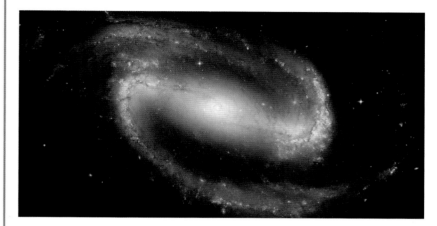

**Barred spiral galaxy NGC 1300**
Seen here in a Hubble view is a classic example of a barred spiral galaxy. NGC 1300 lies about 70 million light-years from us. Large telescopes are needed to see it.

**ERIDANUS (THE RIVER)**

NGC 1535

NGC 1300

Achernar

**Width:**

# LEPUS

Lepus represents a hare scampering under the feet of the hunter Orion. It was one of the constellations known to the ancient Greeks. The name of its brightest star, Arneb, means "hare" in Arabic. An interesting feature in this constellation is Gamma Leporis, an attractive double star that can be divided with binoculars. Another object of interest is NGC 2017, a small group of stars, the brightest of which can be seen through small telescopes.

**SOUTHERN HEMISPHERE**

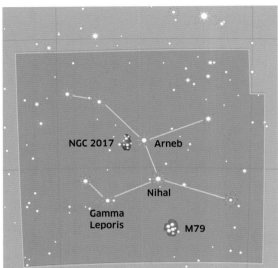

NGC 2017    Arneb

Nihal

Gamma Leporis

M79

**Width:** 

**LEPUS (THE HARE)**

# COLUMBA

This constellation was devised in 1592 by the Dutch astronomer Petrus Plancius, using stars between Lepus and Canis Major that were not part of any Greek constellation. It is said to represent the dove that Noah sent from the biblical Ark to find dry land. Columba's brightest star is called Phact, from the Arabic meaning "ring dove."

**SOUTHERN HEMISPHERE**

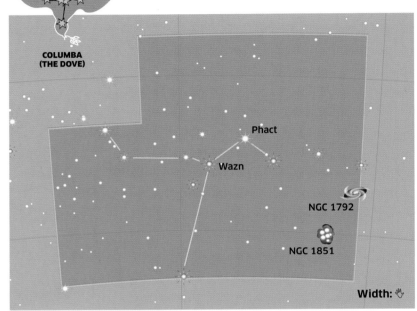

**COLUMBA (THE DOVE)**

Phact

Wazn

NGC 1792

NGC 1851

**Width:** 

# PYXIS

French astronomer Nicolas Louis de Lacaille devised this faint southern constellation in the 1750s during his survey of the southern sky. Pyxis depicts a magnetic compass as used on ships. The constellation's most remarkable star is T Pyxidis, a recurrent nova—a kind of star that brightens from time to time. It has been seen to flare up six times since 1890. Further outbursts could occur at any time.

**SOUTHERN HEMISPHERE**

**PYXIS (THE COMPASS)**

NGC 2613

T Pyxidis

**Width:** 

# PUPPIS

Puppis was once part of a much larger Greek constellation called Argo Navis, the ship of Jason and the Argonauts. It depicted the ship's stern. Puppis lies in a rich part of the Milky Way and contains many bright star clusters. M46 and M47 lie side by side and create a brighter patch in the Milky Way. NGC 2451 and NGC 2477 are two more clusters that lie close together. Binoculars give a good view of them both.

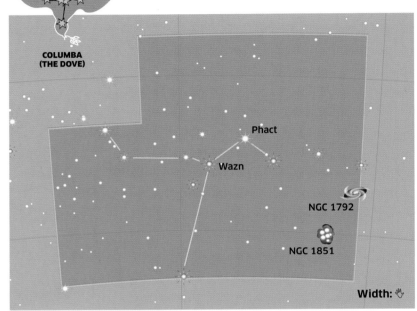

**SOUTHERN HEMISPHERE**

M47

M46

M93

NGC 2571

NGC 2546

NGC 2439

NGC 2451

Naos    NGC 2477

**PUPPIS (THE STERN)**

**Width:** 

**Star cluster M47**
M47 is a large and scattered cluster of a few dozen stars in the north of Puppis, visible with binoculars. The rich view in this image was captured through a large professional telescope.

# VELA

Vela represents the sails of Argo Navis, the ship of Jason and the Argonauts. Argo Navis was a large Greek constellation that was split into three smaller parts. The other two parts are Puppis and Carina. Two stars in Vela combine with a pair of stars in Carina to form the False Cross, sometimes mistaken for the real Southern Cross. Around another star is a large cluster called IC 2391, bright enough to be visible to the naked eye.

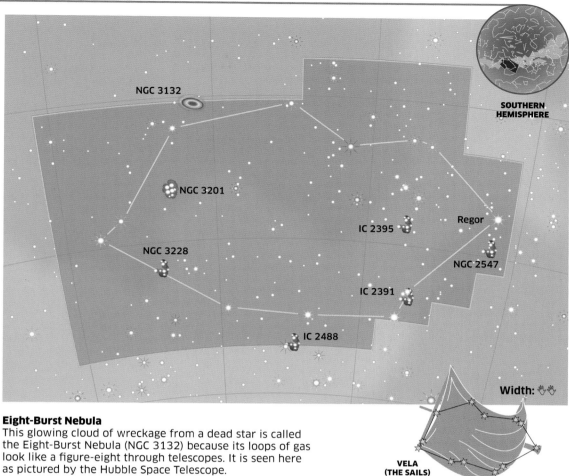

NGC 3132

SOUTHERN HEMISPHERE

NGC 3201

IC 2395

Regor

NGC 3228

NGC 2547

IC 2391

IC 2488

Width: 🖐🖐

VELA (THE SAILS)

**Eight-Burst Nebula**
This glowing cloud of wreckage from a dead star is called the Eight-Burst Nebula (NGC 3132) because its loops of gas look like a figure-eight through telescopes. It is seen here as pictured by the Hubble Space Telescope.

# CARINA

Carina is one of the three parts into which the large Greek constellation of Argo Navis, the ship of Jason and the Argonauts, was split. It depicts the ship's keel, or hull. This constellation contains the second-brightest star in the night sky, Canopus. A pair of stars in Carina form half of the False Cross, completed by two stars in Vela.

SOUTHERN HEMISPHERE

NGC 3293

IC 2581

NGC 3114

Canopus

NGC 3532

NGC 2516

NGC 3372

NGC 2808

IC 2602

Width: 🖐🖐🖐

CARINA (THE KEEL)

**Southern Pleiades**
The large star cluster IC 2602, called the Southern Pleiades, is a glorious sight through binoculars.

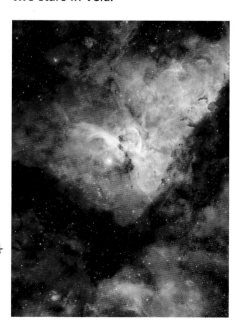

**Carina Nebula**
The Carina Nebula (NGC 3372) is a large, V-shaped cloud of gas visible to the naked eye. Its brightest part surrounds the star Eta Carina, a peculiar variable star that has thrown off shells of gas in the past.

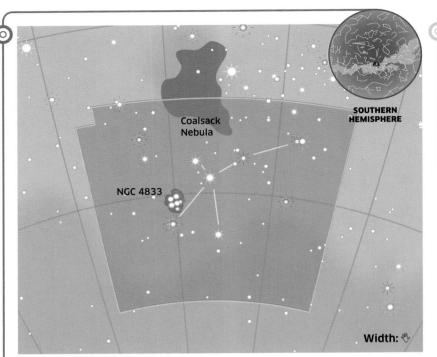

Coalsack Nebula

NGC 4833

Width: ✋

## MUSCA

This constellation of the southern sky was invented at the end of the 16th century by Dutch seafarers. It represents a fly. Part of the dark Coalsack Nebula spills into Musca from Crux, which lies to the north. Of note is NGC 4833, a globular cluster that can be seen through binoculars and small telescopes.

**MUSCA (THE FLY)**

## CIRCINUS

This small southern constellation was created in the 1750s by the French astronomer Nicolas Louis de Lacaille. Most of his constellations represented instruments from science and the arts. He visualized Circinus as the dividing compass used by surveyors and navigators. Its brightest star is a double.

**CIRCINUS (THE COMPASSES)**

NGC 5315

Width: ✋

## NORMA

Norma was introduced in the 1750s by the French astronomer Nicolas Louis de Lacaille. It represents a set square as used by draftsmen and builders. Objects of note include the star Gamma Normae, which consists of a wide pair of unrelated stars, both separately visible to the naked eye, and NGC 6087, a large, rich star cluster visible through binoculars.

NGC 6167

Gamma Normae

NGC 6067

NGC 6087

Width: ✋

**NORMA (THE SET SQUARE)**

**Star cluster NGC 6067**
NGC 6067 is a rich cluster of stars in central Norma, visible through binoculars and small telescopes. It covers an area of sky about half the apparent diameter of the full moon.

## TRIANGULUM AUSTRALE

At the end of the 16th century, Dutch explorers who sailed to the East Indies created a dozen new constellations among the southern stars. The smallest of them was Triangulum Australe, the Southern Triangle. It is smaller than the Northern Triangle, Triangulum, but its stars are brighter. The main object of interest in Triangulum Australe is the star cluster NGC 6025 on its northern border, visible through binoculars.

**TRIANGULUM AUSTRALE (THE SOUTHERN TRIANGLE)**

NGC 6025

Width: ✋

# ARA

The constellation Ara was known to the ancient Greeks. To them it depicted the altar on which the gods of Mount Olympus swore an oath of loyalty before fighting the Titans, their sworn enemies. An attractive star cluster in Ara is NGC 6193. None of the stars of Ara is of particular interest.

ARA
(THE ALTAR)

SOUTHERN
HEMISPHERE

NGC 6352

NGC 6193

NGC 6188

NGC 6397

NGC 6362

Width: ✋

**Starbirth nebula NGC 6188**
Ultraviolet radiation from the stars in NGC 6193 lights up the sulfur, hydrogen, and oxygen atoms in the starbirth nebula NGC 6188, as seen in this Hubble photo.

# CORONA AUSTRALIS

This small constellation lies under the feet of Sagittarius. It represents a crown or wreath, and was one of the constellations known to the ancient Greeks. Although faint, Corona Australis is fairly easy to spot because its main stars form a noticeable arc. An interesting object for small telescopes is the globular cluster NGC 6541.

SOUTHERN
HEMISPHERE

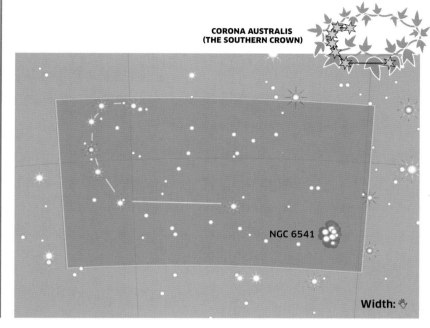

CORONA AUSTRALIS
(THE SOUTHERN CROWN)

NGC 6541

Width: ✋

# TELESCOPIUM

French astronomer Nicolas Louis de Lacaille came up with this faint constellation in the 1750s to commemorate the telescope, the astronomer's basic tool. The constellation has since been reduced in size. Besides a globular cluster and a wide pair of unrelated stars, which can be seen separately with binoculars or even good eyesight, there is little of note.

SOUTHERN
HEMISPHERE

NGC 6584

Width: ✋

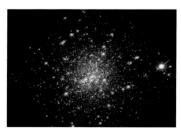

**Globular cluster NGC 6584**
NGC 6584 is a faint and distant globular cluster and can be seen well through a large telescope. It is seen here as photographed by the Hubble Space Telescope.

TELESCOPIUM
(THE TELESCOPE)

# INDUS

Indus is one of the 12 southern constellations introduced at the end of the 16th century by Dutch seafarers. This constellation was visualized as a native hunter brandishing a spear. Indus has an interesting double star that can be divided by a small telescope.

SOUTHERN
HEMISPHERE

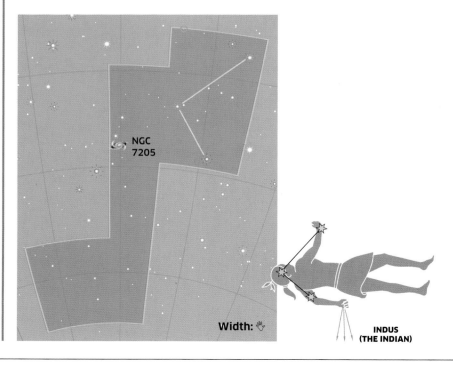

NGC 7205

Width: ✋

INDUS
(THE INDIAN)

## GRUS

Grus represents a crane, a long-necked wading bird. It is one of the constellations invented in the late 16th century by Dutch seafarers. In the bird's neck lie two wide double stars. Both pairs can be divided with the naked eye. The stars in each pair are actually at different distances from us and so not related— they are just optical doubles and not true binaries.

**SOUTHERN HEMISPHERE**

**GRUS (THE CRANE)**

NGC 7582

Alnair

Width: 🖐

## PHOENIX

This constellation lies near the southern end of Eridanus. Phoenix is the largest of the 12 new constellations that were created at the end of the 16th century by Dutch explorers sailing to the East Indies. It represents the mythical bird that was said to be reborn from its own ashes every 500 years.

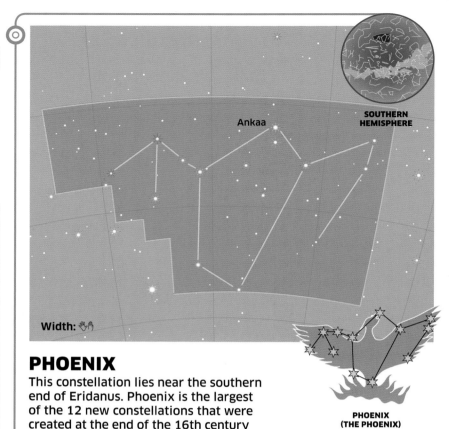

**SOUTHERN HEMISPHERE**

Ankaa

Width: 🖐🖐

**PHOENIX (THE PHOENIX)**

## TUCANA

Dutch navigators came up with this southern constellation in the late 16th century. It represents a toucan, a tropical bird with a large beak. Tucana contains the Small Magellanic Cloud (SMC), a mini-galaxy about 200,000 light-years away from us. To the naked eye, the SMC looks like a separate part of the Milky Way. The globular clusters 47 Tucanae and NGC 362 lie on either side of the SMC but are actually much closer to us.

**SOUTHERN HEMISPHERE**

**TUCANA (THE TOUCAN)**

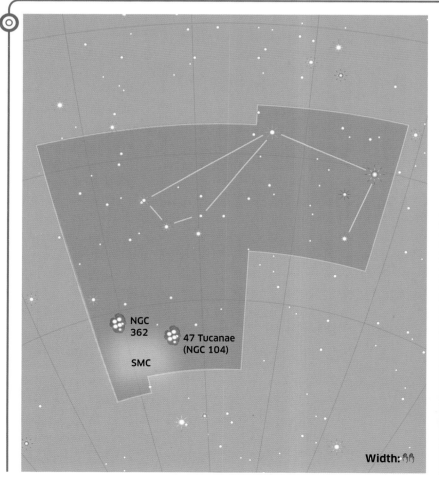

NGC 362

47 Tucanae (NGC 104)

SMC

Width: 🖐🖐

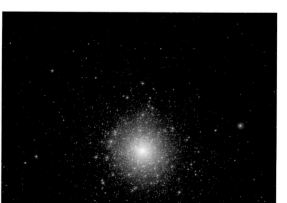

**Globular cluster 47 Tucanae**
To the naked eye, the globular cluster 47 Tucanae (NGC 104) looks like a single fuzzy star, but through large telescopes it breaks up into a swarm of individual points of light, as seen here. It lies about 16,000 light-years away from us.

# HYDRUS

Representing a sea snake, this constellation slithers between the Large and Small Magellanic Clouds (LMC and SMC). Hydrus was created by Dutch explorers in the 16th century. It should not be confused with Hydra, the Large Water Snake, which has been known since ancient Greek times. Hydrus has a pair of red giants, Pi Hydri, that look like a double star but are unrelated and lie at different distances from us. Pi Hydri can be seen separately through binoculars.

**SOUTHERN HEMISPHERE**

**HYDRUS (THE LITTLE WATER SNAKE)**

Pi Hydri

LMC

SMC

**Width:** 🖐

# HOROLOGIUM

Horologium represents a clock with a long pendulum, as used in observatories for accurate timekeeping in the days before electronic clocks. It is one of the southern constellations honoring scientific and technical instruments that were introduced by the French astronomer Nicolas Louis de Lacaille in the 1750s. Horologium is faint and contains few objects of interest for small telescopes.

**SOUTHERN HEMISPHERE**

NGC 1512

AM1

NGC 1261

**HOROLOGIUM (THE PENDULUM CLOCK)**

**Width:** 🖐

**SOUTHERN HEMISPHERE**

Zeta Reticuli

NGC 1313

**Width:** 🤏

# RETICULUM

This small southern constellation is one of 14 invented in the 1750s by the French astronomer Nicolas Louis de Lacaille when he mapped the southern stars from the Cape of Good Hope in southern Africa. Reticulum represents the crosshairs in the eyepiece of Lacaille's telescope, which helped him to measure the positions of stars accurately. Of note is Zeta Reticuli, a pair of yellow stars that can be separated with binoculars.

**RETICULUM (THE NET)**

# PICTOR

This is yet another constellation invented in the 1750s by the French astronomer Nicolas Louis de Lacaille. It represents an artist's easel. Pictor contains an interesting double star, Iota Pictoris, which can be easily separated through small telescopes.

**SOUTHERN HEMISPHERE**

**PICTOR (THE PAINTER'S EASEL)**

Beta Pictoris

Iota Pictoris

**Beta Pictoris**
The second-brightest star in Pictor, Beta Pictoris is surrounded by a disk of dust and gas. Planets are thought to be forming from the disk. This disk can be seen only through large telescopes with special equipment.

**Width:** 🖐

# DORADO

Dutch seafarers created this southern constellation in the late 16th century. It represents a type of tropical fish called a dorado but is also known as the Goldfish. The main feature of Dorado is the Large Magellanic Cloud (LMC), the bigger of the two companion galaxies of the Milky Way. Another point of interest is the Tarantula Nebula (NGC 2070), which appears as a hazy star.

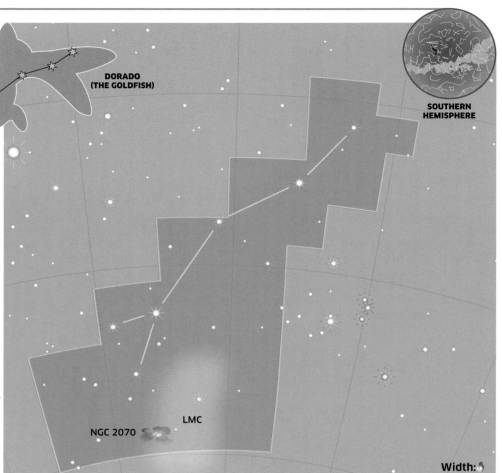

DORADO
(THE GOLDFISH)

SOUTHERN
HEMISPHERE

NGC 2070    LMC

Width: 🖐

**Large Magellanic Cloud**
The Large Magellanic Cloud (LMC) can easily be seen with the naked eye, and looks like a detached part of our galaxy. Binoculars reveal many star clusters and nebulas within it.

# VOLANS

This constellation was invented in the late 16th century by Dutch explorers who sailed to the East Indies, surveying the stars of the southern sky on the way. It represents a flying fish—one of the exotic creatures they saw on their voyages. Gamma and Epsilon Volantis are double stars that can easily be distinguished by small telescopes.

SOUTHERN
HEMISPHERE

VOLANS
(THE FLYING FISH)

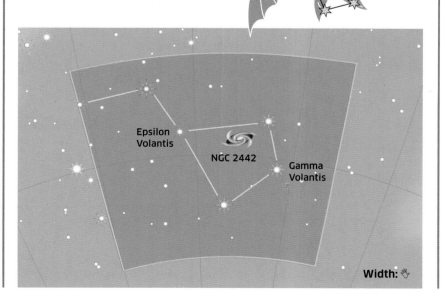

Epsilon
Volantis

NGC 2442

Gamma
Volantis

Width: 🖐

LMC

SOUTHERN
HEMISPHERE

Width: 🖐

MENSA
(THE TABLE
MOUNTAIN)

# MENSA

French astronomer Nicolas Louis de Lacaille devised this constellation in the 1750s. He measured the positions of thousands of southern stars from an observatory near the foot of Table Mountain at the Cape of Good Hope, South Africa. This constellation was named Mensa—which means "table" in Latin—to celebrate the mountain. Mensa contains part of the Large Magellanic Cloud (LMC). All of Mensa's stars are faint, and none of them is of interest for users of small telescopes.

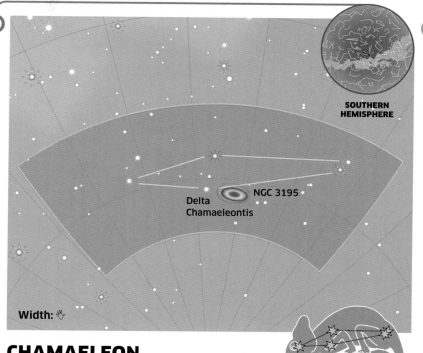

**Width:** 

## CHAMAELEON

Chamaeleon is a small southern constellation invented in the late 16th century. It is named after the lizard that can change its skin color to match its surroundings. Next to it lies Musca, the Fly, which is appropriate because chameleons eat flies. Of interest is Delta Chamaeleontis, a wide double star that is easily seen with binoculars.

**SOUTHERN HEMISPHERE**

**CHAMAELEON (THE CHAMELEON)**

## APUS

Dutch explorers sailing to the East Indies in the late 16th century devised Apus. This constellation represents a bird of paradise, a kind of bird known for its beautiful plumage, which in the past was used to decorate hats and other items of clothing. Delta Apodis is a wide pair of unrelated red giant stars, which can be seen separately with the naked eye or in binoculars.

**SOUTHERN HEMISPHERE**

**APUS (THE BIRD OF PARADISE)**

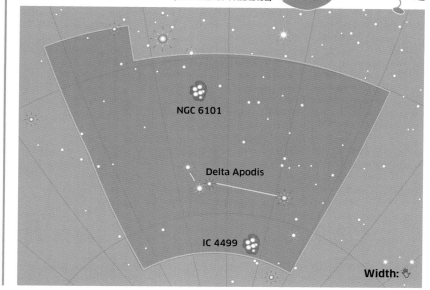

NGC 6101

Delta Apodis

IC 4499

**Width:** 

## PAVO

Pavo represents a peacock, a bird with a glorious, fanlike tail. It is one of the 12 southern constellations introduced by Dutch seafarers at the end of the 16th century. Items of note include NGC 6752, a large and bright globular cluster, easily visible in binoculars; and NGC 6744, a beautiful spiral galaxy with a short central bar, best seen in photographs.

**SOUTHERN HEMISPHERE**

**PAVO (THE PEACOCK)**

NGC 6752

NGC 6744

**Width:** 

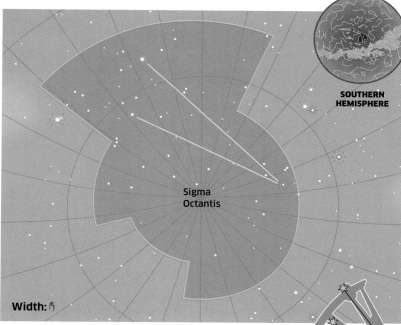

**SOUTHERN HEMISPHERE**

Sigma Octantis

**Width:** 

**OCTANS (THE OCTANT)**

## OCTANS

Octans contains the south pole of the sky. Unlike the northern hemisphere, there is no bright pole star in the southern sky. The closest visible star to the south celestial pole is Sigma Octantis, but it is very faint. Octans was introduced in the 1750s by the French astronomer Nicolas Louis de Lacaille. It represents a navigation instrument known as an octant, the forerunner of the sextant.

# REFERENCE

The reference section is packed with facts and figures about planets, spacecraft missions, stars, and galaxies, and tells you the best time to see shooting stars, comets, and eclipses. A glossary explains many of the terms used in this book.

# Solar system data

Our solar system consists of the Sun and all the objects under its gravitational influence, including the eight planets and their moons, and an unknown number of dwarf planets, asteroids, comets, and smaller objects. The most distant objects—comets orbiting in the Oort Cloud—can be as far as a light-year from the Sun.

**The Sun weighs about 670 times as much as all the planets and other objects in the solar system combined.**

## THE PLANETS

A planet is officially defined as an object in direct orbit around the Sun, with enough mass to pull itself into a ball, and strong enough gravity to force other objects out of broadly similar orbits. Today, astronomers recognize eight planets—four relatively small, rocky (or "terrestrial") worlds close to the Sun, and four much larger giant planets farther out.

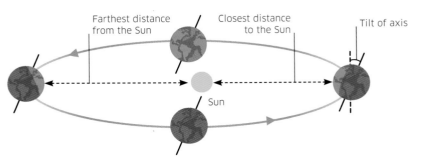

**A PLANET'S ORBIT AROUND THE SUN**

### PLANET DATA

| | Mercury | Venus | Earth | Mars | Jupiter | Saturn | Uranus | Neptune |
|---|---|---|---|---|---|---|---|---|
| Diameter | 3,032 miles (4,880 km) | 7,522 miles (12,104 km) | 7,926 miles (12,756 km) | 4,220 miles (6,792 km) | 88,846 miles (142,984 km) | 74,896 miles (120,536 km) | 31,762 miles (51,118 km) | 30,774 miles (49,528 km) |
| Mass (Earth = 1) | 0.06 | 0.82 | 1 | 0.11 | 318 | 95 | 14 | 17 |
| Time of one rotation | 1,408 hours | 5,833 hours | 23.9 hours | 24.6 hours | 9.9 hours | 10.7 hours | 17.2 hours | 16 hours |
| Surface gravity (Earth = 1) | 0.38 | 0.91 | 1 | 0.38 | 2.36 | 1.02 | 0.89 | 1.12 |
| Tilt of axis | 0.01° | 2.6° | 23.4° | 25.2° | 3.1° | 26.7° | 82.2° | 28.3° |
| Number of moons | 0 | 0 | 1 | 2 | 67+ | 62+ | 27+ | 14+ |
| Closest distance to the Sun | 29 million miles (46 million km) | 67 million miles (107 million km) | 91 million miles (147 million km) | 128 million miles (207 million km) | 460 million miles (741 million km) | 841 million miles (1,353 million km) | 1,703 million miles (2,741 million km) | 2,761 million miles (4,445 million km) |
| Farthest distance from the Sun | 43 million miles (70 million km) | 68 million miles (109 million km) | 95 million miles (152 million km) | 157 million miles (249 million km) | 507 million miles (817 million km) | 940 million miles (1,515 million km) | 1,866 million miles (3,004 million km) | 2,825 million miles (4,546 million km) |
| Time to orbit the Sun | 88 Earth days | 225 Earth days | 365.26 days | 687 Earth days | 12 Earth years | 29 Earth years | 84 Earth years | 165 Earth years |
| Average orbital speed | 30 miles (48 km) per second | 22 miles (35 km) per second | 19 miles (30 km) per second | 15 miles (24 km) per second | 8 miles (13 km) per second | 6 miles (10 km) per second | 4 miles (7 km) per second | 3 miles (5 km) per second |

## METEOR SHOWERS

After being ejected from a comet or asteroid, many grains of rock get concentrated into narrow streams. When Earth's orbit crosses these streams, the grains burn up in our atmosphere as meteors (shooting stars), causing predictable meteor showers.

### MAJOR METEOR SHOWERS

| Name | Peak date | Most meteors | Parent comet/asteroid |
|---|---|---|---|
| Quadrantids | 4 January | 120 per hour | 2003 EH1 |
| Lyrids | 22 April | 10 per hour | C/1861 G1 (Thatcher) |
| Eta Aquarids | 5 May | 30 per hour | 1P/Halley |
| Perseids | 12 August | 100 per hour | 109P/Swift–Tuttle |
| Geminids | 14 December | 120 per hour | 3200 Phaethon |

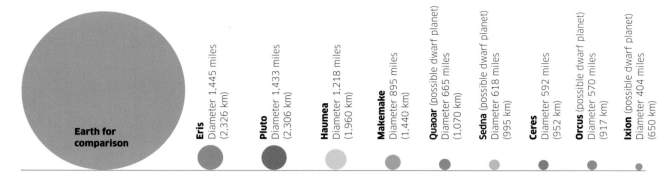

Earth for comparison

**Eris** Diameter 1,445 miles (2,326 km)

**Pluto** Diameter 1,433 miles (2,306 km)

**Haumea** Diameter 1,218 miles (1,960 km)

**Makemake** Diameter 895 miles (1,440 km)

**Quaoar** (possible dwarf planet) Diameter 665 miles (1,070 km)

**Sedna** (possible dwarf planet) Diameter 618 miles (995 km)

**Ceres** Diameter 592 miles (952 km)

**Orcus** (possible dwarf planet) Diameter 570 miles (917 km)

**Ixion** (possible dwarf planet) Diameter 404 miles (650 km)

## DWARF PLANETS

A dwarf planet is a spherical object in an independent orbit around the Sun that lacks the strong gravity required to clear its orbit of other objects. Dwarf planets are mostly found in the Kuiper Belt and scattered disk zones beyond the orbit of Neptune, but they include the largest asteroid in the Main Asteroid Belt, Ceres.

## COMETS

Most comets are deep-frozen, icy objects lurking at the outer edges of the solar system, but a small number have fallen into orbits that periodically bring them closer to the Sun and cause them to burst into life.

COMET HALE-BOPP

### SOME PERIODIC COMETS

| Name | Orbital period | Sightings | Next due |
|---|---|---|---|
| 1P/Halley | 75 years | 30 | July 2061 |
| 2P/Encke | 3 years, 3 months | 62 | March 2017 |
| 6P/d'Arrest | 6 years, 5 months | 20 | September 2021 |
| 9P/Tempel | 5 years, 5 months | 12 | August 2016 |
| 17P/Holmes | 6 years, 8 months | 10 | February 2021 |
| 21P/Giacobini–Zinner | 6 years, 6 months | 15 | September 2018 |
| 29P/Schwassmann–Wachmann | 15 years | 7 | March 2019 |
| 39P/Oterma | 19 years | 4 | July 2023 |
| 46P/Wirtanen | 5 years, 4 months | 10 | December 2018 |
| 50P/Arend | 8 years, 2 months | 8 | February 2016 |
| 55P/Tempel-Tuttle | 33 years | 5 | May 2031 |
| 67P/Churyumov Gerasimenko | 6 years, 4 months | 7 | December 2021 |
| 81P/Wild | 6 years, 4 months | 6 | July 2016 |
| 109P/Swift-Tuttle | 133 years | 5 | July 2126 |

## ECLIPSES

By sheer coincidence, the Sun and Moon appear almost exactly the same size in Earth's skies. As a result, the Moon can sometimes pass in front of the Sun, blocking out its disk to create a solar eclipse. Total solar eclipses, which block the disk completely to reveal the tenuous outer solar atmosphere, are rare and very localized, but partial eclipses are more frequently seen.

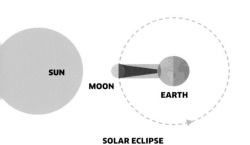

SUN

MOON

EARTH

SOLAR ECLIPSE

### TOTAL SOLAR ECLIPSES

| Date | Location |
|---|---|
| 9 March 2016 | Sumatra, Borneo, Sulawesi, Pacific |
| 21 August 2017 | North Pacific, USA, South Atlantic |
| 2 July 2019 | South Pacific, Chile, Argentina |
| 14 December 2020 | South Pacific, Chile, Argentina, South Atlantic |
| 4 December 2021 | Antarctica |
| 8 April 2024 | Mexico, central USA, east Canada |
| 12 August 2026 | Arctic, Greenland, Iceland, Spain |
| 2 August 2027 | Morocco, Spain, Algeria, Libya, Egypt, Saudi Arabia, Yemen, Somalia |
| 22 July 2028 | Australia, New Zealand |
| 25 November 2030 | Botswana, South Africa, Australia |
| 30 March 2033 | East Russia, Alaska |
| 20 March 2034 | Nigeria, Cameroon, Chad, Sudan, Egypt, Saudi Arabia, Iran, Afghanistan, Pakistan, India, China |
| 2 September 2035 | China, Korea, Japan, Pacific |
| 13 July 2037 | Australia, New Zealand |
| 26 December 2038 | Australia, New Zealand, South Pacific |
| 15 December 2039 | Antarctica |

# Exploring the planets

Since the late 1950s, we have sent dozens of robotic spacecraft beyond Earth's orbit, mostly aimed at other planets. Some perform brief flyby missions en route to another destination, but others stay longer. Orbiters become long-term satellites of planets, while landers and rovers touch down to examine or even explore the surface.

MESSENGER

## Rocky worlds

Earth's immediate neighbors, Venus and Mars, have been subject to intense study by a variety of spacecraft, not all of which can be listed here—those mentioned below include all major successes as well as notable firsts and some interesting failures. The innermost planet, Mercury, moves so quickly in its orbit that it is hard to reach and rarely visited.

**Mercury**

| Mission | Country of origin | Arrival date | Type | Status |
|---|---|---|---|---|
| Mariner 10 | US | 1974 | Multiple flybys | Success |
| MESSENGER | US | 2011 | Orbiter | Success |

Venera

Magellan

**Venus**

| Mission | Country of origin | Arrival date | Type | Status |
|---|---|---|---|---|
| Mariner 2 | US | 1962 | Flyby | Success |
| Venera 4 | USSR/Russia | 1967 | Flyby | Success |
| Mariner 5 | US | 1967 | Flyby | Success |
| Venera 7 | USSR/Russia | 1970 | Lander | Success |
| Venera 9 | USSR/Russia | 1975 | Orbiter/lander | Success |
| Pioneer Venus Orbiter | US | 1978 | Orbiter | Success |
| Pioneer Venus Multiprobe | US | 1978 | Atmospheric probe | Success |
| Venera 11 | USSR/Russia | 1978 | Flyby/lander | Success |
| Venera 15 | USSR/Russia | 1983 | Orbiter | Success |
| Vega 1 | USSR/Russia | 1985 | Flyby/lander/balloon | Partial success (lander failure) |
| Vega 2 | USSR/Russia | 1985 | Flyby/lander/balloon | Success |
| Magellan | US | 1990 | Orbiter | Success |
| Venus Express | Europe | 2006 | Orbiter | Success |

Mariner

Mars Express

**Mars**

| Mission | Country of origin | Arrival date | Type | Status |
|---|---|---|---|---|
| Mariner 4 | US | 1965 | Flyby | Success |
| Mariner 6 | US | 1969 | Flyby | Success |
| Mariner 7 | US | 1969 | Flyby | Success |
| Mariner 9 | US | 1971 | Orbiter | Success |
| Mars 2 | USSR/Russia | 1971 | Orbiter/lander | Partial success (lander failure) |

| | | | | |
|---|---|---|---|---|
| Viking 1 | US | 1976 | Orbiter/lander | Success |
| Viking 2 | US | 1976 | Orbiter/lander | Success |
| Phobos 2 | USSR/Russia | 1989 | Phobos orbiter/lander | Partial success (lander failure) |
| Mars Pathfinder | US | 1997 | Lander/rover | Success |
| Mars Global Surveyor | US | 1997 | Orbiter | Success |
| Mars Odyssey | US | 2001 | Orbiter | Success |
| Mars Express/Beagle 2 | Europe | 2003 | Orbiter/lander | Partial success (lander failure) |
| MER-A Spirit | US | 2004 | Rover | Success |
| MER-B Opportunity | US | 2004 | Rover | Success |
| Mars Reconnaissance Orbiter | US | 2006 | Orbiter | Success |
| Phoenix | US | 2008 | Lander | Success |
| Curiosity | US | 2012 | Rover | Success |
| Mars Orbiter Mission (Mangalyaan) | India | 2014 | Orbiter | Success |
| MAVEN | US | 2014 | Orbiter | Success |

## Gas giants

The giant planets have no surfaces to investigate, but their atmospheres, rings, and moons are all intriguing. After an initial wave of flyby missions that surveyed the giants in the 1970s and 1980s, Jupiter and Saturn have both been surveyed by long-term orbiters. A probe has entered Jupiter's atmosphere, and a lander has touched down on Saturn's largest moon, Titan.

Juno

Galileo

## Jupiter

| Mission | Country of origin | Arrival date | Type | Status |
|---|---|---|---|---|
| Pioneer 10 | US | 1973 | Flyby | Success |
| Pioneer 11 | US | 1974 | Flyby | Success |
| Voyager 1 | US | 1979 | Flyby | Success |
| Voyager 2 | US | 1979 | Flyby | Success |
| Galileo | US | 1995 | Orbiter/atmospheric probe | Success |
| Cassini | US and Europe | 2000 | Flyby | Success |
| New Horizons | US | 2007 | Flyby | Success |
| Juno | US | 2016 (planned) | Orbiter | En route |

## Saturn

| Mission | Country of origin | Arrival date | Type | Status |
|---|---|---|---|---|
| Pioneer 11 | US | 1979 | Flyby | Success |
| Voyager 1 | US | 1980 | Flyby | Success |
| Voyager 2 | US | 1981 | Flyby | Success |
| Cassini/Huygens | US and Europe | 2004 | Orbiter/Titan lander | Success |

## Uranus and Neptune

| Mission | Country of origin | Arrival date | Type | Status |
|---|---|---|---|---|
| Voyager 2 | US | Uranus 1986, Neptune 1989 | Flyby | Success |

# Stars and galaxies

The vast majority of objects in the night sky lie far beyond our solar system. All the individual stars we can see are members of our own Milky Way galaxy, as are most of the star clusters and nebulas visible through amateur instruments. There are also countless other galaxies far beyond our own, most of them too distant to see.

There are about **200 billion** galaxies in the observable universe and about as many stars in the Milky Way.

## Closest stars

Many of the closest stars to Earth are red dwarfs, often in binary or multiple systems and so faint that they are hard to see despite their proximity. There are also a few Sun-like stars, and a couple of brilliant white stars, each paired with a burned-out white dwarf companion. Also close to Earth are many starlike objects called brown dwarfs—failed stars that are not massive enough to trigger nuclear fusion in their core.

**KEY**

- ● Red dwarf
- ○ White main-sequence star
- ○ Yellow main-sequence star
- ○ White dwarf
- ○ Orange main-sequence star
- ● Brown dwarf

| Star type | Designation | Distance | Constellation | Apparent magnitude | Visibility |
|---|---|---|---|---|---|
| ○ | Sun | 8 light minutes | – | -26.7 | Naked eye |
| ● | Proxima Centauri | 4.2 light-years | Centaurus | 11.1 | Telescope |
| ○ ○ | Alpha Centauri A/B | 4.4 light-years | Centaurus | 0.01/1.34 | Naked eye |
| ● | Barnard's Star | 6.0 light-years | Ophiuchus | 9.5 | Telescope |
| ● ● | Luhman 16 A/B | 6.6 light-years | Vela | 10.7 | Telescope |
| ● | WISE 0655-0714 | 7.2 light-years | Hydra | 13.9 | Telescope |
| ● | Wolf 359 | 7.8 light-years | Leo | 13.4 | Telescope |
| ● | Lalande 21185 | 8.3 light-years | Ursa Major | 7.5 | Binoculars |
| ○ ○ | Sirius A/B | 8.6 light-years | Canis Major | -1.46/8.44 | Naked eye/telescope |
| ● ● | Luyten 726-8 | 8.7 light-years | Cetus | 12.5/13.0 | Telescope |
| ● | Ross 154 | 9.7 light-years | Sagittarius | 10.4 | Telescope |
| ● | Ross 248 | 10.3 light-years | Andromeda | 12.3 | Telescope |
| ○ | Epsilon Eridani | 10.5 light-years | Eridanus | 3.73 | Naked eye |
| ● | Lacaille 9352 | 10.7 light-years | Piscis Austrinus | 7.3 | Binoculars |
| ● | Ross 128 | 10.9 light-years | Virgo | 11.1 | Telescope |
| ● | WISE 1506+7027 | 11.1 light-years | Ursa Minor | 14.3 | Telescope |
| ● ● ● | EZ Aquarii A/B/C | 11.3 light-years | Aquarius | 13.3/13.3/14.0 | Telescope |
| ○ ○ | Procyon A/B | 11.4 light-years | Canis Minor | 0.4/10.7 | Naked eye/telescope |
| ○ ○ | 61 Cygni A/B | 11.4 light-years | Cygnus | 5.2/6.0 | Naked eye/binoculars |
| ● ● | Struve 2398 A/B | 11.5 light-years | Draco | 8.9/9.7 | Telescope |
| ● ● | Groombridge 34 A/B | 11.6 light-years | Andromeda | 8.1/11.1 | Telescope |

## Brightest star

Star brightness is measured by apparent magnitude. The brightest stars have the lowest number; 6 is roughly the limit of naked-eye visibility in a clear, dark sky. The Sun, with a magnitude of -26.7, is the brightest object in our skies, but at night thousands of stars are visible to the naked eye, and millions more can be seen through binoculars or a telescope.

Apparent magnitude

| -30 | -25 | -20 | -15 | -10 | -5 | 0 | +5 | +10 | +15 | +20 | +25 | +30 |

The Sun    Full moon    Polaris  Naked-eye limit    Hubble Space Telescope detection limit

## Nebulas

Nebulas are clouds of interstellar gas and dust of various shapes and sizes, ranging from huge star-forming complexes to the smoke rings puffed out by dying stars. Below are a few of the brightest nebulas.

**Name:** Carina Nebula

**Designation:** NGC 3372

**Constellation:** Carina

**Magnitude:** 1

**Distance:** 6,500 light-years

**Type:** Emission nebula

**Visibility:** Naked eye

**Name:** Dumbbell Nebula

**Designation:** M27

**Constellation:** Vulpecula

**Magnitude:** 7.5

**Distance:** 1,360 light-years

**Type:** Planetary nebula

**Visibility:** Binoculars

**Name:** Orion Nebula

**Designation:** M42

**Constellation:** Orion

**Magnitude:** 4

**Distance:** 1,340 light-years

**Type:** Emission nebula

**Visibility:** Naked eye

**Name:** Helix Nebula

**Designation:** NGC 7293

**Constellation:** Aquarius

**Magnitude:** 7.6

**Distance:** 700 light-years

**Type:** Planetary nebula

**Visibility:** Binoculars

**Name:** Lagoon Nebula

**Designation:** M8

**Constellation:** Sagittarius

**Magnitude:** 6

**Distance:** 4,100 light-years

**Type:** Emission nebula

**Visibility:** Naked eye

**Name:** Rosette Nebula

**Designation:** NGC 2237

**Constellation:** Monoceros

**Magnitude:** 9

**Distance:** 5,200 light-years

**Type:** Emission nebula

**Visibility:** Binoculars

## Galaxies

The brightest galaxies in the sky tend to be those closest to the Milky Way. This table lists some of the most interesting galaxies that can be observed with binoculars or the naked eye.

**KEY**

 Irregular   Barred spiral

 Spiral   Elliptical

| Type | Name | Designation | Constellation | Apparent magnitude | Distance | Visibility |
|---|---|---|---|---|---|---|
| Barred spiral | Large Magellanic Cloud | LMC | Dorado/Mensa | 0.9 | 160,000 light-years | Naked eye |
| Irregular | Small Magellanic Cloud | SMC | Tucana | 2.7 | 200,000 light-years | Naked eye |
| Spiral | Andromeda Galaxy | M32 | Andromeda | 3.4 | 2.5 million light-years | Naked eye |
| Spiral | Triangulum Galaxy | M33 | Triangulum | 5.7 | 2.9 million light-years | Binoculars |
| Elliptical | Centaurus A | NGC 5128 | Centaurus | 6.8 | 13.7 million light-years | Binoculars |
| Spiral | Bode's Galaxy | M81 | Ursa Major | 6.9 | 11.8 million light-years | Binoculars |
| Spiral | Southern Pinwheel | M83 | Hydra | 7.5 | 15.2 million light-years | Binoculars |
| Barred spiral | Sculptor Galaxy | NGC 253 | Sculptor | 8.0 | 11.4 million light-years | Binoculars |

# Glossary

**ANTENNA**
A rod- or dishlike structure on spacecraft and telescopes used to transmit and receive radio signals.

**APHELION**
The point in the orbit of a planet, comet, or asteroid at which it is farthest from the Sun.

**ASTEROID**
A small, irregular solar system object, made of rock and/or metal, that orbits the Sun.

**ASTEROID BELT**
A doughnut-shaped region of the solar system, between the orbits of Mars and Jupiter, that contains a large number of orbiting asteroids.

**ASTRONAUT**
A person trained to travel and live in space.

**ATMOSPHERE**
The layer of gas that surrounds a planet. Also the outermost layer of gas around the Sun or a star.

**ATOM**
The smallest particle of a chemical element that can exist on its own.

**AURORA**
Patterns of light that appear near the poles of some planets. Solar wind particles are trapped by a planet's magnetic field and drawn into its atmosphere, where they collide with atoms and cause them to give off light.

**AXIS**
The imaginary line that passes through the center of a planet or star and around which the planet or star rotates.

**BIG BANG**
The explosion that created the universe billions of years ago. According to the Big Bang theory, the universe began in an extremely dense and hot state and has been expanding ever since. The Big Bang was the origin of space, time, and matter.

**BLACK HOLE**
An object in space with such a strong gravitational pull that nothing, not even light, can escape from it.

**BLAZAR**
An active galaxy with a supermassive black hole at its center.

**CHARGED PARTICLE**
A particle that has a positive or negative electrical charge.

**CHROMOSPHERE**
A gaseous layer above the surface of a star, such as the Sun. Along with the corona, it forms the star's outer atmosphere.

**COMET**
An object made of dust and ice that travels around the Sun in an elliptical orbit. As it gets near the Sun, the ice starts to vaporize, creating a tail of dust and gas.

**CONSTELLATION**
A named area of the sky (defined by the International Astronomical Union). The whole sky is divided into 88 constellations. Many are based around distinctive patterns of stars.

**CORONA**
The outermost part of the Sun or a star's atmosphere, seen as a white halo during a solar eclipse.

**COSMONAUT**
A Russian astronaut.

**CRATER**
A bowl-shaped depression on the surface of a planet, moon, asteroid, or other body.

**CRUST**
The thin, solid outer layer of a planet or moon.

**DARK ENERGY**
The energy that scientists believe is responsible for the acceleration in the expansion of the universe.

**DARK MATTER**
Invisible matter that can be detected only by the effect of its gravity.

**DENSITY**
The amount of matter that occupies a certain volume.

**DWARF PLANET**
A planet that is big enough to have become spherical but hasn't managed to clear all the debris from its orbital path.

**ECLIPSE**
An astronomical event in which an object either passes into the shadow of another object or temporarily blocks an observer's view. During a solar eclipse, the shadow of the Moon falls on Earth. In a lunar eclipse, the shadow of Earth falls on the Moon.

**ELECTROMAGNETIC RADIATION**
Energy waves that can travel through space and matter. Visible light, X-rays, and microwaves are all forms of electromagnetic radiation.

**EQUATOR**
The imaginary line around the center of a planet, halfway between its north and south poles.

**ESCAPE VELOCITY**
The minimum speed at which an object has to travel to escape the gravity of a planet or moon. Earth's escape velocity is 7 miles (11.2 km) per second.

**EXOPLANET**
A planet that orbits a star other than the Sun.

**GALAXY**
A collection of millions or trillions of stars, gas, and dust held together by gravity.

**GAMMA RAY**
An electromagnetic energy wave that has a very short wavelength.

**GLOBULAR CLUSTER**
A ball-shaped cluster of stars that orbits a large galaxy.

**GRANULATION**
Mottling on the surface of the Sun or another star.

**GRAVITY**
The force that pulls all objects that have mass and energy toward one another. It is the force that keeps moons in orbit around planets, and planets in orbit around the Sun.

**HABITABLE**
Suitable for living in or on.

**HEMISPHERE**
One half of a sphere. Earth is divided into northern and southern hemispheres by the equator.

**HERTZSPRUNG–RUSSELL DIAGRAM**
A diagram showing a star's temperature and brightness in relation to other stars.

**INFRARED**
Electromagnetic radiation with wavelengths shorter than radio waves but longer than visible light. It is the primary form of radiation emitted by many objects in space.

**LAUNCH VEHICLE**
A rocket-powered vehicle that is used to send spacecraft or satellites into space.

**LIGHT-YEAR**
The distance traveled by light in a vacuum in one year.

**LITHOSPHERE**
The solid, hard outer layer of a planet or moon.

**MAGNETIC FIELD**
A field of force created by a planet, star, or galaxy, that surrounds it and extends into space.

**MAGNITUDE**
The brightness of an object in space given as a number. Bright objects have low or negative numbers and dim objects have high numbers.

**MAIN-SEQUENCE STAR**
An ordinary star, such as our Sun, that shines by converting hydrogen to helium. Main-sequence stars lie on the main band of the Hertzsprung–Russell diagram.

**MANTLE**
A thick layer of hot rock between the core and the crust of a planet or moon.

**MARE**
A large, flat area on the Moon's surface that looks dark when viewed from Earth. These areas were originally thought to be lakes or seas but are now known to be floods of solidified lava.

**MATTER**
Something that exists as a solid, liquid, or gas.

**MESOSPHERE**
The layer of atmosphere 30–50 miles (50–80 km) above Earth.

**METEOR**
A streak of light, also called a shooting star, seen when a meteoroid burns up due to friction on entering Earth's atmosphere.

**METEORITE**
A meteoroid that reaches the ground and survives impact. Meteorites are usually classified according to their composition as stony, iron, or stony-iron.

**METEOROID**
A particle of rock, metal, or ice traveling through space.

**MICROWAVE**
Electromagnetic radiation with wavelengths longer than infrared and visible light but shorter than radio waves.

**MILKY WAY**
The barred spiral galaxy that contains the solar system and is visible to the naked eye as a band of faint light across the night sky.

**MODULE**
A portion of a spacecraft.

**NEBULA**
A cloud of gas and/or dust in space.

**NEUTRINO**
A subatomic particle produced by nuclear fusion in stars as well as in the Big Bang.

**NEUTRON**
A subatomic particle that does not have an electrical charge. It is found in all atomic nuclei except those of hydrogen.

**NEUTRON STAR**
A dense collapsed star that is mainly made of neutrons.

**NUCLEAR FUSION**
A process in which two atomic nuclei join to form a heavier nucleus and release large amounts of energy.

**NUCLEUS**
The compact central core of an atom. Also the solid, icy body of a comet.

**ORBIT**
The path taken by an object around another when affected by its gravity. The orbits of planets are mostly elliptical in shape.

**ORBITER**
A spacecraft that is designed to orbit an object but not land on it.

**PARTICLE**
An extremely small part of a solid, liquid, or gas.

**PAYLOAD**
Cargo or equipment carried into space by a rocket or a spacecraft.

**PENUMBRA**
The lighter outer shadow cast by an object. A person inside this region can see part of the source of light causing the shadow. Also the lighter, less cool region of a sunspot.

**PERIHELION**
The point in the orbit of a planet, comet, or asteroid at which it is closest to the Sun.

**PHASE**
The portion of a moon or planet that is seen to be lit by the Sun. The Moon passes through a cycle of different phases every 29.5 days.

**PHOTOSPHERE**
The thin gaseous layer at the base of the Sun's atmosphere from which visible light is emitted.

**PLANET**
A spherical object that orbits a star and is sufficiently massive to have cleared its orbital path of debris.

**PLANETARY NEBULA**
A glowing cloud of gas around a star at the end of its life.

**PLANETESIMALS**
Small rocky or icy objects formed in the early solar system that were pulled together by gravity to form planets.

**PLANISPHERE**
A disk-shaped star map with an overlay that shows which part of the sky is visible at particular times and dates.

**PLASMA**
A highly energized form of gas. The Sun is made of plasma.

**PROBE**
An uncrewed spacecraft that is designed to explore objects in space and transmit information back to Earth (especially one that explores the atmosphere or surface of an object).

**PROMINENCE**
A large, flamelike plume of plasma emerging from the Sun's photosphere.

**PULSAR**
A neutron star that sends out beams of radiation as it spins.

**QUASAR**
Short for "quasi-stellar radio" source, a quasar is the immensely luminous nucleus of a distant active galaxy with a supermassive black hole at its center.

**RED GIANT**
A large, luminous star with a low surface temperature and a reddish color. It "burns" helium in its core rather than hydrogen and is nearing the final stages of its life.

**ROVER**
A vehicle that is driven remotely on the surface of a planet and moon.

**SATELLITE**
An object that orbits another object larger than itself.

**SEYFERT GALAXY**
An active galaxy, often spiral in shape, with a supermassive black hole at the center.

**SOLAR FLARE**
The brightening of a part of the Sun's surface, accompanied by a release of huge amounts of electromagnetic energy.

**SOLAR WIND**
A continuous flow of fast-moving charged particles from the Sun.

**SPACE-TIME**
A combination of three dimensions of space—length, breadth, height—with the dimension of time.

**SPACEWALK**
Activity by an astronaut in space outside a spacecraft, usually to conduct repairs or test equipment.

**STAR**
A huge sphere of glowing plasma that generates energy by nuclear fusion in its core.

**STRATOSPHERE**
The layer of the atmosphere 5–30 miles (8–50 km) above Earth's surface.

**SUBATOMIC PARTICLE**
Any particle smaller than an atom.

**SUNSPOT**
A region of intense magnetic activity in the Sun's photosphere that appears darker than its surroundings.

**THERMOSPHERE**
The layer of the atmosphere 50–375 miles (80–600 km) above Earth's surface.

**THRUST**
The force from an engine that propels a rocket or spacecraft forward.

**TRANSIT**
The passage of a planet or star in front of another, larger, object.

**TROPOSPHERE**
The layer of the atmosphere 4–12 miles (6–20 km) above Earth's surface.

**ULTRAVIOLET RADIATION**
Electromagnetic radiation with wavelengths shorter than visible light but longer than X-rays.

**UMBRA**
The darker central shadow cast by an object. A person inside this region cannot see the source of light causing the shadow. Also the darker, cooler region of a sunspot.

**X-RAY**
Electromagnetic radiation with wavelengths shorter than ultraviolet radiation but longer than gamma rays.

# Index

Page numbers in **bold** type refer to main entries

## A

Abell 1185 107
Abell 1689 107
Abell 2218 107
accretionary disk 89, 90
active galaxies **100-101**, 104
Albireo 168
Aldrin, Buzz 117, 136
aliens 148-149
Alpha Centauri 158
Alphekka 174
Andromeda constellation **169**
Andromeda Galaxy 96, 105, 106, 119, 201
animals in space 116-117
Antares 84, 96
Antennae Galaxies 105
Antlia **181**
Apollo program 27, 115, 122, 123, **134-137**
    Apollo 11 27, 136, 139
    Apollo 15 137
    Apollo 17 24-25
    lunar landers 136-137
    Lunar Roving Vehicle (LRV) 138-139
    spacesuits 141
Apus **193**
Aquarius 153, **177**
Aquila **176**
Ara **189**
Arecibo radio telescope 148-149
Aries 153, **170**
Armstrong, Neil 117, 136, 137
Asteroid belt 9, **40**, 42, 64, 197, 202
asteroids 9, 10, 21, **40-41**, 64, 65, 202
    impact craters 28
astronauts 113, 202
    first 124-125
    crewed spacecraft 130-131
    spacesuits 140-141
    spacewalks 142-143
astronomers 96
astronomical units 9, 10
astronomy 116

practical stargazing 154-155
Atlantis 114
atmosphere 202
    Earth 20, 22, 23
    Io 48
    Jupiter 45
    Mars 3, 14, 69
    Mercury 17
    Neptune 62
    Pluto 65
    Rhea and Dione 57
    Saturn 50
    stars 70
    Titan 59
    Uranus 60
    Venus 18
atoms 110, 202
Auriga **164**
auroras 202
    Jupiter 45
axis of rotation 202
    Earth 21
    Saturn 51
    Uranus 61

## B

B ring (Saturn) 52
Baikonur Cosmodrome 124
Barnard's Galaxy 107
barred spiral galaxies 101, 106
    Milky Way 100
    NGC 1300 185
    NGC 1365 101, 185
Barringer Crater (Arizona) 29
Beagle 2 lander 36, 37, 199
Beehive Cluster 170
Beta Centauri 158
Beta Pictoris 191
Betelgeuse 81
Big Bang 96, **110-111**, 202
Big Dipper 156, 165
binary systems 90
binoculars 155
black dwarfs 80-81
black holes 70, 81, 84, 86, **88-89**, 90, 92, 100, 102, 103, 202
blazars 103, 202
blue dwarfs 80-81
blue hypergiants 73
blue supergiants 72
Bode's Galaxy (M81) 101, 156, 157, 201

Boeing CST-100 114
Boötes **166**
Butterfly Cluster (Scorpius) 90
Butterfly Nebula **82-83**

## C

Caelum **185**
Callisto **47**
Caloris Basin (Mercury) 16
Camelopardalis **164**
cameras, rovers 129
Cancer 153, **170**
Canes Venatici 104, **166-167**
Canis Major **178**
Canis Minor **178**
Capricornus 153, **184**
carbon dioxide 18
cargo weight, rockets 122
Carina 158, 159, **187**
Carina Nebula 75, 116, 158, 159, 187, 201
Carina-Sagittarius Arm (Milky Way) 101
Cartwheel Galaxy 105
Cassini Division (Saturn) 53
Cassini spacecraft 51, 52, 54, 58, 115, **126-127**, 199
Cassiopeia 156, 157, **163**
Cat's Eye Nebula 121, **163**
celestial sphere **152-153**
centaurs 64
Centaurus 158, **182**
Centaurus A 201
Cepheus 156, **162**
Ceres 40, 64, **65**, 197
Cetus **178**
Chamaeleon **193**
Chandrayaan 1 Moon mission 27
Chang'e Moon missions 27
China, space exploration 27
Cigar Galaxy (M82) 157
Circinus **188**
cliffs, Mercury 16
Clinton, Bill 149
clouds
    Earth 22
    Jupiter 45
    Saturn 50, 51
    Venus 18
colliding galaxies **104-105**
Collins, Michael 136
Columba **186**
Coma Berenices **172**
coma (comets) 66, 67

comets 9, 11, **66-67**, 197, 202
    67P 66
    Encke 66
    Hale-Bopp 66, 197
    impact craters 28
    landing on 117
    periodic 197
    structure of 66
    tails 66
    Tempel 1 127
Command Module (Apollo) 134, 135, 136, 137
constellations 152, **162-193**, 202
    movement of 155
    zodiac 153
continents 21
convection layers, stars 70
Copernicus Crater (Moon) 25
Copernicus, Nicolaus 117, 153
core
    black holes 88
    Earth 22, 23
    Io 48
    Jupiter 44
    Mars 32
    Mercury 17
    Moon 24
    Neptune 62
    red supergiants 85
    Saturn 51
    stars 70, 74, 75, 80, 81
    Sun 14
    Titan 59
    Uranus 61
    Venus 19
corona 30, 202
Corona Australis **189**
Corona Borealis **174**
Corvus **181**
cosmologists 96
cosmos **96-97**
Crab Nebula 171
Crater **181**
craters 202
    asteroids 40, 41
    Callisto 47
    formation of **29**
    impact **28-29**
    Mercury 16, 17
    Moon 25
    transient 29
    Venus 18
crewed spacecraft 15, 117, **130-131**
    first 124-125
    future 146-147

crust
    comets 66
    Earth 22, 23
    Io 49
    Mars 33
    Mercury 17
    Moon 25
    Titan 59
    Venus 19
Crux (Southern Cross) 158, 159, **182**
Curiosity rover 36, 37, 38-39, 115, 127, 199
Cygnus **168**

## D

D ring (Saturn) 53
Dali Chasma (Venus) 18
Daphnis 53, 57
dark energy 96, 202
dark matter 96, **97**, 106, 202
death of stars 70
    black holes 88
    hot Jupiters 79
    planetary nebulas 83
    red supergiants 85
declination, lines of 152
Deep Impact 127
Deimos 33
Delphinus **176**
Delta Cephei 162
density 202
    neutron stars 87
Descent Module 130
deserts 21
Destiny Laboratory 144
Dione 57
distances, cosmic 96
Dorado **192**
Draco 156, **163**
Dragon spacecraft 114, 131
Drake Equation 148-149
Drake, Francis 148
Dumbbell Nebula 176, 201
dust clouds 74, 75, 80
dust torus 102, 103
dwarf galaxies 104-105, 107
    NGC 5195 104
dwarf planets 9, 40, 64, 65, 197, 202
dwarf stars 72

# E

E ring (Saturn) 52
Eagle Nebula 100, 121, 175
Earth **20-23**
  celestial sphere 152-153
  curvature 9
  data 196
  distance from stars 71
  distance from the Sun 9
  human influence 21
  impact craters 28-29
  inside **22-23**
  orbit 11
  rotation of 152-153
  in the universe 108, 109, 153
eclipses 30-31, 197, 202
Eight-Burst Nebula 187
Einstein, Albert 88, 97
ejecta curtains 28, 29
electromagnetic (EM) spectrum 70
elliptical galaxies 101, 106, 107
elliptical orbits 11, 66
Enceladus 52, 57, 149
Encke, Comet 66
energy 70, 96, 110
engines, rocket 123
equator, celestial 152, 161
Equuleus **176**
Eridanus **185**
Eris 9, **64**, 65, 197
ESA, space exploration 27, 36-37, 198-199
Eskimo Nebula 172
Europa **46**, 47, 149
European Extremely Large Telescope (E-ELT) **118-119**
European Space Agency see ESA
event horizons 88
exoplanets **76-77**, 202
exosphere 23
extraterrestrials 148-149
Extravehicular Mobility Unit 141

# F

False Cross 159
Flaming Star Nebula 164
flybys 127, 198-99
forces 110
Fornax **185**
fossils 149

# G

Gagarin, Yuri 117, **124-25**
Gaia 120
galactic center 100
galaxies 95, 96, 97, **100-107**, 202
  active **100-101**, 104
  Andromeda 96, 105, 106, 119, 201
  Antennae 105
  Barnard's 107
  Big Bang 110-111
  Bode's (M81) 101, 156, 157, 201
  Cartwheel 105
  Cigar (M82) 157
  colliding **104-105**
  dwarf 104-105, 107
  elliptical 101, 106, 107
  Great Wall 107
  Guitar 107
  irregular 101
  Large Magellanic Cloud 106, 159, 192, 201
  M81 and M82 101, 156, 157
  Milky Way 80, 90, 92-93, 96, **98-99**, **100-101**, 105, 106, 107, 108, 109, 154-155, 157, 158, 159, 161, 203
  newborn 121
  NGC 1566 103
  Pinwheel 106
  radio 103
  reference 201
  Sagittarius Dwarf 107
  Sculptor 201
  Seyfert 103, 203
  shapes 101
  Small Magellanic Cloud 107, 158, 159, 201
  Sombrero 121, 173
  Spindle 181
  spiral 99, 101, 104, 105, 106, 111, 165, 173, 180
  Triangulum 106, 201
  Whirlpool **104-105**, 166
  Wolf-Lundmark-Melotte 107
galaxy clusters **106-107**
Galilean moons (Jupiter) 47
Galilei, Galileo 47, 54, 117
Galileo spacecraft 45, 115, 127, 199
Ganymede **46**, 47
Garnet Star 156
gas clouds 74, 75, 80, 110

gas giants 8, 11
  birth of 13
  data 196
  exploration 199
  see also Jupiter; Neptune; Saturn; Uranus
Gemini 153, **172**
Gemini spacecraft 131
geysers, Neptune 63
giant stars 72, 90
globular clusters 90, 202
  47 Tucanae 158, 190
  M15 177
  M71 175
  NGC 6584 189
Goddard, Robert 116
GRAIL Moon mission 27
gravitational lensing **107**
gravity 110, 202
  black holes 88, 89
  colliding galaxies 104, 105
  dwarf planets 9
  and formation of planets 13
  galaxy clusters 106
  Io 48, 49
  laws of 97
  Mercury 17
  Moon 24, 137
  multiple stars 90
  Neptune 62, 63
  neutron stars 87
  Saturn 50, 52, 54, 57
  stars 70, 74, 75, 80
  Sun 9, 11, 117
  universe 97, 108
Great Dark Spot (Neptune) 62
Great Globular Cluster 90
Great Red Spot (Jupiter) 44
Great Wall 107
greenhouses, on Mars 147
Grus **190**
Guitar 107

# H

habitable ("Goldilocks") zone 77
Hale-Bopp, Comet 66, 197
Haumea **64**, 65, 197
HD 189733 b 78-79
HD 209458 b 79
heat shield 127
heliocentrism 153
helium 50, 80, 81
Helix Nebula 177, 201
Hercules 90, **166-167**
Hercules A 103
Herschel, William 60
Hertzsprung, Ejnar 73
Hertzsprung-Russell diagram 73, 202

Hiten Moon mission 27
Horologium **191**
Horsehead Nebula 75, 179
hot Jupiters 77, **78-79**
Hubble Space Telescope 74, 97, 116, **120-121**
hurricanes 51
Huygens, Christiaan 126
Huygens space probe 51, 58, **126-127**, 199
Hyades 171
Hydra **180**
hydrogen 50, 70, 74, 75, 80, 81
Hydrus **191**
Hyperion 56

# I

impact craters **28-29**
India, space exploration 27, 199
Indus **189**
infrared 119, 202
infrared telescopes 115
inner planets 8, 9, 10
interacting binaries 90-91
International Space Station 114, 130, 143, **144-45**
  spacesuits 140-41
interstellar dust clouds 99
interstellar gas 74
Io 46, 47, **48-49**
iron 80
irregular galaxies 101
Irwin, James 137
Ixion 197

# J

James Webb Space Telescope 121
Japan, space exploration 27
Johnson Space Center (Houston) 135
Juno orbiter 199
Jupiter **44-49**
  data 196
  missions to 115, 127, 199
  moons 46-49
  rotation 11

# K

Kennedy Space Center (Florida) 123, 134
Kepler 5b and 7b 79
Kepler Observatory 116

Kepler-62 system 76-77
kinetic energy 28, 29
Kuiper belt 9, 11, 64, 65, 197

# L

Lacerta **169**
LADEE Moon mission 27
Lagoon Nebula 201
Laika 117
lakes, Titan 58, 59
landers 127
Large Magellanic Cloud 106, 159, 192, 201
launch sites 114
LCROSS Moon mission 27
lenses, telescope 118, 119, 155
lensing
  black holes 89
  gravitational 107
Leo 153, **173**
Leo cluster 107
Leo Minor **172**
Lepus **186**
Libra 153, **174**
life
  on Earth 20, 21, 22
  on Mars 36, 39
  search for extraterrestrial 148-149
  and water 149
light
  bending 89, 107
  speed of 15
  waves 70
light pollution 154
light-years 71, 96, 202
living conditions, on Mars 147
Local Group **106**
Luna spacecraft 27
lunar eclipses 31
lunar landers 136-137
Lunar Module (Apollo) 134, 135, **136-137**
Lunar prospector 27
Lunar Roving Vehicle (LRV) 27, 137, **138-139**
Lunokhod 1 and 2 26, 27, 117
Lupus **182**
Lynx **164**
Lyra **167**

# M

M81 and M82 galaxies 101, 156, 157
Maat Mons (Venus) 18
Magellan orbiter 198
main-sequence stars 73, 202

Makemake 65, 197
manned spacecraft *see* crewed spacecraft
mantle 203
   Earth 23
   Io 48, 49
   Mars 33
   Mercury 17
   Moon 24, 25
   Neptune 62
   Titan 59
   Uranus 60
   Venus 19
Mariner spacecraft 35, 115, 198
Mars **32-39**
   data 196
   exploration **36-37**, 128-129, 198-199
   future crewed landings 37, 117, **146-147**
   life on 149
Mars 2, 3, and 6 probes 33, 36, 198
Mars Express 37, 199
Mars Global Surveyor 199
Mars Orbiter Mission (Mangalyaan) 199
Mars Pathfinder 199
Mars Polar Lander 36
Mars Reconnaissance Orbiter 34, 199
mass-energy 96
massive stars 80-81
matter 96-97, 110, 203
MAVEN 199
Mensa **192**
Mercury 11, **16-17**
   data 196
   missions to 115, 198
Mercury spacecraft 141
mesosphere 23, 203
MESSENGER space probe 115, 198
meteor showers 42, 196
meteorites 12, **42-43**, 203
   impact craters 28-29
   Martian 149
meteoroids 42, 203
meteors 42, 203
Microscopium **184**
microwave telescopes 115
microwaves 70, 203
Milky Way 90, 92-93, 96, **98-99**, **100-101**, 106, 107, 154-155, 161, 203
   future collision with Andromeda Galaxy 105
   northern night sky 157
   southern night sky 158, 159
   spiral arms 80
   in the universe 108, 109

Mimas 53
minor bodies 9
minor planets **64-65**
Mir space station 116
Miranda 60
mirrors, telescope 118, 119, 121, 155
Mission Control (Houston) 135
Mizar 165
molecular clouds 74, 75
Monoceros **180**
Moon **24-27**
   Apollo program 115, 117, 134-135, **136-137**, 138-139
   eclipses 30, 31
   exploring **26-27**
   formation of 24
   future missions to 146
   impact craters 28-29
   landings 24-25, 113, 115, 117, **136-137**, 138-139
   mementos left on 137
Moon rovers 26-27, 117, **138-139**
moons
   Jupiter **46-49**
   Mars 33
   Neptune 63
   Pluto 65
   Saturn 50, 52, 53, **56-59**
   solar system 9
   Uranus 60
multiple stars **90-91**
Musca **188**
Mystic Mountain (Carina Nebula) 75

Nair al Saif 74
NASA, Apollo program 134-135
near-Earth asteroids 41, 146
nebulas 201
   Butterfly Nebula **82-83**
   Carina Nebula 75, 116, 158, 159, 187, 201
   Cat's Eye Nebula 121, **163**
   Crab Nebula 171
   Dumbbell Nebula 176, 201
   Eagle Nebula 100, 121, 175
   Eight-Burst Nebula 187
   Eskimo Nebula 172
   Flaming Star Nebula 164
   Helix Nebula 177, 201
   Horsehead Nebula 75, 179
   Lagoon Nebula 201
   North America Nebula 168

Orion Nebula **74-75**, 179, 201
Owl Nebula 165
Ring Nebula 167
Rosette Nebula 180, 201
solar 13
Trifid Nebula 183
Veil Nebula 168
Neptune 11, **62-63**
   data 196
   missions to 115, 199
neutron stars 81, 84, **86-87**, 90, 203
neutrons 110
New Horizons mission 65, 199
newborn stars 74, 104
Newton, Isaac 9, 97, 117
night sky **150-193**
   celestial sphere 152-153
   northern star-hopping 156-157
   nouthern star-hopping 158-159
   star maps 160-161
night vision 154
Noctis Labyrinthus (Mars) 34
Norma **188**
North America Nebula 168
northern celestial hemisphere 156-157, 160
northern lights 15
novas 90, 91
nuclear fusion 69, 70, 75, 80, 81, 203
nucleus
   atoms 110, 203
   comets 66, 67

oceans 22
Octans **193**
Olympus Mons 32
Oort cloud 9, 65, 196
open clusters 90
   IC 2391 158, 159
Ophiuchus 153, **175**
Opportunity rover 36, 129, 199
optical telescopes 115
orange giants 72
orange main-sequence stars 71
Orbital Module 130
orbital plane 9
orbiters 127, 198-199, 203
orbits 13, 203
   asteroids 10
   comets 11, 66
   Earth 11, 21
   elliptical 11, 66

hot Jupiters 79
how orbits work 9
International Space Station 144
Mars 10, 33
Mercury 11, 16
Neptune 11
planetary 196
Saturn's moons 56, 57
Orcus 197
ordinary matter 97
Orion 73, **179**
Orion Arm (Milky Way) 101, 109
Orion Nebula **74-75**, 179, 201
Orion spacecraft 114
outer moons (Jupiter) 47
outer planets 8, 9, 11
Owl Nebula 165
oxygen 57

pancake domes 19
parallax 71
particle jets 102
Pathfinder spacecraft 36
Pavo **193**
Pegasus **177**
Pele volcano (Io) 49
Perseus **170**
Perseus Arm (Milky Way) 101
Philae lander 66, 127
Phobos 33
Phobos orbiter/lander 199
Phoenix **190**
Phoenix lander 36, 199
photosphere 15, 203
Pictor **191**
Pinwheel Galaxy 106
Pioneer spacecraft 198, 199
Pisces 153, **178**
Piscis Austrinus **184**
planetary motion 11, 153, 196
planetary nebulas 80, 81, 83, 203
planetesimals 13, 203
planets 8-9, 203
   birth of 74
   data 196
   distance from the Sun 10-11
   exploration **198-199**
   formation of 12, 13, 75
planispheres 154-155
plasma torus 49
Pleiades 171
Pluto 9, 64, 65, 197
polar regions
   Earth 20
   Saturn 51

Polaris (Pole Star) 156, 157, **162**
poles, celestial 152-153, 156
Pollas, Christian 41
Porpoise 105
pressure, stars 70, 80
probes *see* space probes
prominences 14, 203
proplyds 74
Proxima Centauri 71, 96
pulsars 86, **87**, 203
Puppis **186**
Pyxis **186**

**QR**
Quaoar 197
quasars 103, 203
radiation
   Big Bang 110
   stars 70
radio galaxies 103
radio signals, alien 148
radio telescopes 115, 148
radio waves 115, 119
Ranger spacecraft 26, 27
red dwarfs 71, 72, 80
red giants 70, 72, 80-81, 90, 91, 203
red supergiants 73, 80, 81, **84-85**
relativity, theory of 89
Reticulum **191**
Rhea 56
Rigel 73, 179
right ascension, lines of 152-153
Ring Nebula 167
rings
   Jupiter 45
   Neptune 63
   Saturn 10, 50, 51, **52-55**
   Uranus 61
robotic spacecraft 27, 115, 146
rock samples 128
rockets 113, 114-115, 116, **122-123**
rocky planets 8, 10
   data 196
   exploration 198-199
   formation of 12
   *see also* Earth; Mars; Mercury; Venus
Rosetta spacecraft 66, 117, 127
Rosette Nebula 180, 201
rovers 26-27, 127, **128-129**, 146, 198-199, 203

Russell, Henry 73
Russia, space exploration 26-27, 36, 198-199

# S

Sagitta **175**
Sagittarius 153, **183**
Sagittarius Dwarf Galaxy 107
Salyut 1 116, 144
sand dunes 34
Saturn **50-59**
 axial tilt 51
 data 196
 missions to 51, 115, 126, 127, 199
 moons 53, **56-57**
 rings 10, 50, 51, **52-55**
Saturn V rocket 122, 134
science fiction 117
Scorpius 90, 153, **183**
Scott, David 137
Sculptor **184**
Sculptor Galaxy 201
Scutum **175**
Scutum-Centaurus Arm (Milky Way) 100
seasons
 Earth 21
 Mars 33
 Pluto 65
 Uranus 61
Sedna 9, 197
SELENE Moon mission 27
Serpens **174-175**
Service Module (Apollo) 134, 135, 136, 137
Service Module (Soyuz) 130
SETI (search for extraterrestrial intelligence) 148
Sextans **181**
Seyfert galaxies 103, 203
shepherd moons (Saturn) 53
shooting stars **42-43**
shuttle program 133
singularity 88, 89
Skylab 116
Small Magellanic Cloud 107, 158, 159, 201
small stars 80-81
SMART-1 Moon mission 27
Sojourner 36
solar cycle 15
solar eclipses 30-31, 197
solar nebula 13
solar system **6-13**, 100
 birth of 12-13, 111
 data **196-197**
 structure 9
 in the universe 108, 109

solar wind 15, 203
Sombrero Galaxy 121, 173
southern celestial hemisphere 158-159, 161
Southern Cross (Crux) 158, 159, **182**
Southern Pinwheel **180**, 201
Southern Pleiades 158, 159, 187
Southern Pointers 158
Soyuz spacecraft 114, **130-131**
space exploration **112-149**
 future 146-147
 reference 198-199
 timeline 116-117
Space Launch System (SLS) rocket 114, 122-123
space probes 114, **126-127**, 198-199, 203
 Mars 33, 36-37
 Titan 58
space race 26, 124
space, shape of 108
Space Shuttle 114, 116, 131, 132-133
 spacesuits 141
space stations 114, 116, 143, **144-145**
space telescopes **120-121**
space tourism 147
space-time 89, **97**, 203
SpaceShipTwo 131, 147
spacesuits **140-141**, 143
spacewalks 117, 140-141, 142-143, 145, 203
spaghettification 89
spicules 15
Spindle Galaxy 181
spiral galaxies 101, 104, 105, 106, 111
 M101 165
 M66 173
 M83 180
 Milky Way 99
Spirit rover 36, 128-129, 199
Sputnik spacecraft 117, 124
star clouds 92-93
star clusters 90
 M13 166
 M4 183
 M47 186
 NGC 6067 188
star-hopping
 northern **156-157**
 southern **158-159**
stargazing, practical 154-155
starlight 70
stars **68-93**, 203
 Big Bang 110-111
 birth of **74-75**, 80
 brightness 70, 200

colors 73
constellations 162-193
death of 70, 79, 83, 85, 88
distance from Earth 71
forces in 70
formation of 12, **75**
how stars work **70-71**
lives of 80-81
mapping 154
maps 160-161
newborn 74, 104
parts of 70
pattern of movement 155
reference 200
shining 70
studying 70
types of **72-73**
variable-size 70
stellar black holes 88
stellar winds 75
Stonehenge 116
storms
 Earth 22
 Jupiter 44, 49
 Neptune 62
 Saturn 51
 Uranus 61
subatomic particles 110, 203
Sun **14-15**
 birth of 12, 13
 eclipses 30, 31, 197
 mapping 120
 planetary motion 11, 153
 size of 8
 solar system **6-13**, 196-197
Sunflower Galaxy 166
sunspots 14, 15, 203
supercluster filaments 109
superclusters 107, 109
supermassive black holes 88
supernovas 13, 75, 80, 81, 84, 86, 88
 Type 1a 91
Surveyor spacecraft 27
Swanson, Steve 144
Syrtis Major (Mars) 33

# T

tails, comets 66
Taurus 153, **171**
tectonic plates 23
telescopes 117, **118-119**, 155
 how they work 119
 types of 115
Telescopium **189**
Tempel 1 comet 127
temperatures
 Earth 20, 21, 22, 23
 hot Jupiters 79
 Mars 39, 147

Mercury 16
Neptune 63
Venus 18
thermosphere 23, 203
thrust, rockets 122, 203
tidal forces, Io 48, 49
tilt, Earth's 21
time, stretching 89
Titan 51, 56, **58-59**, 127
 missions to 126, 199
tourism, space 147
Toutatis **40-41**
transient craters 29
Trapezium 74, 179
Triangulum **169**
Triangulum Australe 158, **188**
Triangulum Galaxy 106, 201
Trifid Nebula 183
Triton 63
Trojans 40
troposphere 23, 203
Tucana 158, **190**
Tupan Patera (Io) 48

# U

ultraviolet 70, 75, 119, 120, 203
universe **96-97**, **108-109**
 Big Bang 110-11
 composition of 95, **96-97**
 expanding 96-97, 110, 111
 observable 109
 origin of 96
 scale of 109
Upsilon Andromedae b 79
Uranus **60-61**
 data 196
 missions to 115, 199
 rotation 11
Ursa Major 157, **165**
Ursa Minor 157, **162**
US, space exploration 26-27, 36-37, 134-135, 198-199
USSR, space exploration 26-27, 36, 198-199

# V

Valles Marineris (Mars) 32, **34-35**
variable stars 70
Vega spacecraft 198
Veil Nebula 168
Vela 159, **187**
Venera space probe 115, 198
Venus **18-19**
 data 196
 missions to 127, 198

rotation 10
Viking spacecraft 36, 37, 116, 199
Virgo 153, **173**
Virgo cluster 107
Virgo supercluster 109
voids 109
Volans **192**
volcanoes/volcanic action
 Earth 22
 Io 46, 48, 49
 Venus 18, 19
Vostok 1 **124-125**
Voyager spacecraft 49, 59, 60, 62, 63, 115, 116, 127, 199
Vulpecula **176**

# W

WASP-12 79
water
 Earth 20, 21, 22
 Europa and Enceladus 57, 149
 Mars 149
wavelengths 70, 115, 119
Wells, H. G. 117
Whirlpool Galaxy **104-105**, 166
white dwarfs 71, 72, 80-81, 83, 90, 91
white main-sequence stars 71
Willamette Meteorite 42
Wolf-Lundmark-Melotte Galaxy 107
World View balloon 147
wormholes 89

# X

X-ray binaries 90
X-ray telescopes 115
X-rays 119, 120, 203

# YZ

yellow main-sequence stars 71
Yerkes telescope 118
young stars 74-75
Yutu rover 27
zodiac 153
Zubenelgenubi 174

# Acknowledgments

**Smithsonian Enterprises:**
Kealy Gordon, Product
Development Manager
Ellen Nanney, Licensing Manager
Brigid Ferraro, Vice President,
Consumer and Education Products
Carol LeBlanc, Senior Vice President,
Consumer and Education Products
Chris Liedel, President

**Curator for the Smithsonian:**
Andrew Johnston, Geographer, Center
for Earth and Planetary Studies, National Air
and Space Museum, Smithsonian

**The publisher would like to thank the
following people for their assistance
in the preparation of this book:**
Ann Baggaley, Ashwin Khurana, Virien
Chopra, and Rohini Deb for editorial
assistance; Nick Sotiriadis, Bryan Versteeg,
and the Maltings Partnership for additional
illustrations; Steve Crozier for image
retouching; Caroline Hunt for proofreading;
Helen Peters for the index.

**The publisher would like to thank the
following for their kind permission to
reproduce their photographs:**

(Key: a-above; b-below/bottom; c-center;
f-far; l-left; r-right; t-top)

**2 NASA:** Tony Gray and Tom Farrar (cl).
**3 Dreamstime.com:** Peter Jurik (cb). **ESO:**
The design for the E-ELT shown here is
preliminary. http://creativecommons.org/
licenses/by/3.0 (cr). **9 ESA:** OSIRIS Team
MPS / UPD / LAM / IAA / RSSD / INTA /
UPM / DASP / IDA (clb). **ESO:** E. Slawik  http://
creativecommons.org/licenses/by/3.0 (clb/
Hale-bopp). **NASA:** (bl). **Science Photo Library:**
Detlev Van Ravenswaay (clb/Pluto). **10 NASA:**
JPL (tc). **12 Science Photo Library:** Jean-
Claude Revy, A. Carion, ISM (br); Mark Garlick
(clb). **13 NASA:** JPL-Caltech / T. Pyle (SSC) (bc).
**14 BBSO / Big Bear Solar Observatory:** (clb).
**15 Corbis:** Daniel J. Cox (crb). **16 NASA:** (clb).
**17 NASA:** Johns Hopkins University Applied
Physics Laboratory / Carnegie Institution
of Washington (br). **18 NASA:** (tl); JPL (cra).
**19 NASA:** (tr). **20 FLPA:** Chris Newbert /
Minden Pictures (l). **21 Corbis:** Frans Lanting
(cb, bc). **NASA:** Robert Simmon, using Suomi
NPP VIIRS data provided courtesy of Chris
Elvidge (NOAA National Geophysical Data
Center). Suomi NPP is the result of a
partnership between NASA, NOAA, and
the Department of Defense. (crb). **22 Corbis:**
Stocktrek Images (cra). **NASA:** Hal Pierce ,
NASA / GSFC (cl). **24 Getty Images:** Dana
Berry (cla). **NASA:** (br). **25 NASA:** (tr). **29
Corbis:** Jim Wark / Visuals Unlimited (c). **30
Science Photo Library:** Dr. Fred Espenak (tl).
**31 Alamy Images:** Alexey Stiop (bc). **Corbis:**
Brian Cassey / epa (tl). **32 Corbis:** Walter
Myers / Stocktrek Images (bl). **NASA:** JPL /
MSSS / Ed Truthan (tc). **33 NASA:** JPL-Caltech
/ University of Arizona (tr, fcrb). **34 ESA:**
DLR / FU Berlin (cra). **NASA:** JPL / University
of Arizona (ca). **34-35 NASA:** (tl). **Kees
Veenenbos:** (b). **36 NASA:** (bc); Edward A.
Guinness (bl). **37 ESA:** All Rights Reserved
Beagle 2 (bl). **NASA:** JPL-Caltech (br). **38-39
NASA:** JPL-Caltech / MSSS. **41 Science Photo
Library:** Joe Tucciarone (tr). **42 Corbis:**
Bettmann (br). **44 NASA:** (bl). **45 NASA:**
Hubble Heritage Team (STScI / AURA)
Acknowledgment: NASA / ESA, John Clarke
(University of Michigan) (tc); JPL, Galileo
Project, (NOAO), J. Burns (Cornell) et al. (crb).
**47 NASA:** JPL (c). **48 NASA:** JPL / University
of Arizona (tr). **49 NASA:** JPL / University of
Arizona (br). **51 NASA:** (br); JPL-Caltech / SSI
(tl, tc, cr). **52 NASA:** JPL-Caltech / SSI (tr, clb).
**54-55 NASA:** JPL-Caltech / SSI. **58 NASA:** ESA

/ NASA / JPL / University of Arizona (c); JPL-
Caltech / ASI / JHUAPL / Cornell / Weizman
(cl); JPL-Caltech / ASI / USGS (bl). **61 W.M.
Keck Observatory:** Lawrence Sromovsky,
University of Wisconsin-Madison (br). **62
Corbis:** NASA / Roger Ressmeyer (clb). **63
NASA:** JPL (cb). **Dr Dominic Fortes, UCL:** (tc).
**64 NASA:** (tr). **65 ESO:** L. Calçada (tl) http://
creativecommons.org/licenses/by/3.0. **NASA:**
(tr); JPL-Caltech / UCLA / MPS / DLR / IDA (ca).
**66 Corbis:** Andrew Bertuleit Photography
(clb). **ESA:** Rosetta / MPS for OSIRIS Team
MPS / UPD / LAM / IAA / SSO / INTA / UPM /
DASP / IDA (clb/comet). **ESO:** E. Slawik (bc)
http://creativecommons.org/licenses/by/3.0.
**74 NASA:** ESA and L. Ricci (ESO) (cb); K.L.
Luhman (Harvard-Smithsonian Center for
Astrophysics, Cambridge, Mass.); and G.
Schneider, E. Young, G. Rieke, A. Cotera, H.
Chen, M. Rieke, R. Thompson (Steward
Observatory, University of Arizona, Tucson,
Ariz.) http://creativecommons.org/licenses/
by/3.0 (cl). **75 NASA:** ESA, and the Hubble
Heritage Team (AURA / STScI) (crb); ESA, M.
Livio and the Hubble 20th Anniversary Team
(STScI) (crb). **77 ESO:** http://creativecommons.
org/licenses/by/3.0 (tr). **Danielle Futselaar /
SETI Institute (Collaborative work):** (cra). **79
NASA:** ESA / G. Bacon (cra); ESA, Alfred Vidal-
Madjar (Institut d'Astrophysique de Paris,
CNRS) (fcra). **82-83 NASA:** ESA and the Hubble
SM4 ERO Team. **84 Science Photo Library:**
Royal Observatory, Edinburgh (bl). **87 Corbis:**
Chris Cheadle / All Canada Photos (crb).
**88 NASA:** JPL-Caltech (bl). **89 A. Riazuelo,
IAP/UPMC/CNRS:** (cr). **90 Adam Block/Mount
Lemmon SkyCenter/University of Arizona
(Board of Regents):** T. Bash, J. Fox (clb).
**Sergio Eguivar:** (cla). **92-93 Two Micron All
Sky Survey, which is a joint project of the
University of Massachusetts and the Infrared
Processing and Analysis Center/California
Institute of Technology, funded by the
National Aeronautics and Space
Administration and the National Science
Foundation. 94 NASA:** ESA, S. Beckwith
(STScI), and The Hubble Heritage Team (STScI
/ AURA) (cl). **96-97 Science Photo Library:**
Take 27 Ltd. (bc). **97 Alamy Images:** Paul
Fleet (br). **Chandra X-Ray Observatory:** X-ray:
NASA / CXC / CfA / M.Markevitch et al.;
Optical: NASA / STScI; Magellan / U.Arizona /
D.Clowe et al.; Lensing Map: NASA / STScI;
ESO WFI; Magellan / U.Arizona / D.Clowe et
al. http://creativecommons.org/licenses/
by/3.0 (tr). **Dorling Kindersley:** The Natural
History Museum, London / National Maritime
Museum, London (crb). **NASA:** R. Williams
(STScI), the Hubble Deep Field Team (br). **98-99
Mark Gee. 100 CFHT/Coelum:** J.-C. Cuillandre
& G. Anselmi (clb/M16). **NASA:** ESA, SSC, CXC,
and STScI (clb). **101 NASA:** CXC / SAO, JPL-
Caltech, Detlef Hartmann (cra); CXC / MSU / J.
Strader et al, Optical: NASA / STScI (crb); ESA
/ Hubble (br). **SSRO:** R.Gilbert,D.Goldman,J.
Harvey,D.Verschatse,D.Reichart (cr). **103
NASA:** DOE / Fermi LAT Collaboration (br);
ESA, S. Baum and C. O'Dea (RIT), R. Perley and
W. Cotton (NRAO / AUI / NSF), and the Hubble
Heritage Team (STScI / AURA) (cra); ESA /
Hubble & Flickr user Det58 (cr); John Bahcall
(Institute for Advanced Study, Princeton) Mike
Disney (University of Wales) and NASA / ESA
(crb). **105 NASA:** ESA, Curt Struck and Philip
Appleton (Iowa State University), Kirk Borne
(Hughes STX Corporation), and Ray Lucas
(STSI) (cra); ESA and the Hubble Heritage
Team (STScI / AURA) (cr); ESA, and the Hubble
Heritage Team (STScI / AURA) / Hubble
Collaboration (crb); ESA; Z. Levay and R. van
der Marel, STScI; T. Hallas; and A. Mellinger
(br). **106 Adam Block/Mount Lemmon
SkyCenter/University of Arizona (Board of
Regents):** (cl). **CFHT/Coelum:** J.-C. Cuillandre &
G. Anselmi (c). **ESO:** Digitized Sky Survey 2
http://creativecommons.org/licenses/by/3.0

(ca). **NASA:** ESA, the Hubble Heritage
Team (STScI / AURA), J. Blakeslee (NRC
Herzberg Astrophysics Program, Dominion
Astrophysical Observatory), and H. Ford
(JHU) (cla); ESA, Andrew Fruchter (STScI),
and the ERO team (STScI + ST-ECF) (bl). **107
NASA:** ESA / Hubble & Digitized Sky Survey
2. Acknowledgment: Davide De Martin (ESA /
Hubble) (crb); Swift Science Team / Stefan
Immler (tc). **110 NASA:** WMAP Science Team
(tc). **114 Boeing:** (bc). **NASA:** (clb, bl); Tony
Gray and Tom Farrar (ca); JPL-Caltech (cb).
**116-117 Dreamstime.com:** Justin Black (tc).
**116 Dreamstime.com:** Jahoo (cr). **NASA:** (ca,
bl, crb); JPL (cb); Ames / JPL-Caltech (br);
ESA and M. Livio and the Hubble 20th
Anniversary Team (STScI) (bc). **117 Alamy
Images:** DBI Studio (c); Danil Roudenko (br).
**Dorling Kindersley:** The Science Museum,
London (tr). **ESA:** Rosetta / MPS for OSIRIS
Team MPS / UPD / LAM / IAA / SSO / INTA /
UPM / DASP / IDA (bl). **Getty Images:**
Universal History Archive (cla). **NASA:** (tc,
cb); Hubble Heritage Team, D. Gouliermis (MPI
Heidelberg) et al., (STScI / AURA), ESA (bc).
**118-119 European Southern Observatory:**
The design for the E-ELT shown here is
preliminary http://creativecommons.org/
licenses/by/3.0. **119 ESA:** Herschel / PACS /
SPIRE / J. Fritz, U. Gent (br). **ESO:** L. Calçada
http://creativecommons.org/licenses/by/3.0
(tc). **Adam Evans:** (crb/Visible). **NASA:** GALEX,
JPL-Caltech (crb); ROSAT, MPE (crb); JPL-
Caltech / Univ. of Ariz. (fcrb/mid-infrared).
**Science Photo Library:** Dr. Eli Brinks (fbr). **121
NASA:** (tl); Hubble Heritage team, JPL-Caltech
/ R. Kennicutt (Univ. of Arizona), and the
SINGS Team (cr); ESA, HEIC, and The Hubble
Heritage Team (STScI / AURA), R. Corradi
(Isaac Newton Group of Telescopes, Spain)
and Z. Tsvetanov (NASA) (crb); ESA, and the
Hubble Heritage Team (STScI / AURA) (br).
**122 NASA:** (br, br/Earth); Artist concept (tl).
**123 NASA:** (cra). **124 NASA:** F. Espenak , GSFC
(bl). **125 Rex Features:** Sovfoto / Universal
Images Group (c). **128 NASA:** JPL-Caltech /
Cornell (bl). **129 NASA:** JPL-Caltech / Cornell
University (ca). **130 ESA:** T. Peake (br). **NASA:**
Bill Ingalls (cl). **132-133 NASA. 134 NASA:**
(cl). **135 Corbis:** Bettmann (br). **NASA:** (tc).
**137 NASA:** (crb, br). **139 NASA:** J.L. Pickering
(cr). **141 NASA:** (br, cra, tr); JSC (crb). **142-143
NASA. 144 NASA:** (cl). **145 NASA:** ESA (ca).
**146-147 Bryan Versteeg:** (Mars Habitat
artworks). **147 courtesy Virgin Galactic:**
(crb). **World View:** (cb). **148 Ohio State
University Radio Observatory:** North
American Astrophysical Observatory (cr).
**Science Photo Library:** David Parker. **149 ESA:**
DLR / FU Berlin (G. Neukum) (c). **NASA:** (crb);
Galileo Project, JPL, Ted Stryk (bc). **NRAO :**
SETi (bl). **150 Corbis:** Rick Fischer / Masterfile
(cl). **NASA:** NASA, ESA, K. Kuntz (JHU), F.
Bresolin (University of Hawaii), J. Trauger
(Jet Propulsion Lab), J. Mould (NOAO), Y.-H.
Chu (University of Illinois, Urbana), and
STScI, Canada-France-Hawaii Telescope / J.-C.
Cuillandre / Coelum, G. Jacoby, B. Bohannan,
M. Hanna / NOAO / AURA / NSF (c). **Peter
Michaud (Gemini Observatory):** AURA, NSF
(cr). **153 Corbis:** (cra). **154 Dreamstime.com:**
Andrew Buckin (tr). **154-155 Corbis:**
Bryan Allen (bc). **156 Corbis:** Rick Fischer /
Masterfile (cra). **157 Corbis:** Alan Dyer, Inc /
Visuals Unlimited (br). **Peter Michaud (Gemini
Observatory):** AURA, NSF (cr). **Science Photo
Library:** Eckhard Slawik (crb). **159 Corbis:** Alan
Dyer, Inc / Visuals Unlimited (tr, br, cra). **Chris
Picking:** (cr). **Science Photo Library:** Celestial
Image co. (crb). **163 NASA:** J. P. Harrington
(U. Maryland) and K. J. Borkowski (NCSU)
(cr). **NOAO / AURA / NSF:** Hillary Mathis,
N.A.Sharp (bl). **164 NOAO / AURA / NSF:**
Adam Block (bl). **165 NASA:** NASA, ESA
and the Hubble Heritage Team STScI / AURA).
Acknowledgment: A. Zezas and J. Huchra

(Harvard-Smithsonian Center for Astrophysics)
(cl); NASA, ESA, K. Kuntz (JHU), F. Bresolin
(University of Hawaii), J. Trauger (Jet
Propulsion Lab), J. Mould (NOAO), Y.-H. Chu
(University of Illinois, Urbana), and STScI,
Canada-France-Hawaii Telescope / J.-C.
Cuillandre / Coelum, G. Jacoby, B. Bohannan,
M. Hanna / NOAO / AURA / NSF (bc). **NOAO /
AURA / NSF:** (bl). **166 Adam Block/Mount
Lemmon SkyCenter/University of Arizona
(Board of Regents):** (c, br). **NASA:** ESA, S.
Beckwith (STScI), and The Hubble Heritage
Team (STScI / AURA) (bc). **167 NASA:** ESA,
The Hubble Heritage Team (AURA / STScI /
NASA) (br). **168 Adam Block/Mount Lemmon
SkyCenter/University of Arizona (Board of
Regents):** (bl). **NOAO / AURA / NSF:** N.A.Sharp,
REU program (br). **170 NASA:** Stuart Heggie
(br). **171 Corbis:** Rogelio Bernal Andreo /
Stocktrek Images (br); Tony Hallas / Science
Faction (bl). **NASA:** ESA / ASU / J. Hester (bc).
**172 NASA:** Andrew Fruchter (STScI) (cla).
**173 NASA:** The Hubble Heritage Team (STScI /
AURA) (clb). **Science Photo Library:** NASA /
JPL-CALTECH / CXC / Ohio State University /
C. Grier et al. (STScI / ESO / WFI (cr). **174
Corbis:** Roger Ressmeyer (bl). **175 ESO:** http://
creativecommons.org/licenses/by/3.0 (ca).
**NASA:** ESA / Hubble (br). **176 ESO:** http://
creativecommons.org/licenses/by/3.0 (cr). **177
ESO:** VISTA / J. Emerson. Acknowledgment:
Cambridge Astronomical Survey Unit
http://creativecommons.org/licenses/by/3.0
(bl). **NOAO / AURA / NSF:** (cl). **179 ESO:**
http://creativecommons.org/licenses/by/
3.0 (tc). **NASA:** ESA, K.L. Luhman (Harvard-
Smithsonian Center for Astrophysics,
Cambridge, Mass.); and G. Schneider, E. Young,
G. Rieke, A. Cotera, H. Chen, M. Rieke, R.
Thompson (Steward Observatory, University
of Arizona, Tucson, Ariz.) (bl); ESA, M.
Robberto ( Space Telescope Science Institute /
ESA) and the Hubble Space Telescope
Orion Treasury Project Team (br). **180
Corbis:** Visuals Unlimited (cla). **ESO:** http://
creativecommons.org/licenses/by/3.0 (br).
**181 Chandra X-Ray Observatory:** ESO / VLT
(cra). **183 ESO:** http://creativecommons.org/
licenses/by/3.0 (cla). **NASA:** STScI, Wikisky
(br). **185 ESO:** http://creativecommons.org/
licenses/by/3.0 (cl). **NASA:** ESA, and The
Hubble Heritage Team (STScI / AURA).
Acknowledgment: P. Knezek (WIYN) (cra).
**186 ESO:** http://creativecommons.org/
licenses/by/3.0 (bc). **187 Roberto Mura:** (bl).
**NASA:** ESA, N. Smith (University of California,
Berkeley), and The Hubble Heritage Team
(STScI / AURA) (br); The Hubble Heritage Team
(STScI / AURA / NASA) (cl). **188 Meire Ruiz:**
(bl). **189 John Ebersole:** (cl). **Science Photo
Library:** NASA / ESA / STScI (bl). **190 ESO:**
M.-R. Cioni / VISTA Magellanic Cloud survey.
Acknowledgment: Cambridge Astronomical
Survey Unit http://creativecommons.org/
licenses/by/3.0 (br). **191 ESO:** (crb). **192 ESO:**
Y. Beletsky (LCO) http://creativecommons.org/
licenses/by/3.0 (cla). **194 Corbis:** Dennis di
Cicco (cr). **NASA:** JPL-Caltech (cl). **NOAO /
AURA / NSF:** SSRO / PROMPT / CTIO (cl).
**197 Corbis:** Dennis di Cicco (cr). **201 Brian
Davis:** (crb). **ESO:** (cra). **NASA:** ESA, The
Hubble Heritage Team (AURA / STScI) (cla);
ESA, M. Robberto (Space Telescope Science
Institute / ESA) and the Hubble Space
Telescope Orion Treasury Project Team
(cl); JPL-Caltech (cr). **NOAO / AURA / NSF:**
SSRO / PROMPT / CTIO (clb)

All other images © Dorling Kindersley

For further information see:
www.dkimages.com